# Great Australian Mysteries

**Also by John Pinkney**

*Great Australian Mysteries II*

*Greatest Mysteries of the Modern World*

*Unexplained*

*Haunted: The Book of Australia's Ghosts*

*Unsolved: Exploring the World's Strangest Mysteries*

Published by
**The Five Mile Press Pty Ltd**
950 Stud Road
Rowville Victoria 3178 Australia
Email: publishing@fivemile.com.au
Website: www.fivemile.com.au

First published in 2003.
Reprinted 2004 (four times), 2005, 2006 (twice), 2007 (twice)


The mysteries described in this volume were unsolved
at the time of going to press.

Designed by SBR Productions Olinda Victoria
Edited by Emma Borghesi
Printed in China

National Library of Australia Cataloguing-in-Publication data

Pinkney, John
Great Australian Mysteries

ISBN 978 1 74124 024 5

1. Curiosities and wonders – Australia. 2. Australia – Miscellanea.
994

UNSOLVED • UNEXPLAINED • UNKNOWN

# Great Australian Mysteries

JOHN PINKNEY

# Contents

# Preface

The early settlers were unprepared for the sheer *strangeness* of the Australian continent. Silent bush, so dense and labyrinthine that it could snatch the lives of those who lost their way. Mountains from which travellers never returned. Reclusive animals, so bizarre that Europeans courageous enough to draw or describe them were dismissed as hoaxers.

Despite the veneer of ordinariness imposed by urbanisation, Australia has never lost her reputation as a repository of mysteries. These pages examine the profoundest puzzles that have confronted us over the past two centuries.

Included are inexplicable disappearances, on land, at sea and in the air. Some of these vanishings – as in the case of the five Bermagui boatmen – defied logic (in the words of one police investigator) to 'an impossible degree'.

Also analysed are unsolved murders, whose motive and method have defeated the keenest forensic minds ... such mystifying phenomena as the Min-Min globes and the spinning lights which haunt a Victorian valley ... scientific enigmas, including Queensland's 'forgotten footprints' and the stones that rained on a Western Australian farmhouse ... the continent's deadly treasures, with special emphasis on Lasseter's legendary Reef.

There is, also, a catalogue of unanswered questions: Who was the 'respectable rapist' who allowed an innocent Melbourne saloonkeeper to hang for his crime? What really happened to Prime Minister Harold Holt? Was Breaker Morant at the centre of an international hoax? What do the desert carvings signify?

Only one chapter in *Great Australian Mysteries* offers a solution. The rest describe occurrences that remain unsolved and unexplained.

While conducting interviews and research for this book I found myself being forced to abandon some of my comfortable preconceptions about Australia. Perhaps you will have a similar experience.

John Pinkney
*Melbourne, 2003*

# New Year's Day Deaths that Baffled the World
# The Bogle-Chandler Mystery

*Why did America's FBI spend seven months investigating the bizarre deaths of two Australians on a riverbank in suburban Sydney? And why did the agency refuse, on 'national security grounds', to release its file on the case? This is just one of the many mysteries surrounding the strange fate of Dr Gilbert Bogle and Mrs Margaret Chandler...*

**Sydney, 1 January 1963. Morning.**

IT WAS THE BEGINNING of a typical Australian summer day. Already the sun had a sting in it – a hint of the heat to come. Near Fuller's Bridge, on the Lane Cove River, two teenage boys were hunting for stray golfballs. One of the youths, thinking he'd spotted a prize, ran a few steps along the dirt track ... then recoiled in horror.

Spreadeagled before him was a man, partly naked and unmistakably dead. Blood was trickling from the dead man's nose. His body was partly covered by a small piece of carpet.

The distressed boys were sensible enough not to disturb what looked very much like a crime scene. They ran to the nearest house and breathlessly described what they had found.

Detectives reached the dirt track within fifteen minutes. They quickly discovered a second body, that of a woman, lying in a ditch several metres away. Inexplicably, someone had covered the woman's face and torso with cardboard from beer cartons. One of the detectives removed the cardboard. (At the subsequent inquest, police would be criticised for disturbing the body in this way before it could be photographed, and details recorded. They defended themselves by saying they'd had no idea whether the woman was dead, or merely unconscious and urgently needing help.)

Before long, detectives had identified the corpses as belonging to a Dr Gilbert Bogle and a Mrs Margaret Chandler. Police photographers took pictures of the death scene – and the bodies were removed, to be refrigerated overnight. Forensic experts who conducted a preliminary examination of the pair said there was little doubt they had been poisoned – but they could only speculate as to what the deadly substance might have been.

Police began questioning the victims' friends and family. They learned that Dr Bogle, a 38 year-old New Zealand-born Rhodes Scholar, had worked at the Commonwealth Scientific and Industrial Research Organization (CSIRO). A specialist in solid state physics and laser beam technology, he had recently accepted a high-level research position in the United States – and had been preparing to fly to Washington that week with his wife and children. Gilbert ('Gib') Bogle had been fluent in several languages. He was handsome, well-liked and exceedingly popular with women.

Bogle's companion in death, Mrs Chandler, had been 29 years old and had worked as a nurse before her marriage.

On the eve of their deaths, they had both been guests at a New Year's Eve party in Chatswood. They had arrived and left separately.

The detectives decided there were four possible scenarios: a suicide pact; murder-suicide; double murder by a third party; and accidental poisoning.

They ruled out the first two options. Neither the pair's friends nor their families described them as having been the type of people to kill themselves. Either it had been accidental poisoning – or murder by some toxic substance. But what kind of substance might it have been?

Police specialists went to work searching for the poison. They minutely combed the death scene and surrounding vegetation. They checked Dr Bogle's green Ford Prefect which was parked on Millwood Avenue, 150 metres from the dirt track ... and called at the house in 12 Waratah Street, Chatswood, where the two victims, hours earlier, had attended the New Year's Eve party.

Dr John Laing, Director of the New South Wales Division of Forensic Medicine, examined the bodies. He was assisted by two doctors in his department. (Later, at the inquest, Dr Laing would deny that refrigeration of the corpses had in any way hampered the investigation.)

The doctors found that neither Dr Bogle nor Mrs Chandler had had sexual intercourse in the final hours of their lives. The cause of death, in both cases, seemed to have been acute heart failure, associated with pulmonary oedema and anoxia. One of the assistant medical officers, Dr William Brighton, later said he preferred the inclusive term 'cardiac failure', explaining, 'That's because we're unable to say which occurred first.'

Dr Bogle had been the first to die, soon after he left the party. Rigor mortis was less developed in Margaret Chandler. The doctors concluded that she died an hour or two after her fellow-victim.

The examiners ruled out death by violence. The bodies bore no hypodermic marks. There were no signs of asphyxia. Nor had the pair been attacked by a deadly snake or funnelweb spider. The bodies, like the riverside death scene itself, were free of radioactivity. In the tissues, there was no sign of sedatives or monoxides that could have caused death.

Ernest Ogg, the state government analyst, was asked to probe for ever-more tangential solutions to the puzzle. Meanwhile, police were piecing together the final hours in the lives of Gilbert Bogle and Margaret Chandler ...

KEN NASH WAS A COLLEAGUE of Dr Bogle at CSIRO. Ken and his wife Ruth enjoyed giving parties. Not the big, noisy kind, but gatherings of valued friends. Since moving in to 12 Waratah Street in 1956 they'd hosted several New Year celebrations, customarily with a 'theme'. In previous years this usually had been some variation on fancy dress. But for the 1962–63 party, Ken and Ruth asked everyone to bring an 'original artwork' they'd created themselves.

At 9.00 p.m. Dr Bogle walked up the pleasant garden path of his friends' property and knocked at the front door. He was the first of the twenty guests to arrive. As requested, he had brought his 'original artwork' with him. It was a line drawing, in the style of Picasso. He seemed proud of it – announcing that when he left he'd be taking it home, to show his children.

The party was supposed to be a jacket-and-tie affair. But the tall, red-bearded Geoffrey Chandler, who arrived at about 9.30 p.m. with his wife Margaret, appeared to have forgotten the rule. He was wearing a Hawaiian shirt, slacks and sandals.

Chandler also worked for CSIRO. Margaret Chandler

knew many of his colleagues, but she had only met Gilbert Bogle ten days earlier, at a staff barbecue. He made a positive impression. She told her husband that she liked him very much.

Geoffrey Chandler left the Waratah Street gathering at roughly 11.30 p.m., to buy cigarettes. At midnight, everyone linked arms to sing *Auld Lang Syne.* Shortly afterward, Ken Nash noticed for the first time that Geoffrey was not present. Ruth Nash went to look for him, without result.

Several minutes later, Ken Nash glanced through the kitchen window and noticed Margaret Chandler and 'Gib' Bogle standing outside on the grass, a small distance apart, looking at each other. 'Partly in jest, from a point of puckish humour, I switched off the light that spilled onto the lawn,' Nash recalled. The pair immediately re-entered the house.

Dr Bogle was always good value as a party guest. On this occasion, when someone put on the record *In a Little Spanish Town*, he leapt to his feet and danced a mock-flamenco. Guests gathered around him and applauded wildly. Encouraged by the praise, Gilbert Bogle did the Twist.

The first guests to leave (at 2.30 a.m.) were a Lester and Francis Cotton. Ruth Nash urged them to stay for supper, which she was about to serve – but when they politely refused, she insisted they each take a chicken leg to eat on the drive home. When she re-entered the house, after farewelling the Cottons, she noticed that Geoffrey Chandler had reappeared. Ruth Nash finally served supper at 3.00 a.m. – a near- universal time recollection which helped police establish that Geoffrey Chandler returned to

Waratah Street at 2.30 a.m. At 3.30 a.m. Ruth served coffee. Margaret Chandler had one cup, then told her husband that Dr Bogle had offered to drive her home. Geoffrey Chandler said he had no objection to the arrangement.

At 3.45 a.m. Ken Nash went outside to say goodbye to another departing couple. On his return he noticed Bogle and Mrs Chandler sitting together, talking. Geoffrey Chandler wasn't there. (This matches Mr Chandler's subsequent evidence that he left a little before 4.00 a.m.)

At 4.15 a.m., Dr Bogle asked Ken Nash if he could have his 'artwork' (the Picasso-style drawing) back. Ken Nash produced the picture. Dr Bogle said goodnight and bade them a happy New Year – then left. He was alone.

Roughly five minutes later, a guest named Margaret Beavis said her farewells. Ruth and Ken Nash stood on the verandah to see her off. They were surprised to see that Margaret Chandler was outside, standing at the foot of the steps. She looked up at them, then turned slowly and walked away.

The party continued, its mood happy and optimistic. At about 7.00 a.m. the telephoned shrilled. Ruth Nash took the call. It was Mrs Bogle, asking where her husband was. He left quite a while ago, Ruth Nash said.

Ten minutes after that, the last guests went home. Exhausted, Ken and Ruth Nash went to bed. They'd wash up later in the day.

WHAT WAS GEOFFREY Chandler doing, during his three-hour absence from the Chatswood party (11.30 p.m.–2.30 a.m.)?

# DID MYSTERY POISON KILL TWO?

The Sun News-Pictorial
DAILY AT DAWN
Registered in Australia for transmission by post as a newspaper
44 FLINDERS ST. PHONE: MF0211
12,563. Melbourne, Wednesday, January 2, 1963. 40 Pages. 4d.

.OF THE WEEK

## —Scientist, woman found dead in bush

**SYDNEY, Tues. — Detectives are convinced that poisoning caused the deaths of a brilliant scientist and a married woman whose bodies were found at a heavily-wooded spot on the Lane Cove River, Sydney, today.**

**But the detectives have not been able to discover what the poison was, how it was administered, or by whom.**

**The dead man was Dr Gilbert S. Bogle, 38, of Turramurra, Sydney.**

Dr Bogle, a married man with four children, was a specialist in solid - state physics with the Commonwealth Scientific and Industrial Research Organisation, and was a New Zealand Rhodes Scholar. His brother, Professor A. G. Bogle, of Auckland University, was also a Rhodes Scholar.

DR GILBERT BOGLE

**The dead woman was Mrs Margaret Chandler, 29, mother of two children, of Croydon, Sydney. She was formerly attached to the CSIRO.**

## Both were at party

Her husband, **Dr Geoffrey Chandler**, is an experimental officer in the CSIRO Division of Radiophysics.

**Mrs Chandler's body, which was only partly clothed, was in a shallow depression in the ground. It was covered with empty beer cartons.**

He had left to buy cigarettes – but, unable to find a shop open, he'd ranged further and further from Waratah Street. Finally he decided to drop by at the house of a friend, Ken Buckley, in Phoebe Street, Balmain.

Ken was also giving a New Year's party that night – a 100-guest affair that sounded more to Geoffrey Chandler's taste.

Chandler arrived just as the party crowd was singing *Auld Lang Syne*. He chatted with various friends for a while, then left. He was accompanied by a woman of his acquaintance, Pamela Logan. He invited her to follow him to his house in Darlington. Pamela, a beginner driver, was nervous about simultaneously navigating the New Year traffic and keeping Chandler in view. But in the end she had little difficulty keeping her eye on Geoffrey Chandler's distinctive 1924 model silver Vauxhall.

They stayed at the Darlington house for about 30 minutes, after which Chandler drove back alone to the Chatswood party, and his wife.

Chandler testified that he left the Chatswood house a second time at about 4.00 a.m. After sitting in his car for a while, smoking a cigarette, he decided to visit Pam Logan. He drove to the Granville house via the Sydney Harbour Bridge, where he remembered, at around 4.35 a.m., hearing a tollkeeper and a towtruck driver discussing an accident.

Pamela Logan was (unsurprisingly) asleep when Chandler arrived, but she agreed to accompany him to Granville, to pick up his children. A witness, Leo Powling, gave evidence that he had seen Mr Chandler in his distinctive car at about 4.50 a.m., crossing the Parramatta–

Great North roads intersection.

THE INQUEST INTO the deaths of Gilbert Bogle and Margaret Chandler was held in May 1963. One of the witnesses, Ernest Stanley Ogg, the state government analyst, testified that he had examined the pair's brains, hearts, livers, spleens, kidneys and blood. Using ultraviolet and infrared rays and radiation monitors he had sought 'ionising influences'. *No result.* He had tested hair for arsenic. *No result.* Ogg suspected possible fluoride poisoning – but his tests with rabbits, guinea pigs, cats' heads and chick organs had again produced *no result.*

Ogg said he had also looked for aconite, atropine, strychnine, carbolic acid, cocaine, henbane, phenyl, mercury, phosphorus, opium, nicotine, the effects of poisonous mushrooms and almonds, durata seeds (a toxin used by Asian criminals) and Queensland conefish venom. All with *no result.*

His scrapings from the victims' nails and muscles also proved unproductive.

Police testified that on New Year's morning they had visited the Nash house in Waratah Street, where the remains of the party still lay undisturbed. They had taken everything, from the unwashed glasses, cups and plates to the ashtrays, liquor bottles (empty and full) and pest sprays. In a vast and dedicated effort, forensic experts tested the lot. *Result: negative.*

By this time the investigators were leaning strongly toward the belief that the deaths were the result of an overdose of the hallucinogenic drug LSD – either voluntarily ingested, or (more likely) used as a murder weapon. It would be 25 years before a controversial tissue test seemed to support their theory.

Another inquest witness was Professor Roland Thorpe, occupant of the Chair of Pharmacology at the University of Sydney. He testified that on 15 January he had tested the stomach contents of both victims, *without result.*

Every test for poisons proved negative – but police kept tissue samples in the hope that new scientific developments might produce a breakthrough.

In 1998 the *Sydney Morning Herald* announced a controversial test by Dr Frederick Rieders which, supporting the 1963 police theory had shown traces of LSD.

But even if this finding proved definitive, it would not answer the array of seemingly unanswerable questions surrounding the riverside deaths. Just one of those questions was: *who covered the bodies?*

SOON AFTER THE CORPSES were found, detectives searched Dr Bogle's green Ford Prefect, which was parked on Millwood Avenue, a short walk from the death scene. Under the driver's seat they found a case containing the physicist's clarinet. On the back seat lay his drawing – the 'artwork' he had created for his friends' New Year's Eve party. The ignition key was hidden behind the sun visor. A museum expert checked the car for traces of poisonous spiders, insects or snakes, but found nothing.

However, the carpet was missing from the boot. Police surmised this was probably the same carpet that had been found partly covering Dr Bogle. They showed it to his service station mechanic, Graham Digby, who confirmed that it was indeed from the Prefect.

Nothing at the scene seemed to make a great deal of sense ...

*Why* had Dr Bogle hidden his key in the car, when he could have kept it in his pocket?

*Who* had placed the scrap of carpet over him? And again, why?

Might he and Mrs Chandler have taken it down to the dirt track, so they'd have something to sit on? Unlikely. The carpet measured only 68 x 91 centimetres.

*Had* Mrs Chandler (proved forensically to have died at least an hour later than Dr Bogle) gone to the car to fetch the carpet when he became ill? Also unlikely. Why would she merely have covered him when she could have called an ambulance from one of the houses on the other side of the bridge? As a trained nurse she would surely have realised that he needed immediate medical help.

*Why* did they go to the rubbish-littered dirt track in the first place?

Nearby was an uncluttered, park-like stretch of riverbank – a far more pleasant and private spot for an assignation. Besides, why hadn't they driven straight to the Chandlers' house? At the party, Geoffrey Chandler had made it clear he wouldn't be home that night.

*And who* had placed the mouldy sheets of beer carton cardboard over Margaret Chandler's body and face? It couldn't have been Dr Bogle, because he died first. Had Mrs Chandler covered herself, then? Probably not, in the opinion of police. At the inquest, counsel assisting the coroner asked a detective whether Mrs Chandler would have had to be 'a contortionist' to cover herself in that fashion. The detective agreed that it would have been 'exceedingly difficult'.

Geoffrey Chandler had more to say about the mouldy cardboard. He insisted his wife would have found its texture 'repulsive' on her bare skin. He didn't believe for a moment that she'd have placed the cardboard sheets over herself – particularly not on her face.

The inquest explored every scenario the police and anyone else could imagine. What if the pair had intended to go to the Chandlers' house, but had fallen ill on the way? A possibility – but why, after parking in Millwood Avenue, had they walked down to that dirt track? Surely, if one or both of them were sick, they'd have knocked at someone's door and asked the householder to ring an ambulance. It all defied reason.

In his official finding, Coroner Loomes said the couple had died of 'acute circulatory failure'. He added: 'But as to the circumstances under which that failure was brought about, the evidence does not permit me to say.'

A prominent laser physicist and a nurse, who had known each other for only ten days, were dead. But how? Why? In the months and years that followed, the speculation increased.

The Hong Kong police department's Director of Forensic Medicine publicly opined that the couple must have died after overdosing on the aphrodisiac yohimbine.

The Sydney *Daily Mirror*'s crime reporter, Bill Jenkings, published an interview with Detective Sergeant Jack

Bateman, who said he was convinced the couple had been poisoned with arecoline hydrobromide, the chemical used in dog-worming tablets. Mrs Chandler owned dachshunds. Police enquiries confirmed she had bought worm medicine for the dogs two days before she died.

Around the world, journalists and other theorists intrigued by this strangest of cases offered a bewildering variety of 'explanations', ranging from shellfish toxin and nerve gas to some newly-developed untraceable poison that self-destructed after completing its deadly task.

In the months following the deaths, rumours swept Sydney about a 'mystery woman' who had been expected to give evidence at the inquest, but failed to appear. Had she been silenced? Murdered?

One widely repeated story suggested that Dr Bogle had been recommended as an agent for ASIO during the 1950s. In 1980, Geoffrey Chandler was quoted in Sydney newspaper articles as saying that Bogle might have been murdered by the CIA. The killing, he said, was possibly linked to Bogle's support of a recommendation by Australian Atomic Energy Commission member Dr Clifford Dalton. The gist of that recommendation was that a fast-breeder nuclear reactor Dalton had developed should not go to the Americans.

Most analysts agreed that whoever committed the murders (if murders they were) would have been 'after' Dr Bogle. Margaret Chandler had simply been unlucky enough to be present when the assassin or assassins struck.

During the 1980s a journalist using the United States Freedom of Information Act obtained declassified state department documents showing that FBI chief J. Edgar Hoover had discussed the case with New South Wales police. The upshot was that the FBI conducted its own investigation of the Bogle-Chandler mystery. When the Australian *National Times* and Melbourne's *Sun News-Pictorial* asked that the FBI file be released, their applications were refused.

The first journalist to break the story about the top-secret FBI dossier was Brian Toohey of the *National Times*. He revealed that the United States Consul in Sydney had sent a telegram to the American embassy in Manila in October 1980. The telegram said that, during discussions with United States officials, New South Wales police inspector Frank Travis asked if it was true that the FBI had created a file on the Bogle-Chandler case. If so, he wanted it handed to Australian authorities. The telegram said there had been speculation in the Australian press about Bogle's 'involvement in international espionage activities and that this connection may have led to his death'.

Authorities, both Australian and American, have been unusually secretive about the Bogle-Chandler case. The results of tests on the couple's clothing were not revealed. During the 1980s, New South Wales police refused newspaper requests to release details of their dealings with the FBI. 'Any discussions between the police department and the FBI are confidential,' a police spokesman said. When the Melbourne *Sun* spoke to former inspector Frank Travis (by that time retired) he said New South Wales police had received evidence from the FBI – but he 'couldn't remember' what it was.

And in a letter to the same newspaper the FBI said it would not release its Bogle–Chandler file on 'national security grounds – and in the interest of national defence'.

One of the detectives at the death scene was Keith Paull who would subsequently become chief superintendent of the New South Wales police force. In an interview after his retirement he told a journalist: 'Of all the possible explanations I'm inclined to think LSD might well have been a cause. But whether it was self-administered or administered by force or trickery, it's hard to say. At this stage, I suppose, we'll never know for sure. There may still be someone out there who knows what happened – but it's unlikely they'll come forward now.'

How did Dr Gilbert Bogle and Mrs Margaret Chandler die? Are powerful people concealing the truth from us? Conceivably, the answer is yes.

POSTSCRIPT: A controversial new theory about the Bogle-Chandler deaths was proposed in an independent documentary shown on the ABC TV in September 2006. Writer-director Peter Butt speculated that hydrogen sulphide ('rotten-egg gas') rising from the polluted Lane Cove River had killed the pair. Forensic toxicologist Thomas Milby told the interviewer that after reading the autopsy reports he saw 'nothing that would exclude the possibility of hydrogen sulphide being the culprit'. No evidence of this kind was presented to the May 1963 inquest.

# Do 'Man-monsters' Hide in the Bush?

*When the first settlers invaded Australia, Aborigines advised them to beware of the gigantic 'man-animals' that inhabited the brooding continent's remote lakes and bushland. The new arrivals shrugged off the warnings as the superstitions of a primitive people. But slowly, attitudes began to change. From the Australian colonies' earliest years government reports, newspaper articles and private letters abound with descriptions of encounters with hominid creatures of a nightmarish kind. Such encounters are still being reported by reliable witnesses today...*

IN FEBRUARY 1997 a listener rang ABC regional radio station 2NR with remarkable news. He told biologist and talkback presenter Gary Opit that while picnicking in the Guy Fawkes National Park he and his daughter had found a trail of enormous footprints.

The impressions (which bore some resemblance to human prints) were deeply embedded in the sandy alluvial soil of a dry creekbed. Each was 60 centimetres (23.6 inches) long. The big toes on what were clearly left and right feet were distinct from the smaller toes, which had impressed together so they were impossible to count. The heels had made the deepest depressions at about two centimetres (0.7 inches).

And whatever it was that had left the footmarks had been taking huge strides. Gaps between the prints were up to 1.5 metres (4.9 feet).

The family followed the remarkable trail for about a kilometre until it petered out at a rocky outcrop. There were no fallen leaves or any other debris within the prints – indicating they were fresh. It was plain that something – some huge, heavy two-legged creature of unknown provenance – had been at the picnic spot shortly before the family arrived. It was a frightening thought.

Gary Opit conducted a regular native wildlife program for the ABC. This was not the first time a witness had confronted him with evidence that not all of the animals dwelling in the Australian bush have been formally named and classified. When he first read newspaper reports about gigantic furry primates lurking in bushland, he was inclined to disbelieve them. But his views had begun slowly to change in 1973, when he visited Papua New Guinea to study rainforest fauna with a team of biologists from the Wau Ecology Institute.

On five separate days, he recalls in his website report, 'we heard, during daylight, very loud and powerful mammal calls'. The cries consisted of a series of bass notes, repeated over a five-second period. The sounds were clearly audible through the rainforest for a distance of about one kilometre.

'Having spent some time listening to the vocabulary of chimpanzees, gibbon and other primates at Taronga Zoo I was forced to the conclusion that I was listening to the calls of a very large and powerful primate,' he says. Knowing that Papua New Guinea has an Australian faunal assemblage, with no primates, he found it hard to believe a creature like the one he was hearing could possibly exist.

In November 1973 Gary Opit got his first glimpse of what might have been one of the rainforest noisemakers. While walking along an old logging track toward a bird hide on Mount Massim he saw 'a dark bipedal figure' cross the track 200 metres ahead. At first he thought it was a native Melanesian – but then realised the figure had neither clothing nor weapons. It did not even glance or walk along the track, but moved instead, arms swinging, straight into the dense vegetation.

Back in Australia, his curiosity sparked, Opit learned of other cases. Typical was the testimony of a national park ranger who, on an early afternoon in 1978, saw a startlingly alien creature in rainforest near Springbrook, south-eastern Queensland. From a distance of four metres, in strong light, the ranger caught sight of a 'gorilla-like primate standing 2.5 metres [8.2 feet] tall'. The hominid was grunting to itself. It had a 'distinctive odour', flat, shiny-black face, yellow eyes and large hands. Its body was covered with long black hair. Local newspapers described similar sightings on the same mountain.

The author of this book has interviewed numerous people who claim to have encountered 'the hairy men of the bush'. In 1992 two residents of remote Shark Bay, 650 kilometres north-west of Perth, described a series of frightening encounters with one of the creatures. 'It's enormous – and it leaves a sickening stench behind it,' John, a former councillor, told me. The reeking entity seemed particularly fond of a water tank on the old dirt road into Denham. 'It was set up for travellers who needed a drink,' John said, 'but locals won't stop there any more.

'The creature's been seen around that tank quite often – and it's not the sort of being you'd like to share a drink with. It's also terrified a few visitors to a rock-soak waterhole nearby. A bloke pulled up and was about to get himself some water when his dog started bristling and whimpering. He's a pretty tough ex-soldier, but the pet's fear infected him and he drove on. Quite a few dogs have vanished around this area and it's widely believed the creature has eaten them.'

John saw the malodorous being in 1977, when he was working on Dirk Hartog Island. 'My wife and our new baby were living at the homestead with me, so I was always careful to shut the doors against snakes,' he recalled. 'One night I heard a tremendous clatter from the kitchen. I rushed out and found the door open and cans of food scattered all over the floor. I glimpsed something huge and black running off into the night. It was shaped like a man, but it would be impossible for a man to be such an enormous size. One of the worst things was the smell it left behind – a strong sweet odour like rotting meat.'

The intruder also tried to steal a meal from a local naturalist, Barry. 'In 1965 I was writing a paper on sharks for the Museum of Western Australia,' he said. 'I was camping on a coral beach 25 kilometres from town. The place was a hell-hole – the hottest spot on earth. One night, just after I'd managed to get to sleep, I was woken by a rustling noise. Against the canvas I saw an absolutely huge shape, around eight feet [2.4 metres] tall and it seemed as wide as a car.

'I should have lain quiet, but I let out an involuntary scream instead. This seemed to scare the animal – and it leapt to one side, bringing the tent down around it. It ran in one direction and I ran in the other. I spent the rest of the night sweating in my car with the doors locked.'

NEXT MORNING BARRY INSPECTED the collapsed tent. 'There were bottles and tins everywhere,' he said. 'It was obvious the thing had been foraging for food. To try and calm myself down I went for a walk along the beach – and that, I think, is when I got the biggest jolt of all. There was a long chain of absolutely enormous footprints stretching along the seafront. The beach is very soft in that area, with coarse coral sand. A man's feet don't make much impression at all – but this creature had left deep holes, like an elephant running. I estimated that its feet must have been double the size of mine. And the prints were so far apart that I couldn't even jump from one to the next.

'That thing, whatever it was, needn't have run away. It could have killed me with one blow.'

The author and broadcaster Liz James spent many years of her life studying evidence of 'man-monsters' in Queensland's outback. On one field trip she discovered a claw which she believed had belonged to one of the hominids. Zoologists were unable to associate the extremity with any known animal.

Liz became grimly accustomed to farmers showing her the mutilated remains of cows and horses – often with the legs torn from their sockets. 'Most of the people I spoke to believed that some kind of bush creature was to blame – a creature that was savage and incredibly strong,' Liz told me.

She described the experiences of a farming couple living on a property near Rannes. 'One day they heard an animal screaming. When they raced out of the house they saw their cows were standing stock-still, as if they'd been hypnotised. In the paddock they found huge deep footprints. The marks made by the claws alone were about seven centimetres long.

'Later, when the couple moved to another farm, the wife

heard noises in the night. She went outside with a flashlight and was confronted by an enormous shaggy creature at least three metres tall. She screamed and it ran off.'

A similar shaggy giant was described to me in 1986 by a Melbourne lineman, Bill Johnstone and his companion Stella. While camping one night near Lake Dulverstone in central Tasmania, the couple heard a crashing in the reeds. 'Then we saw a gorilla-like animal about two and a half metres in height tramping through the water toward us,' Stella said. 'We rushed to our car and drove as fast as we could to a police station. They said they'd had no other reports. But a few days later a taxi driver told us two boats had vanished on that lake. The wreckage had never been found.'

Geoff Nelson had two brushes with anomalous animals – the first when he was driving along a dirt road near Taree, New South Wales. 'I stalled the car when a thing about seven feet tall [2.1 metres] and on two legs crossed the road in a few bounds,' he said. 'It sailed – quite effortlessly – over a four-foot [1.2-metre] fence.'

On the second occasion he was out shooting with a friend: 'We were walking by the river when something huge and shaggy came running up the bank. 'We hit it with the spotlight and saw it was a human-like figure, covered in jet-black hair.

'It looked straight into the light, seemingly very curious – and we saw it had bright orange eyes. Then it bolted.'

In 1994, Queensland newspapers reported multiple sightings of a smaller variety of so-called 'hairy men' in the area of Carnarvon Gorge. Over a period of several weeks the hominids – known to Aborigines as *junjuddis* – terrified tourists and local workers alike. Most of the witnesses' descriptions tallied. The *junjuddi* was about one metre tall with an elongated head and long trailing arms – and like its larger 'cousins' seemed extremely timid.

Paddy O'Connor, a retired timber worker, told me: 'I saw two of them outside my camp at dawn. They were pointing at my billycan and seemed to be exchanging comments about it. I wasn't in much doubt they were using some type of language. It was a kind of chirping, but seemed to have a shape to it.

'The light wasn't good enough for me to see the colour of their fur, but their reddish eyes were very visible – and they gave off a smell that made me want to throw up. I was so scared by these creatures that I was about to run. But to my relief they seemed just as frightened to see me – and they bolted first.'

Grahame Walsh, a former Carnarvon National Parks and Wildlife Officer, commented: 'There's strong evidence that something is living out there. Witnesses are quite consistent in describing the creatures' terrible smell. And I know of quite a few bushmen who refuse to camp in *junjuddi* country.' Walsh is convinced he has seen tracks made by the 'man-animals'.

'I found them near the headwaters of the Maranoa River. They were fresh and looked at first glance like the tracks a five year-old child might make. But closer inspection showed they weren't human. I followed them up a hill, but then I lost them.'

Leo Denton, a timber worker in Injune, said he and his

wife had found similar tracks, 'like bare feet in the dust'. They had also heard cries, 'resembling the cackling of chooks', in places where there were no hens. Another timberman, Graham Rigg, was kept awake at night by *junjuddis* leaping playfully in the shadows outside his bush camp. 'They were jumping between the tent and the fire,' he said. 'I don't think they'd realised I was there. It was bloody unnerving and I went back to town that night.'

It seems unlikely that the numerous modern reports of this kind are, without exception, misidentifications or freaks of the imagination.

If they are, our forebears were mistaken, also. Similar hominid encounters have been described since the earliest days of settlement. And the drawings and word-pictures of 'hairy men', published in Australia from the 18th to 20th centuries, are persuasively consistent.

On 17 April 1871, for example, the Sydney *Empire* described a census collector's encounter with what it called 'a monster in human form':

> *The following particulars have been supplied to us by Mr George Osborne of the Illawarra Hotel, Dapto, concerning a strange-looking animal which he saw last Monday and believes was a gorilla. It is to be hoped the animal may be captured, as it is evident it is one of the greatest natural curiosities yet found in the colony.*
>
> *Mr Osborne was doing his rounds collecting the census. The following are his remarks:*
>
> *'On my way from Mr Matthew Reen's, coming down a range at Avondale after sunset, my horse was startled*

*at seeing an animal coming down a tree, which I thought at the moment to be an Aboriginal. When it got to within about eight feet [2.4 metres] of the ground it lost its grip and fell. Although my horse was restless I endeavoured to get a good glimpse of the animal as it retreated until it disappeared into a gully. It was slender-proportioned, arms long, legs like a human being, only the feet being about 18 inches [45 centimetres] long and shaped like an iguana's, with long toes. The muscles of the arms and chest were well-developed, but the front of face projected forward, with monkey features.*

*'Every particle of the body except the feet and face was covered with black hair, with a tan streak from the neck to the abdomen. While looking at me, its eyes and mouth were in motion, after the fashion of a monkey. It walked quadruped fashion, but at every few paces it would turn around and look at me, supporting the body with two legs and one arm, while the other arm was placed across the hip. It had no tail.*

*The query is, where did it come from?*

An indication that hairy bushmen may, like humans, grow old was offered to the *Sydney Morning Herald* (24 October 1912) by a George Summerell. He said he had watched one of the beings, covered with long grey hair, drinking from a creek near Bombala in New South Wales. At first the witness imagined it was a kangaroo – but then it stood up, revealing itself to be a hominid more than seven feet [2.1 metres] tall. The face was 'like that of an ape or man, minus forehead and chin, with a great trunk all one size from shoulders to hips, and with arms that nearly reached its ankles.'

Having finished its drink the creature picked up a stick and ambled off into the bush. Next morning a friend of Mr Summerell's rode out to the creek, where he found huge footprints. These, he wrote, resembled 'an enormously long and ugly human foot in the heel, instep and ball with only four toes, each of them nearly five inches [13 centimetres] long'. Even in the prints which had sunk most deeply into the mud, there was no trace of the 'thumb' found on an ape's 'foot'.

Less than a month later (10 November 1912) Sydney's *Sun* described a dramatic encounter on the Currickbilly mountain range. The report came from Sydney surveyor Charles Harper and several colleagues. When they were just about to go to sleep the men heard peculiar scratching noises near their campsite. They threw dry sticks onto the embers to illuminate the scene – and were immediately confronted by a chilling sight. Charles Harper said:

> *A huge man-like animal stood erect not 20 yards [18 metres] from the fire growling, grimacing and thumping his breast with huge hand-like paws. I looked round and saw that one of my companions had fainted. The creature stood in one position for some time.*
>
> *Its body, legs and arms were covered with long brownish-red hair, which shook with its every quivering movement. What struck me as most extraordinary was the apparently human shape, but still so very different*

*... The body frame was enormous, indicating immense strength and power of endurance. The arms and forepaws were extremely long and very muscular. The head and face were small, but very human. The eyes were large, dark and piercing, deeply set.*

*A most horrible mouth was ornamented with two long canine teeth. When the jaws were closed they protruded over the lower lip. The stomach seemed like a sack hanging halfway down the thighs. All this observation occupied a few minutes while the creature stood erect as if the firelight had paralysed him.*

*After a few more growls he made off, the first few yards erect, then on all fours through the low scrub. Nothing would induce my companions to continue the trip, at which I was rather pleased than otherwise. We returned as quickly as possible, out of the reach of Australian gorillas, rare as they are.*

From 1795, when the first known description of an Australian hairy man was published, there has been an interesting degree of uniformity in diverse witnesses' statements:

- The creature is covered from head to toe in long black hair.
- Its facial features resemble a gorilla's, but its body is on a far greater scale than that of any known gorilla.
- It exudes a sickening stench.
- Despite its fearsome and threatening appearance it is timid – and seems unwilling to attack humans.

(Domestic animals and native creatures are another matter, however. In 1987 a Queensland farmer told me he had watched two hairy hominids 'herding' a small group of kangaroos into dense bush. It was not the first such report.)

- The hairy man (or woman!) sometimes leaves a trail of deep footprints, roughly similar to human prints but of far greater size.
- The behaviour of these gigantic animals has sometimes betrayed a considerable degree of self-awareness and intelligence.
- For more than two centuries – and ongoingly today – sightings have been reported from remote regions of Australia.
- In some Aboriginal languages the creature is known as the *yowie* or *yewhoo.* It has been a part of Aboriginal lore and art for thousands of years.
- By human standards the *yowies* are giants – sometimes reportedly three metres tall. But in Queensland and northern New South Wales a dwarfish sub-species, the hair-covered, humanoid *junjuddis* are sporadically reported. The *junjuddi* is child-size – about one metre tall. It is intensely curious and indiscriminately hungry. According to witnesses, *junjuddis* have invaded campsites in search of food. They have been described as making a noise like hens, where there are no hens.

To many an urban Australian the notion that such 'monsters' lurk in the bush may seem merely fanciful. Most people see their country's wildlife in national parks and on television – and it's easy to take it for granted that any species which hasn't been trapped, tamed, filmed or photographed can't possibly exist.

British naturalists of the early 19th century were similarly sceptical about the fauna Down Under. The black swans reportedly seen in Australia were either an illusion or a lie, they pronounced. Everyone knew that swans were white – just check the reference books.

The body of the first platypus imported into London produced comparable disbelief. Plainly, sneered some newspapers, it was a simple needle-and-thread job – a duck's beak attached to the body of a large antipodean rodent.

The Australian *yowie* taxes belief to an even greater degree. But our hairy man is not entirely lacking in scientific respectability. Hominids, sometimes known as wildmen, have been reported for centuries in Asia, Africa and the Americas. Crypto-zoologists and scientists who have analysed sightings of America's *Bigfoot*, the *Yeti* of the Himalayas, China's *Yeren* and Australia's *yowie* or *Doolagaal* tentatively believe they could all be members of the same species – descendants of the *Gigantopithicus*, whose fossil remains were found in China last century.

Why are these creatures – if indeed they are real – so elusive?

Theoretically, they might be survivors of a species almost eliminated by the onslaught of humanity. As in all evolutionary selection the individuals who weather the destruction of forests and natural habitat are those best-equipped to improvise, conceal themselves and continue to breed. There are plenty of examples of species thought not to exist that were simply in hiding. Typical, as investigator Gary Opit points out, was the American mountain lion (eastern puma), thought for most of the 20th century to have been hunted into extinction. While the United States Fish and Wildlife Service denied the animal's existence, scores of eyewitnesses insisted they'd seen it. Finally, Canadian authorities officially confirmed the puma's continuing presence on earth. It had simply been smart enough to travel incognito.

Assume for a moment that the innumerable witnesses who came forward over two centuries were not simply liars – and that *yowies* and *junjuddis* are a part of our reality. Is it not logical that most sightings of them occur on densely-forested mountains and in remote gorges and bushland? (Parts of the Carnarvon Gorge, for example, are so rugged that the only means of human entry is by rope down a cliff face.)

The advance of man (beginning with Aboriginal hunters and accelerated by land-clearing Europeans) might arguably have driven the hairy hominids into increasingly inaccessible areas of the Australian continent.

Here's one example (recorded by Opit) of how an individual hominid fled the increasingly urbanised scene during the second half of the 20th century. As a boy in the 1960s Larry Edwards lived at Blunder Creek, south of Brisbane, Queensland. At the beginning of spring each year he and his family would hear roaring, bellowing calls emanating from the bush. The calls would usually occur on nights of full moon and would increase in volume as the family watched the vociferous animal run down a dry creek bed in the gully below the house. They would hear the sound of the beast's feet as it made huge leaping steps. The calls decreased in volume as the creature continued on its way.

The manager of the nearby Blunder repeater station tape-recorded the calls and made plaster casts of the animal's large, human-like foot and claw prints.

When developers began to build houses in the area, the calls ceased – and the footprints never reappeared.

### Bush 'Panthers' that Strike by Night

Something was killing – and savagely mutilating – Ron Jones's cattle. Between January 2000 and December 2002 the Binginwarri (Victoria) dairy farmer lost almost 200 cows to huge predators that attacked under cover of darkness.

Ron Jones shot at several of the beasts without success. But he was convinced they were panthers, or a closely related species. 'I've seen around a dozen of them now,' he said in an ABC radio interview. 'When they're sitting they're about three feet six [1.07 metres] tall. Standing, they're roughly eight feet (2.4 metres) from the tip of the nose to the end of the tail. And when they take off they go in big loping bounds.

Each of those bounds carries them about 20 feet [6 metres].'

The cattle had been despatched in a chilling fashion. 'The latest, a Friesian cow, had its brain eaten,' Mr Jones said. 'The cats go in through the ear to get to it. They also go to the back to eat out the bag [udder] area. It's definitely big cats that are doing it. The wounds are much cleaner than a dog would leave. A dog would tear at the flesh, leaving a jagged wound. But when these cats are finished there's not a bit of fat left on the skin. It's licked perfectly clean.'

Ron Jones is not alone in making such claims. On 4 August 2002 Melbourne's *Sunday Herald Sun* reported that it had obtained a leaked state government dossier listing 59 'black panther' sightings in Gippsland alone between 1998 and 2001. One farmer told the Department of Natural Resources and Environment that big cats had wounded 20 of his sheep. A dogcatcher wrote that he had seen 'a huge black puma-size cat' near Heyfield on 29 July 1999. 'I got a shot at it with my rifle from about 300 yards [275 metres],' he recalled. 'I hit the animal but didn't stop it. It disappeared into a thick patch of blackberries.'

Other witnesses quoted in the government report included a school bus driver and his passengers, who watched a 'huge fawn panther' on the Glenmaggie–Seaton Road – and a Driffield West farmer who saw an 'enormous panther-like creature' walking with its kittens.

The enigmatic attackers have consistently eluded attempts to capture or even photograph them – but there is some pictorial evidence. Particularly valuable to researchers is a sketch, executed from memory, by wildlife artist Jahne Hope-Williams (see photograph). Jahne, sitting in her car at Mt Macedon, was afforded a long look at a 'panther' crossing the road mere metres away.

Some encounters have engendered more terror than academic interest. In January 2003, 15 year-old cousins Chris and James McLaren were walking horses on their grandparents' Healesville (Victoria) property when they were startled by a 'gruesome yowling noise'. The source of the din was a large panther-like creature which appeared to be attacking another animal, not visible in the grass. The horses bolted and the boys ran, fearing for their lives. Chris's father, airline pilot Mark McLaren, said he had never seen his son so disturbed.

The elusive 'Big Cats of the Bush' have been decimating livestock across Australia for a long time. One of the predators even achieved international notoriety. On 2 March 1969 Britain's *Sunday Express* published an investigation into the perplexing 'Emmaville Panther' which for many years had created havoc in the district of that name on the New South Wales–Queensland border. In another report

Clive Berry, who farmed 2,023 hectares near Uralla, testified that 'huge black cats' had killed 350 of his sheep. Neighbours joined Berry in a massive hunt for the predators. Although several saw – and managed to shoot at – the cats, they melted, characteristically, into the undergrowth. No fur or blood was found.

Farm families are not the only witnesses. Peter Chapple, a former Victorian State Opera tenor with six albums to his credit, was confronted by one of the cryptic creatures in 1981. He was walking at night in the Olinda State Forest when his torch beam fell on 'something' standing in the middle of the track. Staring into the beam, several metres from him, was a big grey puma-like cat.

'It growled,' Peter Chapple recalled, 'and I remember its eyes glinting angrily when the bright light hit them.'

The singer thought it wisest to stand his ground – and after a tense 30 seconds the 'puma' turned and ambled off into the dark forest.

This encounter so stirred Peter Chapple's curiosity that he founded Victoria's Rare Fauna Research Association. The society's 60 members investigate as many puma sightings and cattle mutilations as time and budget allow. The organization's database now catalogues more than 5,000 big cat encounters in Victoria alone.

Where do the pumas come from?

Some theorists say they are the descendants of caged cats which escaped from travelling zoos and carnivals. Others believe (without documentary evidence) that a black circus panther and her cubs were rescued by American servicemen during World War II and released into the Grampians.

There are even those who speculate that the mega-cats – savage, shy and impossible to catch – might have lived in Australia longer than man.

## Strange Life-forms of Lakes and Creeks

The English convict William Buckley (1780–1856) was transported to a Port Phillip penal colony at age 22. He so detested life in the Indented Head prison camp that in 1803 he escaped to take his chances in the wilderness. Buckley would almost certainly have perished in the bush had not an Aboriginal tribe found and taken pity on him. Buckley lived with the kindly Aborigines for 32 years, eventually becoming a fully-fledged tribal member. In 1835 an exploration party led by John Batman discovered him – after which he was pardoned and eventually given a government pension.

In his biography, written with John Morgan, Buckley describes his encounters with the lake monster the Aborigines called *bunyip* – their word for 'devil' or 'evil spirit':

*We lived very sumptuously and in peace for many months at Kironomoat and then went to the borders of another lake called Moodewarri; the water of which was perfectly fresh, abounding in large eels, which we caught in great abundance. In this lake, as well as in most of the others inland, and in the deep water rivers, is a very extraordinary amphibious animal which the*

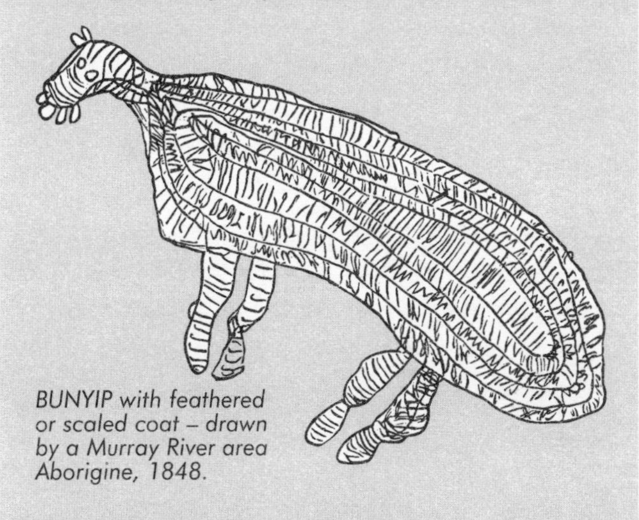

BUNYIP with feathered or scaled coat – drawn by a Murray River area Aborigine, 1848.

*natives call Bunyip, of which I could never see any part except the back, which appeared to be covered with feathers of a dusty grey colour. It seemed to be about the size of a full-grown calf, and sometimes larger. The creatures only appear when the weather is very calm and the water smooth. I could never learn from any of the natives that they had seen either the head or the tail, so that I could not form a correct idea of their size, or what they were like ...*

*The extraordinary animals were often seen by the natives, who had a great dread of them, believing them to have some supernatural power over human beings, so as to occasion death, sickness, disease and such-like misfortunes. They also have a superstitious notion that the great abundance of eels in some of the lagoons are ordered for the Bunyip's provision; and they therefore seldom remain long in such neighbourhoods after having seen the creature.*

*... When alone I several times attempted to spear a Bunyip; but had the natives seen me do so, it would have caused great displeasure. And again, if I had succeeded in killing, or even wounding one, my own life would probably have paid forfeit – they considering the animal, as I have already said, something supernatural.*

*– From Life and Adventures of William Buckley, by John Morgan. Hobart, 1852.*

Water monsters similar to the *bunyip*, but with such names as *kajanpratic*, *kianpratty* and *tumbata*, were described to white settlers by Aborigines in most parts of the Australian continent. Fear of the creatures was universal. They lived, said the Aborigines, in burrows with underwater entrances. They laid large pale-blue eggs (bigger than emu eggs) and were aggressive –

using long claws to kill their prey, which sometimes included an incautious swimmer or fisherman.

Many zoologists believe *bunyips* were no more than seals which strayed inland through the river systems. Fur and elephant seals were plentiful off Australia's southern coast in the early 19th century. However, Aborigines were very familiar with these seals – hunting them for food. And the zoologists' theory does not explain the cave art found in such remote places as Lake Galilee in far-western Queensland.

The lake is surrounded by dense, mountainous bush and is only accessible in a four-wheel drive vehicle. Local Aboriginal legend says that tribes long ago abandoned their camps on the shores because of the marauding 'devil-creatures' that emerged from the waters at night. Archaeologists who visited the site discovered a trove of cavern art showing tribesmen hunting the local animals.

They also found two large ochre paintings that were out of character with the commonplace nature of the other pictures. The paintings depicted a bizarre water creature, long-necked, flippered and closely resembling a plesiosaur. According to local lore, several 'white' people have died at the lake. One unconfirmed story says that in 1870 a farmer vanished while fishing. His boat was subsequently found, reduced to splinters, on the opposite shore.

Many early settlers were completely convinced that

water monsters existed – even to the point of taking care not to disturb a lake's waters when they were filling billycans.

In a letter to the *Sydney Gazette* of 27 March 1843, an E.S. Hall of Lake Bathurst claimed he had seen a terrifying water monster with a head like a bulldog. In 1847, Sydneysiders queued to inspect an alleged '*bunyip* skull' which several purported experts had declared to be part of a creature 'unknown to science'. The skull, retrieved from the Murrumbidgee riverbank, was placed on display in the Australian Museum, which was then located in Sydney's Supreme Court building. The display prompted a spate of letters to the *Sydney Morning Herald* from readers claiming to have seen and heard immense unidentified animals in rivers and lakes. One reader described a wailing sound emerging from a lagoon. Whether the '*bunyip* skull' that prompted this response was genuinely part of a cryptic creature will never be known. After several months on show, it was stolen.

But belief in the *bunyip* persisted long beyond the 19th century. On 7 January 1927 the New South Wales newspaper *Windsor and Richmond Gazette* published an extraordinary article about a local landmark that had long been a focus of fear and speculation:

> *Wingecarribee Swamp holds a mystery of which the outside world has never heard. When the long*

*cold months are over, with the first returning warmth of spring, the swamp awakes from its frozen winter sleep, and the call of night birds innumerable and millions of frogs can be heard in the village. But these are not the only denizens of old Wingecarribee, for there lives the Bunyip, so-called by local people, but by Aborigines in earlier days 'Debil Debil'.*

*Mr H. Mackie, a farmer living almost on the banks of the swamp, states that there are several creatures. He has noticed their sound proceeding from as many as five different stations on the swamp, as though one called and another answered. The sound is best described as a hollow roar as loud as a bull, and yet it is also a kind of hooting 'mump'. It roars every spring and summer, usually in the early part of night until midnight.*

*Forty years ago three men, Schofield, Mansfield and Bunt (whose descendants still live in the district) went out with dogs to secure this animal. They returned terrified and related that they came across the thing basking in the sun on the side of a hole. The creature was approximately the size of a two year-old steer and appeared to possess two short broad fins or flippers. It took fright and plunged into the hole. The dogs ran away and so did the men.*

Many distinguished figures in Australian history believed such water monsters were far more than figments. Charles La Trobe, first Governor of the Port Phillip district, was so overwhelmed by settlers' descriptions of large aquatic animals that he began to classify and analyse them. By 1847 he was convinced there were two major types of *bunyip*: the pig-like *banib* and the *Tooroodon*. The latter animal was represented in one drawing as having an emu-like head and four legs, each ending in three emu-like webbed toes.

The explorers Hamilton Hume and James Meehan found bones and skulls on the edge of Lake Bathurst and concluded that they had belonged to a 'native hippopotamus'. From the shores of the same lake, E.S. Hall, founder of the Bank of New South Wales, spotted an animal that filled him with wonder. In a letter to the *Sydney Gazette*, 27 March 1823, he wrote:

> One fine morning *in November 1821, I was walking by the side of the marsh which runs into Lake Bathurst when my attention was attracted by a creature casting up the water and making a noise, in sound resembling a porpoise, but shorter and louder: the head only was out of the water. At the distance I stood, it had the appearance of a bulldog's head, but perfectly black. The head floated about as though the animal was recreating itself ...*

In December 1822 Hall and a friend were granted a longer and closer look.

> *Mr Forbes and I were bathing at the eastern end of the lake, where an arm runs among the honeysuckles. As I was dressing, a creature, at a distance of about 130 yards [117 metres] suddenly presented itself to my view ... It was gliding on the smooth surface with the rapidity of a whaleboat. Its neck was long, apparently three feet [90 centimetres] out of the water, and about the thickness of a man's thigh; the colour a jet black. The head was rather smaller in circumference than the neck and appeared surrounded by black flaps, which seemed to hang down and gave it a most novel and striking appearance. The body was not seen, but from the rippling of the water I judged it to be longer than the neck. I turned to ascertain if Mr Forbes had also seen it, and on looking again it had dived and was seen no more.*

Settlers' dogs and horses were terrified of the *bunyip*. A typical incident was described in the Melbourne *Argus*, 19 December, 1853:

> *A gentleman writing from Rocky River, near Mount Remarkable, says, 'About four nights ago, I was camped close to a large and exceedingly deep waterhole here ... I was startled by hearing a curious noise in the water. I jumped up and looked*

*towards the place from which the noise seemed to proceed, and as the moon was very bright, I was enabled to perceive a large blackish substance advancing towards the bank and which, as it approached, raised itself out of the water. I crept towards it and perceived that it had a large head and a neck something like that of a horse, with thick, bristly hair.*

*'I suppose it must have seen me, for it proceeded down the river, keeping a few yards from the bank, towards which it made again, nearly abreast of my horse, which no sooner saw it than it made a rush, breaking the tether rope and bolting. The noise occasioned by my horse running away caused my strange visitor to disappear immediately ... From what I saw, I should think its entire length would be from fifteen to eighteen feet [4.5–5.5. metres].'*

*Bunyips* seldom receive much publicity nowadays. But in the first 150 years of European settlement they were accorded hundreds of columns of newspaper space and numerous cautiously speculative articles in such learned organs as the *Australian Museum Magazine* and the *Tasmanian Journal of Natural Science*. Occasional *bunyip* reports were still appearing in the 1960s and 1970s – but most emanated from far-flung areas of Australia not yet devastated by man.

Did *bunyips* ever actually exist? Do a few stragglers survive? The biologist Gary Opit has the last word:

'The identity of the *bunyip* has to be addressed. In the past it has been pushed aside with explanations that the Aboriginal people, who inhabited the land for something like 50,000 years, were a superstitious and ignorant lot who still had not worked out what lived in their own supermarket. European settlers who had observed the *bunyip* were regarded as obviously of the same ilk. Consequently the *bunyip* has been turned into a children's fairytale character.

Perhaps more likely it was a remarkable remnant of Australia's megafauna, a solitary aquatic herbivore on the edge of extinction, surrounded on all sides by predatory humans. With the arrival of Europeans and their cattle competing for forage, the massive habitat destruction with widespread wetland drainage and silting up of the waterways, yet another ancient life form departed this rapidly emptying continent.'

# Mystery of the Naked Giant

*When the huge, uncanny image of an Aboriginal huntsman mysteriously appeared in a South Australian desert, the entire world took notice. The etching, sprawled across four kilometres, was big enough to be visible from space. Despite a tantalising series of clues, no-one could discover who had carved the picture. Or how, or why ...*

**26 June 1998. Morning.**

FOR A MOMENT, pilot Trec Smith thought it was a trick of the light. While flying a routine charter mission from Coober Pedy to the quiet outback town of Marree, South Australia, he noticed, from the corner of his eye, something strange – something very strange – spread vastly across the plateau far below him.

He had to keep flying for a short while before he could make sense of what he was seeing. Finally he realised it was an immense 'drawing', gouged into the red desert earth. It depicted a naked Aboriginal huntsman holding a club, ready to strike his prey. The image was so painstakingly detailed, from headpiece and bearded face to traditional chest scars and classically positioned feet, that Smith assumed it must be part of some elaborate tourist campaign, unknown to him until now.

As he flew on, he wondered why the tourist people had decided to place their immense picture here, in the state's remote and sparsely-visited north. When he arrived in Marree he asked locals that very question. To his surprise, people gave him strange looks. No-one seemed to have heard about the nude giant in the desert.

But then, in the days that followed, unsigned faxes began to arrive in Marree's shops and offices. The letters, purporting to have been written by the huntsman's anonymous creators, urged locals to fly out over the desert to see the astonishing sight for themselves. The people of Marree were suspicious, but also consumingly curious. Several business owners followed the faxed advice and chartered a plane.

They returned to their tiny township full of wonder. The figure, gouged into the red soil, was on a breathtakingly huge scale, they reported. It seemed impossible to believe that anyone could have performed handiwork that was simultaneously so immense and so intricate.

The faxes kept arriving. The Aboriginal warrior, the authors claimed, was the biggest artwork on the planet – four kilometres long and dwarfing even the largest earth drawings at such ancient sites as Nazca, Peru.

Senior Constable Paul Liersch drove out to the site, accompanied by several townsfolk and the first media crews. He offered a matter-of-fact assessment of the riddle: 'Someone's gone to tremendous effort out there. And they've spent a lot of money, too. It's fairly obvious they've used some kind of navigational equipment to get the scale and perspective right. The picture is extremely well mapped-out on the ground and we've found survey markers right through the area.'

Experts in disciplines ranging from sculpture to engineering soon concurred that the geoglyph, ploughed 30 centimetres deep into the red earth, could only have been formed by earthmoving equipment, using computer technology combined with a global positioning system. Police checks showed that no-one in the previous two years had hired such machinery for 'unspecified reasons' within a 200-kilometre radius of Marree. Therefore, said theorists, the gouging equipment must secretly have been flown into the desert site, then quietly removed when the work was complete.

The high-tech artists had probably chosen the area because of the presence of white chalk (starkly visible from the air) centimetres beneath the soil.

But what motivation would anyone have had for carving such a picture at what plainly must have been enormous expense?

An apparent breakthrough (subsequently dismissed by some commentators as a practical joke) came when a preservative bottle was found near the site. Inside was a note said to contain the words 'Stuart's Giant' and a reference to the Branch Davidian cult, linked with the mass deaths at Waco, Texas, in 1993. Whether the note was genuine or not, police promptly confiscated it and refused to comment further.

Three local Aboriginal tribes – the Dieri Mitha, the Kuyani and the Arabunna – were angered by the picture. They pointed out that it had appeared in the middle of a native title claim, had destroyed swathes of native vegetation – and was 'a mockery' of their culture.

For the six months following his public debut the Marree Man was the subject of rumour and speculation in media around the world. Some academic commentators said the picture bore a strong stylistic resemblance to the ancient hill figures found in several parts of Britain.

These pictures of men and horses – some dating as far back as 100 BC – were (like Marree Man) seen most plainly from the air. Their creators had formed them by cutting away the topsoil and rock on hill slopes to expose the stark white chalk below. Historians described the ancient artworks as 'signals to the gods'.

In January 1999, six months after the discovery of Marree Man, its mysterious makers began to send signals directly to the media. In a fax to major newspapers and television networks, the anonymous writers urged investigators to dig into a particular section of earth near the warrior's nose. There they would find something of great significance ...

Half expecting that the message would prove to be a hoax, reporters and television crews rushed back to the site. But they were pleasantly surprised. Officials from the Aboriginal Affairs Department retrieved a small plaque from the precise spot predicted. Its inscription read:

> *In honour of the world they once knew.*
> *His attainments in these pursuits are extraordinary:*
> *a constant source of wonderment and admiration.*

In a corner of the plaque was the flag of the United States of America.

In one of their letters the desert-carvers mentioned the Cerne Abbas Giant, an ancient hillside figure in Dorset, England. Anthropologists were quick to point out the giant's points of resemblance to Marree Man – particularly the exposed genitals and the killing weapon held high.

Australian academics were bitterly divided about how accurate the depiction of the Aboriginal warrior might be. An anthropologist at the South Australian Museum described the figure as 'cartoon-like', culturally incorrect and brandishing a boomerang.

A second anthropologist, who (like so many of the drama's players) preferred to remain anonymous, wrote to Melbourne's *Age* newspaper insisting that the weapon was not a boomerang. It was a throwing stick which, according to historical records, some South Australian tribal hunters had hurled into flocks of birds.

The anthropologist wrote: 'Considering the size of the object, many details are astonishingly accurate, such as the perfect posture of the non-throwing hand in standard Aboriginal throwing technique, the perfect placement of chest initiation scars and the excellent representation of the hair ties. This level of knowledge points either to Aboriginals (as the artists) or people familiar with details of Aboriginal culture.'

But perhaps the makers of Marree Man were simply familiar with an old book: the classic *The Red Centre* by anthropologist H.H. Finlayson. Among the photographs in this volume are pictures of tribesmen hunting wallabies with throwing sticks almost identical to the stick depicted in the desert carving.

Investigators are now certain that *The Red Centre* is, at the least, the source of the inscription on the plaque buried near the giant's nose. A passage on page 57 of Finlayson's book reads:

> *Ritual ceremonies, magic and the interchange of traditional lore may play a big part in the brief life of his corroborees and gatherings. But when the semi-solitary wandering which makes up most of his life is resumed, he takes up again the absorbing problem of food-getting, and becomes of necessity an intensely keen student of all that makes up the animal life of his environment. His attainments in these pursuits are extraordinary: a constant source of wonderment and admiration.*

Before long, the enigmatic giant was bringing a flood of tourists to Marree – and local business people began pressing for his outline to be carved deeper. But Aborigines were against the idea. Garnet Wilson, chairman of the Aboriginal Lands Trust which administered the area, announced: 'We have no plans to preserve the figure. We'll let the elements do their work and it'll disappear off the face of the earth ... that's a promise.'

Meanwhile, in Broken Hill, New South Wales, an artist who had trained as a mining engineer set out to outdo the creators of Marree Man. Without using satellite or navigational aids Peter Anderson (who paints under the name of Ando) carved the world's biggest artwork – a 4.3 million-square kilometre image of a smiling stockman. He used as his canvas the Mundi Mundi Plains, about 30 kilometres outside Silverton, north of Broken Hill.

Anderson took a year to complete the astonishing task – starting with line drawings, then flying above the site to ensure that all the elements would fit. Using a tractor as a chiselling tool he then created a stockman's image so huge that every tooth in its smiling mouth is bigger than a football field.

When he had completed the carving, he seeded every chiselled line, ensuring that the outline would grow into a living picture visible from the air.

But it was Marree Man – and his secretive creators – who continued to tantalise the world. Several artists were publicly 'accused' of being responsible for the drawing – but all denied it, even though the police had now announced that no crime was committed.

The person most strongly rumoured to have carved the Marree warrior was a giant of a man himself – painter Bardius Goldberg. In the late 1990s, he had moved from his Alice Springs home to Hahndorf, South Australia. To friends he revealed that an Adelaide Hills businessman had offered him $10,000 to create an artwork on 'strictly confidential terms'.

Goldberg's associates now believe that the $10,000 was payment for Marree Man.

'Whenever the subject of that desert figure was raised, he'd clam up,' said Goldberg's closest friend, Reg Harris. 'It was quite out of character for him to be silent about anything.'

Several compelling clues link Goldberg to the carving:

- He had already created two artworks of immense size: a huge green cross which dominates a turn of the Todd River, and the world's largest dot painting which dominates more than a hectare in the Achilda Valley, west of Alice Springs.
- He had expert knowledge of satellite global positioning systems.
- He could operate earthmoving equipment – another of the prerequisites necessary to create a vast picture visible from 700 kilometres in space.
- And, as had always been the case throughout his life as an artist, he sorely needed money.

Bardius Goldberg consistently refused to talk to reporters about his alleged role in the Marree project. In September

2002, aged 61, he died of a heart attack – taking his secret (if indeed it was his secret) with him to the grave.

## Mystery People 'Lived in Kimberley Caves'

Strange cave pictures, which pre-date the Pyramids by 12,000 years, are baffling anthropologists in Western Australia's Kimberley region. The ancient paintings – one of which shows bizarrely-costumed warriors propelling a boat through water – have prompted rock art expert Grahame Walsh to propound a controversial theory.

These artworks, says Walsh, clearly depict a race of people who are quite distinct from the Aborigines. Possibly they reached Australia by sea in the distant past. Rock art created by the mystery race dominates hundreds of obscure caverns in the Kimberley. Other investigators are at a loss to say who created the starkly individual images.

In 1977 researchers from the Commonwealth Scientific and Industrial Research Organization (CSIRO) dated one of the pictures: a painting of a mulberry-coloured human figure wearing an elaborate headdress.

By using tiny grains of quartz trapped in the mud as an atomic clock the scientists proved that the painting was created during or before the last Ice Age, *circa* 15,000 BC. Grahame Walsh, who participated in the experiment, believes the archaic artists may have sailed to north-west Australia from the Indonesian islands. Their garments are suggestive of a 'rainforest culture', he says.

One of the paintings shows the mystifying Ice Age people engaged in what is thought to be the world's first battle scene.

So far, no bones or artefacts belonging to the long-ago cave artists have been found.

## Ancient 'Map' pre-dates the Dinosaurs

About 500 million years ago a near-perfect outline of modern Australia was imprinted by chance on a slab of rock.

The extraordinary 'space-eye view' of the continent – randomly formed by immense tectonic forces – lay encased in a vein of siltstone near what would become Bacchus Marsh, Victoria.

In 1967 the long-buried map was exposed to the light when workmen dynamited a quarry wall. First to notice the fluke of natural cartography (see photograph) was a stoneworker, Jack Martin. He took photographs of his discovery and showed them to earth scientists at Melbourne and Monash universities.

They generally agreed that the outline had been etched by a freak of chance. A mineralogist opined that the continent's image might have been created by iron sulphide, when the stone surface was exposed to oxygen.

Whatever the explanation, Nature had long-ago imprinted upon the rock an eerily accurate representation of a future Australia – millennia before the island continent broke away from the ancient land mass of Gondwanaland.

# Tragedy of the Trio who Never Came Home
# The Beaumont Children

*Adelaide in the 1960s was a big, trusting country town. People left their doors unlocked and their windows open. They allowed their children to walk to school unaccompanied and to go to the beach alone. Then, one nightmare morning, three youngsters simply vanished. Police could never discover who had abducted them or what their fate had been. Australians mourned the Beaumont children – and began to buy deadlocks and window-bars ...*

JIM AND NANCY BEAUMONT'S pleasant house in the Adelaide suburb of Somerton Park was an ideal place to bring up a family. The back garden, massed with peach and nectarine trees, had room aplenty for cubbyhouses and games of hide-and-seek – and a safe beach was only minutes away.

The Beaumonts had three children. The eldest, nine year-old Jane, was top of her class at nearby Paringa Park primary school. The teachers thought highly of the imaginative stories she was forever writing – and believed she might well fulfil her ambition of becoming an author one day. Seven year-old Arnna (the unusual spelling was her mother's idea) was affectionate and dependent and not quite such a scholar as her older sibling. The smallest Beaumont was Grant, aged four. He was a precocious booklover, just as Jane had been. He loved to tag along with his sisters, wherever they went.

Australia Day, 26 January 1966, was hot and still. The children begged their mother for permission to ride their bikes to the beach. Nancy Beaumont vetoed that idea. She didn't like the thought of her kids negotiating the holiday traffic. Briefly she thought of going swimming with them – but she didn't want to hold them up. They could be very impatient when a beach visit was in the offing. She told them they could take the bus to Glenelg. She gave Jane a handful of coins to cover the fares and ice-creams and told her they must be back by midday, for lunch. Jane was jokingly known in the Beaumont household as 'the little mother'. Nancy knew she could be trusted to get her brother and sister home on time.

At 8.40 a.m. the three children, tanned like most of their contemporaries by the harsh South Australian sun, walked hand-in-hand to the front gate. Nancy Beaumont followed them and bent down and kissed them goodbye.

It was the last time she would ever see Jane, Arnna and Grant.

Jim Beaumont was a commercial traveller. He had spent the morning of 26 January driving through rural towns selling linen. He arrived home at about 3.00 p.m. to find his wife very worried. The children were three hours late home.

The couple began a search that would extend into decades to come. Within 24 hours it would be headline news all over Australia.

Glenelg Beach had been crowded with hundreds of people on that fateful Australia Day. When South Australian police asked to hear from anyone who might have seen the young Beaumonts they were overwhelmed by witnesses, most of whom had noticed three children 'playing' on a beachside lawn with a tall man in his thirties. The consensus was that they had seemed happy and confident in his company.

A woman said she had seen a man dressing the youngsters. She thought this was strange, because they were plainly old enough to dress themselves. A tourist from Broken Hill recalled a man leaving the grass reserve with the children in tow.

Reports of this kind – and scores of others directed to them by television and radio stations – enabled detectives, aided by a newspaper artist, to produce what they regarded as a reliable picture of the mystery man. He was tall, lean and gaunt-faced, with untidy light-brown hair. He had been dressed only in navy blue bathers.

Not all the sightings had occurred at Glenelg beach. A postman told detectives that the three children had said hello to him as they crossed a road. They were cheerful – and appeared to be unaccompanied by any adult.

Staff members at a cakeshop reported that the youngsters (whom they knew well) had come in to buy their customary order: pies and pasties in a single bag. They had also bought a second lunch in a separate bag – tendering a £1 note in payment. The police regarded this as sinister news. Nancy Beaumont had given Jane only seven shillings and sixpence. The note must have been provided by someone else.

The disappearance generated a national wave of sympathy for the Beaumonts. Thousands of letters arrived at their silent, grief-riven house. Police forces in all states issued an alert for the abductor, while in Adelaide, detectives searched cars, barns, drains and back yards for bodies. Most of the investigators were privately convinced that Jane, Arnna and Grant had been murdered by a brutal pervert – probably on the day they vanished.

People were desperate to help; to do something, anything, that might ease the parents' grief. Con Polites, a wealthy businessman, asked the Dutch clairvoyant Gerard

Croiset to help in the search. Croiset agreed, on condition that no-one tried to pay him for his work. 'The only reward I seek is to help find the children,' he said. After spending hours meditating over clothes and toys that had belonged to the young Beaumonts, Croiset had a vision that told him where they were. He led searchers to a recently concreted warehouse in Paringa Park, near Jane and Arnna's school. He said the killer had buried the three children in a disused brick kiln.

The warehouse owners were loath to allow their new floor to be dug up on nothing more than a psychic's hunch. But a hastily-formed action group finally persuaded them it was the right thing to do. While police stood watching, Monsieur Croiset's followers smashed the concrete and dug down. They found nothing. Nevertheless, Jim and Nancy Beaumont were grateful that the Dutchman had cared enough about their plight to travel around the world. They bought him a small gift: a writing set covered with kangaroo skin.

South Australian detective sergeant Stan Swaine was one of a small group of policemen who did not believe the children were dead. The evidence, in his view, pointed to them being captives of a religious cult. In 1968 Swaine received two letters from Dandenong, Victoria, which, he believed, might bear out his theory. One of the letters purported to have been written by Jane, to her parents. The other was from a man who claimed he had appointed himself as the children's guardian, but was now prepared to hand them over, without condition, at a Victorian post office.

Swaine, accompanied by Jim and Nancy Beaumont, drove to the meeting place. The detective, disguised as a window cleaner, watched while Jim Beaumont anxiously waited for the letter-writer to appear. Nobody turned up. Twenty-four years later, using new forensic methods, police would establish that the cruel hoax letters had been written by a teenage boy.

Evidence that excited even the most cynical police surfaced in March 1968 when a man scavenging on a suburban rubbish tip found a bulging suitcase. Its contents prompted him to take it straight to the Homicide Squad. The case was stuffed with newspaper clippings covering the Beaumont disappearance. In the margins, someone had scrawled comments in red ink. Beside one news story, about a police hunt in the sandhills, were the words: '*Not in sandhills. In sewerage drain.*' Across a picture of Jane Beaumont the writer had scribbled, '*She used to comb my hair.*' And a drawing of the wanted man was defaced by the words '*Lies – all bluff!*'

Within 24 hours detectives had the writer's name. Relatives sheepishly came forward to say she was an elderly aunt who had become insanely obsessed with the Beaumont case. When she died they had sent many of her effects – including the suitcase – to the tip.

Police followed every possible lead. Acting on an anonymous letter from Sydney they searched for alleged 'burial places' on Swan and Mud islands. Two detectives flew to New Zealand where they fingerprinted an entire ship's crew. The vessel had been berthed in Adelaide on the day the Beaumont children vanished – and in

Melbourne in August 1968, when a young girl disappeared from a St Kilda amusement park. Result: *negative.*

In increasingly desperate attempts to discover the truth, detectives unsuccessfully:

- Searched a sealed shipping container for remains.
- Tracked down and interviewed a fair-haired Tasmanian surfie who had been speaking to a child on the phone about Adelaide. (By chance a policeman overheard the conversation on a crossed line – and considered it suspicious).
- And grilled a Kalgoorlie couple who had 'jokingly' told neighbours they had abducted the children.

The false alarms kept sounding. In August 1997 a 41 year-old Canberra woman claimed in a women's magazine that she had been brought up by a cult and had vague memories of having been Jane Beaumont. The publication engaged a retired detective to check the woman's story. In his report the former policeman said the woman could well be Jane. She was the same age the abducted child would now have been, had the same colour eyes and – most significantly – possessed a birth certificate issued in 1966, *after* the Beaumont children's disappearance. Cults, he pointed out, had often faked their victims' birth details.

Police immediately spoke to the woman and her parents. They established that she had never belonged to a cult and that her birth documentation was genuine.

For years following the loss of their beloved children Jim and Nancy Beaumont continued, understandably, to clutch at any straw of hope that presented itself. In an interview with the Adelaide *News* Nancy revealed that her husband wanted them to escape Somerton Park and its pall of grief and start again somewhere else.

*'But I can't go in case the kiddies come home,'* she said. *'You see, I'm waiting for them to come back here. I never know. Perhaps someone could drop them at the front gate. Wouldn't it be dreadful if I wasn't here.'*

But in the end the Beaumonts did leave their silent house and its peach and nectarine trees and all its memories. The police knew their whereabouts, but the information was held back from the media. Jim and Nancy wanted privacy now. They could speak no more about the evil that had destroyed their family.

# Conundrum of the Corpse on the Sand

*It had all the elements of an espionage thriller: the body of a tall handsome man found propped against a wall on an Adelaide beach. No wallet. No papers. His expensive clothing carefully stripped of identifying labels. But – forgotten in a fob pocket – a tiny roll of paper containing two words that pointed police to a missing book of poetry. A book inscribed with an indecipherable code …*

JEWELLER JOHN LYONS and his wife were possibly the first people to notice the man-with-no-name. It was 7.00 o'clock on the evening of 30 November 1948 and they were strolling along Adelaide's Somerton Beach, enjoying the mild air of the last day of spring.

They saw him just as they were passing the old, cruelly-named Crippled Children's Home. He was half-lying, half-sitting in the sand, his head resting against the beach wall. 'We didn't take much notice at the time,' Mr Lyons recalled. 'We assumed he'd had a few drinks and was resting. And he seemed OK because, as we walked by, he moved his right arm, as though he was trying to light a cigarette.'

A young couple who walked along the promenade 30 minutes later had the same impression. 'We assumed he was drunk,' the girl told police. 'We climbed down to see if anything was wrong, but he just seemed to be asleep. When I think back, though, he certainly didn't seem bothered by the mosquitoes.'

Next morning John Lyons visited the beach again with a party of friends, to enjoy his first swim of the summer. The man was still there, leaning against the beach wall. It was obvious to everyone in the party that he was dead. Mr Lyons hurried to a pay phone and called the police. Within minutes a young constable was at the scene. The corpse was fully clothed. There were no signs of disturbance or violence. A half-smoked cigarette lay balanced on the jacket's right collar.

A police ambulance took the man to the Royal Adelaide Hospital, where doctors opined that he had died, possibly of cardiac arrest, at about 2.00 a.m. He was transferred to the morgue. There is nothing unusual about deaths in public places – and the police assumed that someone would soon identify the corpse.

Meanwhile they began to compile a report on the case. The dead man had been tall, of European appearance, about 45 years old and in apparently excellent physical condition. He was blond, and clean-shaven, with hazel eyes. He was expensively dressed, in a brown double-breasted coat and brown trousers, socks and fashionable shoes, with a white shirt and red-and–blue tie. But any hope the police might have had of using his clothes to identify him was dashed when they found that his garments had been meticulously stripped of identifying labels. Nor was there a wallet, or any personal papers that might offer a clue to who he had been.

And on the cadaver itself there were no scars or other identifying marks.

However, not everything drew a blank. The investigators were at least able to reconstruct some of the man's intentions and movements in the hours preceding his death. In an inside pocket of his jacket they found an unused rail ticket to Henley Beach and a punched bus ticket to Glenelg. These clues would later fit into a tantalisingly incomplete jigsaw puzzle.

The post-mortem only deepened the mystery. The man's

stomach was found to be hugely congested with blood and his heart had failed – symptoms consistent with poisoning. But no trace of poison could be found.

Police distributed a photograph of the body to major newspapers around the world. They provided fingerprints to any police force that requested them. In the weeks that followed, numerous people applied to see the body. A Melbourne woman feared it might be the corpse of her missing son. A Rockhampton man thought the photograph showed a friend with whom he'd co-owned a fishing trawler years before. A sailor believed the man was a Bulgarian sea captain. Two people were convinced the body was that of a South Australian timberman, Bob Walsh. At age 63, however, he didn't fit the profile. The police investigated all leads – but their efforts proved negative.

In January 1949 there was a breakthrough – of sorts. Detectives found an unclaimed suitcase (its baggage label removed) at the Adelaide Railway Station cloakroom. The clothes inside matched those of the dead man – and a forensic investigation showed that some threads, in type and colour, matched threads in the coat on the mystery corpse. Even more excitingly, there were tags – bearing the name T. Keane – on three items of clothing. When this information was published, a ship's master rang police to say the suitcase could have belonged to Tommy Keane, a local sailor. But when Tommy's employers and shipmates visited the morgue to view the corpse, all agreed it was not him.

However, the suitcase did yield other clues. Inside, detectives found slivers of zinc, a stencilling brush, a knife with a sharpened point and a pair of honed scissors.

Implements of this kind were used by third officers on merchant ships, for stencilling cargo. The only problem was that police could find no missing third officer to fit their description of the body on the beach.

In April 1949 a forensic expert again painstakingly inspected the corpse's clothing – and found something startlingly new. From an obscure fob pocket in the trousers he retrieved a tiny, rolled-up piece of paper, scarcely bigger than a ball of lint. On it were printed two words: 'TAMAN SHUD'.

Police asked the University of Adelaide for a translation – but a learned local newspaper reporter beat the academics to it by announcing that the words were ancient Persian for 'THE END'. They appeared, he said, in the 1859 translation of *The Rubaiyat*, a volume of verses by the 12th century astronomer and poet Omar Khayyam.

Detectives promptly issued an appeal for a copy of *The Rubaiyat* with its final page missing. Their press release – sent to newspapers and radio stations throughout the world – produced one result, albeit an invaluable one. A Glenelg doctor presented himself next day at South Australian police headquarters with the very book they were seeking.

He told investigators that on 30 November (the day before the beach body was discovered) someone had tossed *The Rubaiyat* onto the front seat of his car while it was parked, unlocked, outside his house. He had attached no importance to it until he heard the police appeal on radio.

The forensic experts went to work again. Only a *part* of the final page had been ripped away – the section containing the Persian words. The paper scrap and the remainder of the page fitted together exactly. And there were further clues. On the volume's back cover, detectives found a series of faint pencil markings which, under magnification, proved to be a series of what seemed to be telephone numbers. They were followed by rows of capital letters forming some kind of coded message or cryptogram.

This was an era when the Western powers and the Soviet Union were perilously confronting each other in Europe – and the planet seemed to be on the brink of another world war. Australian police forces were under instruction to report any suspicious activity to defence authorities – and in South Australia, with its new Woomera rocket range, such precautions were deemed particularly vital.

The South Australian police sent the suspected code book to Canberra. Army and naval intelligence experts spent months trying to break its suspected cipher – without result. Like every other set of clues in this most baffling of cases, the only result was a blank.

In June 1949, Adelaide Museum taxidermist Paul Lawson made a plaster cast of the dead man's head and shoulders. Police hoped that a three-dimensional image might prove more powerful than a photograph in jogging memories. Lawson told reporters that the body was 'beautifully formed', with wide shoulders and a narrow waist. The Somerton man had been strong and robust. His hands and nails showed no sign of having performed manual work – and his large and little toes met close together in a wedge shape, like the toes of a dancer. Adelaide's tireless detectives acted on this latest tip, but could find no dancer to fit the dead man's description.

Shortly after the plaster cast had been made, the mystery man's body was buried in West Terrace Cemetery, under a headstone inscribed:

> *Here lies the unknown man who was found at Somerton Beach, 1st Dec 1948.*

To keep sightseers away, police ensured the service was conducted in secret. And to spare the man a pauper's burial, members of South Australia's Grandstand Bookmakers' Association generously chipped in to provide him with a dignified farewell.

In June 1949, three days after the burial, the City Coroner, Mr T. Cleland, resumed his adjourned inquest into the death. Expert witnesses offered their testimonies for three days. At the end of the hearing the Coroner announced he was unable to say who the man was or how he had died.

The Somerton Beach death has remained a mystery for more than half a century. The questions it raises will probably never be answered.

- Was he a scientist – murdered by Cold War agents (either of the East or West) because he knew too much?
- Did he commit suicide, perhaps in the aftermath of a failed love affair?
- What was the poison that killed him – leaving no trace?
- Who wrote the suspected codes on the back cover of his book of verse? Were they his work – or his killer's?
- And who threw the book into the doctor's car?

If it was the man of mystery himself, we can only speculate on his state of mind when he alighted from the bus in Glenelg and perhaps read, for the last time, the final stanza of his *Rubaiyat*:

> *And when yourself with silver foot shall pass*
> *Among the Guests star-scattered on the grass*
> *And in your joyous errand reach the spot*
> *Where I made One – turn down an empty glass!*

POSTSCRIPT: Thirty-four years after the man-with-no-name was buried, a woman came forward with evidence she had 'not liked' to reveal at the time. While working as a receptionist at the Strathmore Hotel on North Terrace, she had become suspicious of a male guest who was well-dressed and well-spoken. So worried was she by his behaviour that she ordered a search of his room. The only item found by staff was a black medical case, containing what looked like a hypodermic syringe.

The man checked out the day before the discovery of the body on the beach.

In a 1982 interview a newspaper reporter asked why she hadn't contacted police when they were begging for clues. The woman said, 'I had no conclusive proof. And hotel receptionists had to be discreet.'

# Puzzle of the Disappearing Pilot

*On a summer evening in 1978 Melbourne pilot Frederick Valentich radioed flight authorities that he was being 'orbited' by an unidentified aircraft. He said it was radiating a green light. The transmission ended abruptly – with a metallic scraping sound. Neither Valentich, nor any trace of wreckage from his Cessna, were ever found. The young pilot's disappearance is mystery enough. But the Australian government's secretive behaviour has only intensified it ...*

IT WAS A PERFECT EVENING for flying. Wind, light. Cloud high and streaky. Visibility flawless.

Young Fred Valentich couldn't wait to get back into the air. That morning, at the Moonee Ponds disposal store where he worked part-time, he'd told friends (yet again) that the only career he would ever want was to be a commercial pilot. At the age of 20, with a Class Four instrument rating and 200 solo flying hours already on his record, he was well on the way to realising that ambition.

Fred parked his Fiat at Melbourne's Moorabbin airport and walked across to the administration building. He had already filed a flight plan with the briefing officer. It would be a relatively short, simple trip: across Port Phillip Bay to Cape Otway, then over Bass Strait to King Island, where he planned to buy crayfish as a surprise for his parents. He'd flown to the island three times before.

It was 6.15 p.m. on Saturday 21 October 1978. Fred climbed into the cockpit of the VH DSJ Cessna he had rented for the flight. At 6.19 he waved a cheerful farewell, taxied and took off. Everything seemed normal. No-one – Fred undoubtedly included – had an inkling that within hours, this routine journey would become front-page news around the globe.

At 7.00 p.m. Fred radioed Melbourne Flight Service at Tullamarine (Melbourne Airport) to say he was over Cape Otway. Everything was normal and going to plan.

At 7.06 p.m. he radioed again, with a question. Below is what Australian authorities say is the 'complete transcript' of the conversation between Frederick Valentich (DSJ) and Flight Service (FS):

**1906:14**

DSJ: *Melbourne, this is Delta Sierra Juliet. Is there any known traffic below 5,000?*

FS: *Delta Sierra Juliet – no known traffic.*

DSJ: *Delta Sierra Juliet, I am ... seems to be ... large aircraft below 5,000 feet.*

**1906:44**

FS: *Delta Sierra Juliet, what type of aircraft is it?*

DSJ: *I can't confirm. It's four bright – it seems to me like landing lights.*

**1907:00**

FS: *Delta Sierra Juliet.*

**1907:31**

DSJ: *Melbourne, this is Delta Sierra Juliet. The aircraft has just passed over me. At least a thousand feet above.*

FS: *Delta Sierra Juliet, roger – and is it a large aircraft, confirming?*

DSJ: *Unknown, due to the speed it's travelling. Is there any air force aircraft in the vicinity?*

FS: *Delta Sierra Juliet, no known aircraft in the vicinity.*

**1908:18**

DSJ: *Melbourne, it's approaching now, from due east towards me.*

FS: *Delta Sierra Juliet.*

**1908:41**

DSJ: *[Open microphone for 2 seconds]*

**1908:48**

DSJ: *Delta Sierra Juliet. It seems to me that he's flying over me, two, three times at a time, at speeds I couldn't identify.*

**1909:00**

FS: *Delta Sierra Juliet, roger, what is your actual level?*

DSJ: *My level is four and a half thousand ... four five zero zero.*

FS: *Delta Sierra Juliet – and you confirm you cannot identify the aircraft?*

DSJ: *Affirmative.*

FS: *Delta Sierra Juliet, roger, stand by.*

**1909:27**

DSJ: *Melbourne, Delta Sierra Juliet – it's not an aircraft, it's ... [open microphone for 2 seconds].*

**1909:42**

FS: *Delta Sierra Juliet, Melbourne – can you describe the aircraft?*

DSJ: *Delta Sierra Juliet, as it's flying past it's a long shape ... [open microphone for 3 seconds] ... can't identify more than that. It has such speed ... [open microphone for 3 seconds] ... before me right now, Melbourne.*

**1910:00**

FS: *Delta Sierra Juliet, roger. And how large would the object be?*

**1910:19**

DSJ: *It seems like it's stationary.*[1] *What I'm doing right now is orbiting and the thing is just orbiting on top of me also. It's got a green light and sort of metallic [like] it's all shiny on the outside.*

FS: *Delta Sierra Juliet.*

**1910:46**

DSJ: *Delta Sierra Juliet [open microphone for 5 seconds] ... it's just vanished.*

FS: *Delta Sierra Juliet.*

**1911:00**

DSJ: *Melbourne, would you know what kind of aircraft I've got? Is it a military aircraft?*

FS: *Delta Sierra Juliet, confirm the aircraft just vanished?*

DSJ: *Say again?*

FS: *Delta Sierra Juliet, is the aircraft still with you?*

1. Dr Richard Haines, a former NASA research scientist who later investigated the incident, believes Valentich did not say the unidentified craft was 'stationary' – but that it was 'chasing me': an interpretation (albeit a sinister one) that seems more compatible with the pilot's use of the word 'orbiting'.

DSJ: *Delta Sierra Juliet, it's not ... [open microphone for 2 seconds] ... now approaching from the south-west.*

FS: *Delta Sierra Juliet.*

**1911:50**

DSJ: *Delta Sierra Juliet, the engine – it's rough-idling. I've got it set at 23-24 and the thing is ... [coughing].*

FS: *Delta Sierra Juliet, roger. What are your intentions?*

DSJ: *My intentions are – ah – to go to King Island, ah, Melbourne. That strange aircraft is hovering on top of me again. It's [open microphone for 2 seconds] ... hovering and it's not an aircraft.*

FS: *Delta Sierra Juliet.*

**1912:28**

DSJ: *Delta Sierra Juliet. Melbourne ... [open microphone for 17 seconds, accompanied by 'unidentifiable noises' – subsequently described as 'metallic'].*

*End of transmission.*

The foregoing 'complete transcript' was only released after the media had placed intense pressure on Australia's Department of Transport.

Frederick Valentich's disappearance sparked a massive official response. Within minutes of his final radio transmission the Rescue Coordination Centre at Melbourne Airport had sent a light aircraft to conduct a night search of his route. By daybreak, a RAAF Orion (cost $15,000 per hour) and seven other aircraft had joined the operation.

The Australian Coastal Surveillance Organization alerted all ships and fishing vessels to watch for an oil slick, wreckage, or any other sign that the Cessna had crashed into the sea.

Nothing was found.

And this, as many pilots observed, was remarkable in itself. The Cessna was constructed from modular units, specially designed to float in the event of a crash into water. The plane was equipped with four polystyrene lifejackets, coloured orange so they'd easily be seen from the air. Installed aboard was a VHF emergency beacon which, upon impact, automatically transmits a distress signal.

No signal was received.

Most governments go to bizarre lengths to deny the possibility that unidentified flying objects (UFOs) might exist – and the Australian government is no exception. Less than 12 hours after Valentich's disappearance, television and radio news services broadcast the Department of Transport's theories about what probably had happened. The young pilot, the department, surmised, had in all likelihood been flying his plane upside-down. The unidentified craft he imagined he saw was no more than a pattern of reflections in the water, created by light from his own cabin.

This explanation probably satisfied some people – but professional pilots and aviation experts weren't buying it. Typical was Arthur Schutt of Schutt Aviation Company, who told Melbourne's *Sun* newspaper: 'Valentich would have known if his plane had turned upside-down. The carpets would have come off the floor.' Also sceptical was

Valentich's father Guido. 'My son is good at aerobatics,' he said. 'He'd have known immediately if his flight position was wrong.'

And pilots were quick to point out that the Cessna 182L has a gravity-fed fuel system with a vertical carburettor float. This would have blocked fuel flow to the engine within 60 seconds of a pilot inverting the plane. The allegedly complete transcript has Valentich talking to Melbourne for more than six minutes. This conversation could not have occurred if the plane were upside-down, because it would have crashed into the sea long before.

The fruitless search for Fred Valentich and his Cessna lasted five days and covered 5,000 square nautical miles. The disappearance was not an isolated incident.

On Sunday 22 October 1978, less than 12 hours after Valentich's final transmission, a passenger aircraft with nine passengers aboard vanished over the Solomon Islands. The RAAF helped in an intensive search – but no trace of the plane was found.

AS THE ARCHIVES of the Melbourne *Age*, *Herald* and *Sun News-Pictorial* confirm – strangely similar aircraft disappearances had occurred over Bass Strait more than 40 years earlier. On 19 October 1934 the mailplane *Miss Hobart*, carrying ten passengers across Bass Strait from Launceston to Melbourne, inexplicably vanished from the sky. The aircraft, a DH 86 fitted with four Gipsy V1 engines, was one of the most powerful planes in Australian service. The owners, Holyman's Airways Pty Ltd, said that even if two of the engines had failed, the pilot could have maintained height with a full load.

As in the Valentich case, the weather was perfect. At 10.20 a.m., when *Miss Hobart* was 13 kilometres from Wilson's Promontory, the co-pilot, Gilbert Jenkins, radioed: 'Everything OK. Captain Holyman requests that Captain Haig of the Vacuum Oil Company meet him at Laverton at 11.30 a.m.' The rendezvous was never kept.

An intensive search by four aircraft, among them a flying boat, and several ships, including the battleship HMAS *Australia*, produced no result.

The newspapers described peculiar phenomena surrounding the disappearance. Two Public Works Department surveyors, A.C. Campbell and R. Henry, told the *Age* that at about 10.20 a.m. they were working 20 kilometres north of the Wilson's Promontory Lighthouse when they heard the drone of a plane suddenly stop. 'We often saw the mailplane pass,' said Mr Henry. 'We expected it, as usual, to come around a point of Mt Oberon. But instead, the engine sound ceased abruptly and we saw nothing. We're positive it was the sound of an aeroplane engine because everything was so still and the sky was clear and sunny.'

On 22 October 1934 the *Age* published an interview with J. Millington, of the collier Kooliga. At 7.30 p.m. on Friday, nine hours after *Miss Hobart* vanished, he had been at the vessel's helm when he and the crew saw 'a flare' – huge, white and motionless – over the sea. This 'flare' burned for about four seconds. Ten minutes later a second light, with a 'distinct pinkish colour' appeared – vanishing after about two seconds. The ship changed course in the hope of helping survivors, but found nothing. On the same page the *Age* ruled out any possibility survivors had been signalling. 'Pilot K. Frewin, who has piloted the *Miss Hobart*, was positive last night that no flares were carried in the missing liner,' the paper reported. He was equally definite that emergency flares could not have been improvised from petrol and paper ...'

That evening the Melbourne *Herald* described another mysterious phenomenon. A witness in Mount Best said that at about the time of the plane's disappearance she saw 'a peculiar cloud low down near the water, some distance out at sea'.

On 2 October 1935, less than a year after the loss of *Miss Hobart*, another airliner, *The Loina*, was lost over Bass Strait. The plane left Melbourne's Essendon Airport for Western Junction, Tasmania, at 8.15 a.m. The lighthouse-keeper saw her over Wilson's Promontory at about 9.00 a.m.

At 9.35 a.m. the captain, A.N. Evans, radioed: 'Due to arrive Flinders Island 9.55.' At 9.51 a.m. he radioed again: 'Approaching Emita [a small Flinders Island township]. Height 1,000 feet. On course.136 degrees closing down.'

It was the last message *Loina* would ever send.

Later that day, mystified searchers retrieved, from south-west of Settlement Point, three twisted chairs and a petrol tank so extraordinarily telescoped that it suggested the plane had nose-dived at colossal speed, shattering to splinters on impact. Despite air and sea searches lasting almost a week, the rest of the aircraft, and its two pilots and three passengers were nowhere to be found.

On 3 October 1935 the *Age* published an interview with Mr Murray Jones, managing director of the De Havilland Company. When the reporter asked if he had any explanation for *Loina*'s fate, Mr Jones said: 'There is no explanation'.

In the disappearances of the *Miss Hobart* (1934), *The Loina* (1935) and Frederick Valentich's DSJ Cessna (1978), there is a pattern that spans the decades:

All the vanishings occurred in the month of October. All were surrounded by bizarre phenomena – and characterised by a radio transmission, followed by silence. Aboard the three planes that disappeared was a total of 18 people. Their bodies were never found. No clothes or personal possessions were ever recovered.

When Frederick Valentich disappeared, I (the author of this book) was a special writer with the *Australian* newspaper. Like many other journalists at that time I was looking for a breakthrough in the mystery. One scrap of intriguing – but, as it transpired, unprovable – information was offered to me by a pilot I knew socially. 'I believe the public should know this,' he said. 'One of my best friends works at Moorabbin airfield. He says personnel were approached by government officials who told them a pilot had been lost and that there might be rumours about a UFO, and they were not to talk to the press or anyone else about those rumours. And particularly, they weren't to disclose the plane's registration.

'This all happened, remember, before someone leaked the news to a radio station. My friend asked one of the officials what had happened. The official would only say that the pilot had gone missing after reporting that he was being chased by a UFO – *and that the conversation between him and Flight Service Unit had lasted half an hour.'*

Several weeks after this talk, I was presented with something closer to hard evidence in the Valentich case. Paul Norman, an American engineer who was devoting his retirement years to UFO investigation, came to my office with six photographs.

The pictures had been taken by a plumbing contractor, Roy Manifold, on the evening of Saturday 21 October 1978 – 20 minutes before Frederick Valentich radioed that an unidentified aircraft was orbiting him. Roy had walked down to the beach from his cabin to capture images of the sunset over the water. Using an Olympic tripod camera he took his shots at intervals of roughly 20 seconds – an estimate borne out by the sun's position in the six photographs.

Roy Manifold had no idea there was anything unusual on his negatives – until his wife Brenda collected the prints from a Kodak outlet several weeks later.

The first three pictures showed a normal sunset. On the fourth picture a sudden turbulence erupted from behind a rock in the calm sea. In the fifth picture the water was seemingly calm again. In the sixth picture a strange object could be seen streaking upward from the ocean and into the sky in a visible blur of speed.

Brenda immediately recalled that her husband had taken the photographs on the same evening Frederick Valentich disappeared, just two kilometres away from the Manifold family's holiday cabin. She wondered whether the object streaking across the frame could be the same UFO the young pilot had reported.

Roy Manifold, an experienced amateur photographer with thousands of pictures to his credit, looked for a more mundane explanation. He took the prints and negatives back to Kodak and asked whether there might have been a technical glitch. Kodak investigated – and pronounced that there were no faults in either the negatives or the emulsion. He took his snaps to fellow photographers and friends in photo stores. Most tended to agree that his picture showed a solid object, moving extremely fast. An object from whose 'nose' flowed a trail of 'blue stars'.

I took the Manifold negatives to Mike Arthur, the *Australian*'s chief photographer. After producing a series of 300-magnification prints he said: 'I have to agree with Kodak. There's no fault in the negative. No flaw in the emulsion.' He called to his fellow photographers. 'Come and see this. It's some kind of solid object, moving through the sky.'

Next morning the sixth Manifold photograph appeared on page one of the *Australian* and in newspapers around the world. The RAAF promptly debunked the picture, saying it was nothing more than 'a cumulus cloud in its dying stages'. (There were stratus clouds over the Strait that night – none of them moving in a blur of speed.)

A group of aerospace engineers and physicists with the American organization Ground Saucer Watch did considerably more work in analysing the pictures and had the final say. Their critique, based on computer analysis including digital densitometry, concluded: 'The object is extremely bright when compared with other features in the photographs. Judging from the intensely reflective area at its "top" it was possibly metallic in construction. Distance factoring shows the object was about 1.6 kilometres from the camera and about six metres in diameter. This is an image of a bona fide unidentified flying object of moderate dimensions, apparently surrounded by a cloudlike exhaust or vapour residue.'

Rumours proliferated in the days that followed Fred Valentich's disappearance. One journalist theorised that he might have been the unwitting casualty of a secret weapons test. Others suggested that he had committed suicide – or flown off to start a new life somewhere. The scuttlebutt saddened and angered his family and the people who had known him. In a newspaper interview, one of Fred's RAAF supervisors, Squadron Leader Ronald Grandy, said he was a happy young man of excellent character, who had been 'handpicked as an air training instructor, because he was no fool'. As he had been consumed with ambition to become a commercial pilot, it was hard to see why he'd suddenly give it all away. And the suicide theory failed for even more compelling reasons. If Valentich had crashed the Cessna into Bass Strait, its buoyant modules – and probably his body – would quickly have been recovered.

From the beginning the Australian government played an elusive and enigmatic role in the affair:

- Valentich's devoted girlfriend Rhonda Rushton told me (and other journalists) that officials had ordered her not to speak to the media ... She ignored this instruction –

believing, along with the Valentich family, that publicity might, somehow, help Frederick to return. Rhonda and the family continued for years to believe he might still be alive.

- Authorities refused to allow journalists or other outside observers to listen to, or analyse, the actual tape of Valentich's final radio transmission. The official argument was that details of an interchange between a pilot and Flight Service Unit had never been released before – and that the typed transcript had only been made public because of unprecedented public concern. But many pilots and other aircraft personnel were unconvinced. They believed the typed sheets were probably a drastically shortened and censored version of what Frederick Valentich actually said.
- Puzzlingly the Department of Transport did not release its official report on the Valentich case until 1981 – two and a half years after his disappearance.
- And the Valentich family were unable to access Frederick's bank account until 1988 – 10 years after he vanished.

In science, a single experiment demonstrates nothing. Only repeated experiments can prove a case. By analogy, a similar rule applies to the Valentich disappearance. It was not a one-off incident. I've already enumerated two long-term historical precedents for the 1978 case – but there are others, much closer in time:

## The Green Light

In the official transcript of his conversation with FSU Frederick Valentich says: '... the thing is just orbiting on top of me also. It's got a green light ...'

Five years earlier (19 October 1973, 2.05 p.m. Melbourne time) Captain Lawrence J. Coyne and three crew members were flying in a US Army helicopter over Mansfield Ohio, en route to Cleveland at about 450 metres when a long object suddenly approached them from the south-east – zooming toward their craft on an apparent collision course. Just as Coyne and his companions were preparing for disaster the UFO stopped in front of them. It had a red light on its nose, a white light at the tail and a green light below.

The long object shone the green light on the helicopter. A pyramid-shaped green glow lit up the cabin. The object itself also glowed green. In a subsequent debriefing Coyne and the crewmen said the UFO was about 18 metres long and 5.4 metres wide. When Coyne checked his altimeter it showed 3,000 feet (900 metres). 'We'd gone from 1500 feet [450 metres] to 3000 feet in a matter of seconds, without knowing it,' Captain Coyne said. The helicopter was jolted and buffeted by turbulence before he regained control and was able to bring it down.

All observers – in the helicopter and on the ground – agreed that the green object had been exerting some kind of 'pull' on the craft. Seconds later, it vanished.

## A Previous Attack on a Cessna

Frederick Valentich was not the first 20-year-old Cessna pilot to be confronted by an unidentified craft. Seventeen months earlier (5 May 1977) Manuel Jose Ojeda, 20, a flying student at Bogota, Colombia, managed to land after being blinded by lights from a UFO. His 50-minute ordeal in a Cessna 150 was followed by an estimated 150,000 radio listeners as control tower operators talked him down.

The drama began at 10.00 a.m. when Ojeda began training manoeuvres. During a tight turn his Cessna began to vibrate violently. Hovering beside him was an oval object about 18 metres in diameter, ablaze with high-intensity phosphorescent light. All the plane's instruments swung to zero. The object, which now resembled 'an aluminium mass' moved beneath the Cessna's landing gear. After an initial radio failure, Ojeda managed to describe the emergency to the control tower. As he did so, the UFO swung up into his field of vision (*Valentich: The thing is just orbiting on top of me ...*) The young pilot began to lose his sight and to fly wildly in circles.

From the airfield, aerodrome personnel watched the object streak away. Then, as the city held its breath, ground controllers, helped by two Aero Andes planes, guided Ojeda to the runway – but not before he had twice come close to colliding with the tower. The pilot was taken to hospital, where he regained his sight after several hours.

## The King Island Overture

Frederick Valentich's destination had been King Island. For several weeks before his disappearance, the local paper, *King Island News*, was full of reports from residents describing strange lights and shapes in the sky. Many of these incidents were reported to Sergeant Jack Woodward at Currie police station and Sergeant Bruniewood at Grassy. A typical article appeared in the weekly's 27 September issue, 24 days before the alleged Bass Strait encounter. Under the heading 'More Strange Sightings' the newspaper described how fisherman George Newman and his sons Peter, 20, and Neil, 16, had chased a 'bright white oval light' until it vanished behind the butter factory.

On 20 September the *King Island News* had published a letter from a family who claimed that a glowing object had 'paced' their car along an island road.

## Mysteries Over the Sea

A study of major Victorian newspapers in the year preceding the Valentich disappearance reveals an unusually large number of 'unidentified object' reports.

On 1 January 1978 Melbourne's *Sunday Observer* described a series of perplexing sightings of a 'bright white light' hovering about 30 kilometres out to sea from Cape Otway Lighthouse. The appearances began in early December 1977 and continued for two months.

Witnesses included holidaymakers, fishermen, schoolteachers and local police. Among the first people to notice the apparently huge object were a group of teachers on vacation at Lorne. They phoned the keeper of Otway Lighthouse to say the light was hovering at what seemed to be 30 kilometres out to sea. The lighthouse keeper saw it too.

The crew of the fishing boat *Random Harvest* subsequently reported that they had been 'buzzed' by the light which they said was of 'gigantic size'. An Apollo Bay man said he had found large areas of flattened grass shortly after he saw a pattern of strange lights in the sky.

On 2 October 1978, Melbourne dailies reported that Jim Dillon, a security officer at Renison Limited tin mine, had seen a reddish ball with a long tail moving swiftly across the sky on Wednesday night and early Saturday morning. He said that at about 11.15 p.m. that Wednesday he was driving to work along the Zeehan Highway when the object appeared, flying to his right. It disappeared behind Mt Dundas.

On 20 October, the day before the engine in Frederick Valentich's Cessna began to rough-idle, a glowing object interfered with the electrical system of Bill Guest's motorbike. Mr Guest, of Poowong, Victoria, reported that he first glimpsed the object – which was sitting in a paddock – at about 2.30 a.m., as he was riding to Wonthaggi. 'The thing was in the grass, about 15 metres from the Loch Road,' he said. 'I stopped my bike and turned the headlight onto it. It was big – about 20 metres long – and phosphorescent and glowing in the darkness. I couldn't see any markings on it. I stood there staring for about 20 minutes, trying to get up the courage to go closer.

'Then I heard a car approaching and turned to look down

the road. When I turned back the thing had risen into the air and seemed to be moving toward me. My bike's headlight began to flicker. Now the object had become disc-shaped and was kind of spiralling in front of me. I got out of there!'

## Airliner 'Under Threat'

On 10 September 1978 a commercial airliner had a close aerial encounter near Engadine, New South Wales. The plane had taken off only minutes earlier from Kingsford Smith Airport. The captain suddenly found himself on a collision course with what he described as a UFO. He reported that it veered aside at the last moment. The captain was debriefed at considerable length. Air Traffic Control would provide no further details, but did confirm that the RAAF was investigating the case.

## The October 21 Witnesses

Did anyone see anything unusual on the day Frederick Valentich vanished? Melbourne's *Herald* newspaper, helped by investigators from the Victorian UFO Research Society, asked this question several days after the disappearance. The response was large.

Dozens of people, unknown to each other and in widely-separated areas around Victoria's coast, offered similar descriptions of one round object and two silvery cigar-shaped objects, apparently joined together, moving slowly through the air with no apparent means of propulsion. On the day Frederick Valentich reported his 'unidentified aircraft', these UFOs were reported from Currie, King Island

(2.00 p.m.), Geelong (2.55 p.m.), Cape Otway (4.15 p.m.), Frankston (7.15 p.m.), and Warrnambool (9.00 p.m.)

The objects over Geelong were described by 14 witnesses on a tennis court, a woman and her son in a car near Cape Otway and all members of a cricket team.

In the coastal suburb of Frankston a mother was driving with her children across railway lines. They saw something enormous in the sky – 'like an overblown skyrocket'. This was at 7.15 p.m. – three minutes after Valentich's radio transmission ceased.

What really happened to Frederick Valentich?

Did he fake his own death – miraculously managing to conceal the Cessna so perfectly that it would never be found?

Was he the victim of a secret weapon test that went wrong?

Or was he ensnared by some dark force whose nature and motivation we can only imagine?

No one can honestly claim to have a definitive answer to these questions.

In Australia's federal parliament on 26 October 1978 the then-Transport Minister, Peter Nixon, was asked what he knew about the young pilot's fate. He replied: *'This is one of the few times I am caught short for words ... All I can say is that is it a mystery and looks like remaining a mystery.'*

## Did a Regiment Really Vanish at Gallipoli?

Something exceedingly strange happened at Gallipoli, the scene of Australia's most celebrated battle. Or so the believers insist ...

The uncanny incident allegedly occurred on 28 August 1915 – and was witnessed by the 22 members of the New Zealand Engineers Number One Field Company. Three of the men, Sappers F. Eichardt, J. Newman and R. Newnes, swore an affidavit describing what they claimed to have seen. They wrote:

> *The incident happened ... in the morning, during the final days of the fighting at Hill 60, Suvla Bay.*
>
> *The day broke clear as any beautiful Mediterranean day could be expected to be. The exception was six or eight loaf-of-bread-shaped clouds, all exactly alike, hovering over Hill 60. Despite a four-to-five mile an hour breeze, these clouds did not drift away.*
>
> *Also stationary, and resting on the ground underneath these clouds, was a similar cloud. It was grey and almost solid-looking, straddling a dry creek bed.*
>
> *A British regiment, the First Fourth Norfolk, was then seen marching up the creek bed towards Hill 60. When they arrived at the cloud, they marched*

*straight into it, without hesitation. After the last of the file had disappeared into it, this cloud very unobtrusively lifted off the ground, and, as any fog or cloud would, rose until it joined the other clouds.*

*At this time, the group of clouds had been hovering in one place, but as soon as the 'ground' cloud had risen to their level, they all moved away northward towards Thrace (Bulgaria). In 45 minutes they had all disappeared from view.*

When Turkey surrendered in 1918 Britain (assuming the missing regimental members had been taken prisoner) demanded they be returned. However the Turks insisted that they knew nothing about the men. This claim was supported by the New Zealand witnesses, who wrote: 'Those who observed the incident vouch for the fact that Turkey never captured that regiment, nor made contact with it.'

# Was Tubby Tom a Baronet – or a Butcher?

*Tom Castro was a fat, roughly-spoken butcher from Wagga Wagga, New South Wales. For having the effrontery to claim that he was heir to one of England's richest estates, he was found guilty of perjury – and jailed for 14 years. But Castro went to his grave insisting that he was indeed the true Sir Roger Tichborne, lost at sea in 1854. Lady Henrietta Tichborne passionately believed he was her son – and the family doctor (braving the fury of money-hungry relatives) testified in court that 'a rare defect of the penis' proved the meat-vending pretender's right to the family fortune. Today, some scholars wonder whether the disgraced Tichborne claimant was genuine after all ...*

THE NEWSPAPER ADVERTISEMENT, authorised by Lady Henrietta Felicite Seymour Tichborne, was placed in several dozen Australian newspapers. It read:

> *A handsome reward will be given to any person who can furnish such information as will discover the fate of ROGER CHARLES TICHBORNE. He sailed from Rio de Janeiro on the 20th of April 1854 in the ship La Bella and has never been heard of since, but a report reached England to the effect that a portion of the crew and passengers was picked up by a vessel bound to Australia, Melbourne it is believed. It is not known whether the said Roger Charles Tichborne was among the drowned or saved. He would at the present time be thirty-two years of age, is of a delicate constitution, rather tall, with very light brown hair and blue eyes. Mr Tichborne is the son of Sir James Tichborne, now deceased, and is heir to all his estates.*

Among the journals in which this announcement appeared was the Melbourne *Argus*. It came to the attention of Stephen Gibbes, a New South Wales solicitor, who in turn showed it to one of his clients, a bankrupt butcher who called himself Tom Castro. The pair conferred, reportedly at some length. Next day Gibbes guardedly replied to the advertisement, revealing that he had 'spotted R.C.

Tichborne', who was in good health and residing in Wagga Wagga.

Thus, in October 1865, began the greatest case of disputed identity in British legal history.

Roger Tichborne's mother, Lady Henrietta, was descended from the Bourbon dynasty. Like many of her class she detested England and the English – not least her husband's family. As a young wife, after learning that she was pregnant, she had insisted on giving birth to the child in her native Paris. While his disgruntled father got on with managing the vast Tichborne estates, young Roger grew up as a Parisian, speaking little other than French for the first 15 years of his life. When, at Sir James Tichborne's insistence, Roger finally returned to England to attend a strict Jesuit school, he spoke in a thick foreign accent.

This fact was to play a crucial role in the controversy which, in the years ahead, would consume and almost bankrupt the Tichborne family.

Roger Tichborne grew up to be a rebel, with scant interest in living the easeful life of a baronet-in-waiting. At 25, against his distressed family's wishes, he bought himself a ticket to Chile. He spent two years exploring South America – describing his adventures in long letters to his anxious mother, to whom he also sent parcels containing stuffed birds and the skins of exotic animals.

Then, tiring of primitive locales, he bought a second ocean ticket, this time aboard the schooner *La Bella*, which on 30 April 1854 set sail from Rio de Janeiro for New York. The vessel was never heard from again. The sole trace of her was an upturned long boat surrounded by floating furniture and packing cases. An inquest declared that *La Bella*'s passengers and crew had been lost at sea. Like all the others, Roger Tichborne was presumed dead.

But no-one could convince Lady Henrietta that the court's finding was correct. She knew, sensed, felt it in her bones that her son had escaped the wreck – and was still alive. Somewhere. By 1862, the year her husband died, she was expecting Roger to arrive home at any moment and had ordered the servants to keep a welcoming light burning every night at the entrance to Tichborne Hall.

This was the emotional maelstrom into which Tom, the Wagga butcher, was about to launch himself.

Solicitor Stephen Gibbes was not promoting his client's cause on a whim. Since his arrival in the tiny provincial town three years earlier, Tom Castro had been telling virtually anyone who would listen that he was heir not only to a title but to a vast fortune. He had assumed a pseudonym and settled in Australia, he claimed, because the duties imposed upon him by his exalted position were too onerous to bear. He preferred to live as a simple working man. Most people, including Gibbes, had dismissed these assertions as mere snobbish fantasies. But when the *Argus* published Lady Henrietta's advertisement, everything seemed suddenly to fit. Castro must, without a shadow of doubt, be the wealthy young baronet, Sir Roger Tichborne.

If Gibbes needed further assurance, it was provided by his client. During a series of long, argumentative meetings, Castro adamantly refused to say whether he was or was not the 10th baronet. His whole reluctant and elusive demeanour suggested that he was anxious to retain his Australian anonymity – and was alarmed at the thought of returning to his illustrious duties in England. At one point, in a rough, grating accent – an accent which Gibbes now believed to be assumed – he enquired, 'If I was a baronet, would I have wed a serving girl?' (Castro had married an illiterate domestic, Mary Ann Bryant, and had three children by her.)

Convinced that coarse, boozy, toothless Tom was trying to deny his aristocratic destiny, Gibbes dogged him daily around Wagga. He begged him to accept his responsibilities; to write to Lady Henrietta to say that this was Roger, her beloved son, who had survived the shipwreck and was now living incognito above a meat shop. There was nothing selfless about the solicitor's actions. Butcher Tom owed him a great deal of money – and here was a chance to see the debt repaid. With interest.

At last, under the solicitor's intense pressure, Tom Castro cracked. Painfully, he composed a semi-literate letter to the Dowager lady, sending his love and claiming the title and the Tichborne estates. He revealed that he was bankrupt and needed money to return to England. He signed the letter, 'Your dutifull [sic] son Roger'. The message, accompanied by a covering note from solicitor Gibbes and bearing his wax seal, was despatched to Tichborne Hall by sailship and swift horse courier.

The Dowager was unimpressed. She did not reply to Tom Castro, but instead wrote a sharp note to Gibbes and his associate Ronald Cubitt, owner of a 'missing friends' agency:

*You give no details whatever about the person you believe to be my son. You do not name even the town where he resides, and you say nothing about the way he was saved from the shipwreck.*

If the pair could provide these details, she added, she might send £200 to buy a passage to England for Castro and his family. But she would settle none of his debts. First, she would require proof that they were mother and son.

Gibbes told the butcher he would have to do better. He must write Lady Henrietta a letter that contained less about his desperate need for cash and more about his filial devotion to her. Castro, who, by this time, had begun to look forward to inheriting the ninth-largest fortune in England, took the advice. He wrote again to the Dowager, saying that a ship named *Osprey* had rescued him from the wreckage of *La Bella*, bringing him to Melbourne in July 1854. Dazed and ill, he had changed his identity, hoping that by so doing he might forget the horrors he had suffered. But now, touched by his mother's need as expressed in her advertisement, he wanted to become Roger again – and return to the bosom of the Tichborne family.

Lady Henrietta, desperate to believe her son had been found, responded more warmly than before. She wrote again (still not to Castro, but again to Gibbes and Cubitt) recommending that they introduce 'the Claimant' to a former family servant, an African named Andrew Bogle. This trusted retainer, rescued from slavery by Edward Doughty Tichborne, had been a valet to young Roger's uncle

– and would be able instantly to identify him. Bogle was living in Sydney, on a pension provided by the Tichborne family.

Convinced that they were making a sensible investment, Gibbes and Cubitt gave Tom Castro the fare north. The result exceeded their expectations. Sydney's newspapers, which had learned (or been tipped off) that a baronet was on the way from Wagga, splashed the story. From the moment he arrived, Castro, his butcher's apron superseded by an expensive suit, was feted by socially ambitious colonials.

At dinner parties given in his honour the fat aristocrat told his hordes of new friends that he could hardly wait to go 'home' and to take up his 'responsibilities' – the vast estates he had inherited from his illustrious father, the ninth baronet, Sir James Tichborne. The infatuated circle of sycophants revelled in this grand talk – even though it was delivered in an accent more redolent of the gutter than of the mansion. And when Castro–Sir Roger mentioned that he was temporarily embarrassed for money, admirers mobbed him with cheques and fistfuls of cash.

Solicitor Gibbes soon learned about the relative riches being pressed upon his client – and hurried to Sydney to place everything on a legal basis. Through banks and merchants he arranged thousands of pounds in lines of credit for Sir Roger Tichborne (accompanied by a handsome solicitor's commission each time). It seemed that nobody could do enough for the visiting baronet. If he drank at an inn, it was 'on the house'. Restaurant owners refused to accept payment for meals. It was their privilege to serve a member of the aristocracy – and it would be reward enough to erect a sign saying he had dined at their tables.

But the best was yet to come. When Tom Castro was introduced to Andrew Bogle, the elderly Tichborne retainer immediately recognized him. The claimant's knowledge of the Tichborne family and of their estates was so precise and detailed, Bogle wrote to Lady Henrietta, that only a fool would think him a mountebank.

Was the old man telling the truth? The majority of historians, who dismiss Castro as a fraud, say no. Although he had been generously pensioned off by the Tichbornes, Andrew Bogle felt that they had cruelly discarded him at the end of his working life. After decades of service in one of England's finest mansions, surrounded by sweeping parkland, he regarded Sydney as a squalid, depressing place. He saw Castro as a means to return to England and the grand lifestyle to which he was accustomed. He offered Castro his services as a valet (and, insist the sceptics, a tutor in the Tichborne family's affairs). Castro hired him.

By contrast, Castro's supporters believe Bogle was sincere. He was only one of scores of people who would eventually testify that the ballooning butcher was the young Sir Roger. Among the earliest of those witnesses was Tichborne Park's former head gardener Michael Guilfoyle, who had also retired to Sydney. In a letter to the Dowager he wrote: 'I will swear upon all things that this is the Sir Roger I knew well.'

That was enough for the Dowager. In a ferment of maternal emotion she wrote to Castro accepting him as her son.

On 2 September 1866, Tom Castro, his wife Mary Anne

and their children sailed out of Sydney, first-class, for the Old Country. Behind them they left £18,000 in bad debts, run up in a mere 14 weeks of extravagant living.

On arrival in London, the claimant to the baronetcy and his family moved into luxurious accommodation provided by the Dowager: Essex Lodge in Croydon. Lady Henrietta was not there to greet them. She sent word that, after they were rested, they should sail to France (where she preferred to live) for the longed-for reunion. She advised Castro–Sir Roger to stay away in the meantime from her late husband's relatives, who were unanimously disgruntled about losing their share of the family fortune.

The Dowager arranged to meet her long-lost son at a Paris hotel. Castro, almost disabled by the gross weight-gain his recent high living had brought about, tried at the last moment to cancel the confrontation. Only that morning, he had passed a tapeworm 14 metres long – and he was feeling nervous and queasy. Optimistic though his nature was, this quivering man-mountain of fat gravely doubted that Lady Henrietta could possibly believe he was her once-slim young son. He instructed a servant to tell his mother he was too ill to see her. The avid Dowager took no notice. Bursting into the hotel room, closely followed by her senior legal adviser, she shrieked with joy at the sight of the sick butcher sprawled on the bed. 'It is Roger!' she announced, as she stooped to embrace him. 'See? He has his father's chin and forehead and his ears are exactly like his uncle's!'

Excitedly, Lady Henrietta began to chatter at her 'son' in French – the language Roger had solely spoken for the first 15 years of his life. Apart from the occasional 'oui' or 'non' Castro was unable to reply – but he had a ready excuse. In the aftermath of *La Bella*'s sinking, he explained, he had suffered 'brain fever', possibly exacerbated by a fall aboard the *Osprey*, the ship that had rescued him. This, combined with a fall from a horse during his first weeks in Australia, had affected his concentration. Over time he had realised that the blow to his skull must have erased large parts of his memory, along with any knowledge of French.

The Dowager was deeply sympathetic. Her poor boy had suffered so much. But from today she would do all in her power to restore him to a happy and privileged life and to the full possession of his memories. She would begin the process by reintroducing him to Parisian friends who had known him as a young man. Thus began a bizarre procession of visitors to the flinching Tom Castro's room. Not one of them believed that the bulky butcher was the handsome young Roger they had known. Typical was the reaction of the aristocrat's tutor, Monsieur Chatillon. The moment he entered and glimpsed the flabby giant panting on the bed he turned to Lady Henrietta and exclaimed: 'It is not he, madam! This person could never have been Sir Roger.'

But the Dowager refused to listen – defending Tom Castro far more ably than he could have done himself. 'What did you expect?' she asked the objectors. 'To find in this bed the same young man you knew so many years ago? He has been in a terrible shipwreck, he has lived among the savage people of Australia, his failure of memory and his distress have driven him to excessive use of drink. Of course he looks different! Of course his body is ruined. But he is still my son – and I love him.'

In the face of Lady Henrietta's almost religious belief that her boy had been restored to her, the doubters fell silent. But members of the great Tichborne family were not to be similarly cowed. When Tom Castro returned to London, the happy recipient of a £1,000-per-annum bridging allowance from his doting 'mother', he came under almost immediate legal bombardment. Solicitors representing various branches of the Tichborne family pestered him daily with legal questionnaires, letting him know that they would, as soon as practicable, be instituting court proceedings to prevent him, an impostor, succeeding to the baronetcy. If family members had their way he would not be receiving one penny of Sir James Tichborne's money.

Additional threats were rained upon Castro by his disillusioned former admirers in Sydney. These disgruntled creditors employed their own squads of solicitors and collectors to dun him for settlement of the huge debts he had run up while strutting about as a baronet-to-be. A lesser man might have been tempted to flee from all this hostility. But the embattled butcher not only stood his ground – he began a crusade to prove to the British population that he was the rightful heir to the Tichborne estates.

As a tactic to sway any future jury, Castro employed writers to place glowing articles about him in the yellow press. Many of these stories quoted witnesses who swore on their lives that they recognised him as Sir Roger. Other articles pointed an accusing finger at the Tichborne family, claiming they had promised to call off their threatened legal proceedings if Castro shared the fortune with them.

This was the first major public relations campaign ever conducted in England. And it succeeded brilliantly. The Tichborne case quickly became much more than a mere squabble over money and a title. The man in the mean street began to see it as a struggle between a ruthlessly powerful aristocracy and a lonely, courageous fighter (Castro) who had dared to desert his class and join the underdogs.

The Tichbornes became nervous. The popular press was overwhelmingly against them. Some family members complained they had been booed in the street. And the powerful Lady Henrietta had threatened several vulnerable relatives with the withdrawal of financial privileges.

To add to the family's problems, the evidence supporting Tom Castro continued to grow. The MP Gilbert Onslow, who had known Sir Roger as a boy, announced to a newspaper, 'I have had the privilege of meeting the person who has adopted the name of Mr Castro and can say without the smallest shadow of doubt that he is the Roger Tichborne that I knew intimately in his youth.'

But the clincher was the pretender's peculiar penis.

In June 1867 Tom Castro agreed to undergo a complete physical examination by one of the Tichborne family's principal physicians, Dr Lipscombe. The doctor, who had often attended Sir Roger before his departure for South America, wrote a medical report that set prim Victorian-era journalists scrambling desperately for euphemisms.

Lipscombe attested that he had known every scar and

blemish on the young Roger's body. The same imperfections (albeit stretched) were present on the fat butcher's flesh. But even more conclusive was the fact that Sir Roger had been afflicted by 'a rare defect of the penis.' Like a horse's member, it nestled inside the patient's body – only becoming visible when erect. Tom Castro was cursed by precisely the same penile problem. The two men were one and the same.

With almost daily 'proofs' of Castro's claims appearing in the press, the nobly-born Tichbornes began to despair. How could they ever hope for a fair trial when the matter was constantly pre-judged in the newspapers? Lawyers urged that a case be launched as soon as possible. But the family procrastinated. Lady Henrietta was in poor health. The strain of court proceedings might kill her. And if she survived, she would seek vengeance. Best to wait. To think. To do nothing just yet.

In March 1868, Lady Henrietta resolved the dilemma by dying of heart failure. With the Dowager's dying breath Tom Castro lost his most important ally and the £1,000 a year she had been paying him. The family moved in for the kill. They instructed their solicitors to begin a Chancery suit, Tichborne versus Castro, to prevent the upstart from taking possession of Lady Henrietta's property. It was open to Castro to launch counter-proceedings – but family members were sure he wouldn't dare.

They had reason to be confident. For the previous 14 months, Tichborne-funded private detectives had been scouring Australia and South America in search of evidence against the fortune-hunting butcher. They found plenty – and it seemed damning. Tom Castro, the investigators reported, was actually a Londoner named Arthur Orton, who had migrated to Tasmania in the 1850s. After running up several hundred pounds in unpaid debts he had fled to Wagga Wagga – changing his name to Castro to throw creditors off the trail.

The detectives even produced a man who (for a fee) would testify in court that he was the claimant's brother, Charles Orton. This unpleasant individual claimed that he had been blackmailing his sibling for a 'hush' fee of £5 per week. When the £1,000 annuity dried up, Arthur Orton, alias Castro, had been unable to continue the payments, so Charles had sought a reward elsewhere. With the Dowager safely dead, the Tichbornes gleefully released these damaging details to the press.

But Tom Castro was not defeated yet. His tame journalists sent stories to the newspapers claiming that the greedy Tichbornes had had Lady Henrietta poisoned to prevent him, her true son, inheriting the estates. Castro's legal advisers subsequently arranged a public meeting between their client and the man who claimed to be his brother. To the Tichborne family's dismay, Charles Orton stared searchingly at Castro, then announced: 'No, this man is not my brother. I was mistaken.' He then signed an affidavit to that effect.

The claimant's lawyers and press-manipulators stuck firmly by him – less out of loyalty than in the hope of being well-rewarded when he gained control of his fortune. But in the interim, money was an increasing problem. Castro had considerable daily expenses and no income – a problem his advisers temporarily solved by persuading the public to invest in his future prospects. At rallies around the nation, the claimant, red-faced and sweating, urged working people to buy Tichborne Bonds, which would yield them rich dividends when he won his inheritance. The crowds, who had been tutored to see the affair as a political struggle between the lower classes and the aristocracy, bought bonds by the tens of thousands.

On 23 June 1868, counsel for a cashed-up Castro launched litigation in the Court of Common Pleas. Its purpose: to determine whether or not the claimant was Sir James Doughty Tichborne's heir. Appearing for Thomas Castro was Dr Edward Kenneally QC. The Tichborne family's team was headed by the Solicitor-General of England, Sir John Coleridge.

It would be the longest-running legal action in British history – holding that record for more than a century, until it was exceeded by the even-more protracted McLibel Case of 1996.

The proceedings aroused such intense interest that would-be spectators queued for hours in the hope of obtaining a seat in the public gallery. Lyricist W.S. Gilbert obsessively collected all the press clippings and used them as the basis for his and Sir Arthur Sullivan's operetta *Trial by Jury.* American author Samuel Clemens, writing as Mark Twain, used several witnesses as models for characters in *Huckleberry Finn.*

From the beginning the hearings seemed to demonstrate the imprecise and shifting nature of 'truth'. Dr Kenneally argued that every mother knows her own child – and that Lady Henrietta had been adamant that 'Tom Castro' was the son to whom she had given birth. How could she – or any mother – be mistaken? Sir John Coleridge promptly raised doubt about the Dowager's mental fitness. In her advertisements she had described her son's hair as 'light brown', whereas photographs (and witnesses) attested that it was black. The Dowager had asserted that Sir Roger disappeared at age 32, when he had, in fact, been 36.

Sir John had a field-day with the dead Dowager's credibility – but he was less successful with certain other affirmative witnesses – particularly the valet Andrew Bogle, who unshakeably insisted that Castro was, 'of course', Sir Roger. Bogle denied that he had ever coached the claimant – and withstood all of the opposing counsel's attempts to discover him in a lie.

Many other witnesses and providers of affidavits were equally adamant. There was simply no doubt, they testified, that Castro was the 10th baronet.

The ball volleyed back and forth between the brilliant opposing counsel – but increasingly it seemed that Castro's case was failing. Particularly damaging was the testimony of young Roger's tutor, Monsieur Chatillon, who told the court that Castro was not only unable to speak more than a word or two of Roger's mother-tongue, French, but was also lost for words when questioned – in English – about his boyhood friends, the name of his dog, and the rules of chess: a game which the young Roger had played from an early age. Sir John also raised doubt that the claimant had been rescued by a ship named *Osprey*. The Tichborne family's detectives had been unable to confirm that a vessel of that name ever existed.

Another deadly blow to Castro's case came when Sir John introduced a witness who said she had been one of the claimant's youthful sweethearts – at a time when he, like herself, had been a member of the 'lower classes'. She had seen his penis on several occasions – and had noticed that when not in use it was retracted into his body. Who was telling the truth, the newspapers speculated: the young woman – or the family physician, who had claimed that the retracting member was a physical characteristic of the young baronet? Castro angrily denied that he had ever met the woman – but after hearing her damning testimony and others like it, the predominantly working class jury decided they had heard enough. A spokesman told the judge that he and his fellow jurors felt 102 days of testimony was sufficient to guide them to a decision.

The jury found in favour of the defendant. Tom Castro was immediately charged with perjury and forgery of the Tichborne Bonds. After a trial that dragged through 188 days, Justice Mellor sentenced him to 14 years jail with hard labour. He served ten.

Castro, who had converted to Christianity during his imprisonment, emerged from prison a lonely man. His friends and supporters had long ago deserted him – and the only people interested in his plight were entrepreneurs who believed he could make them a profit. Desperate for money, he accepted a publisher's cash offer to put his name to a quick book, *The Confessions and Story of Arthur Orton*: a work he immediately disclaimed – and which even his opponents concede is a concoction.

For several years (until he was too ill to continue) Castro

appeared in music halls as the Tichborne Claimant, speaking in a cultivated accent and continuing to announce that he was the real Sir Roger. Until he died on April Fool's Day 1898, he unwaveringly insisted, as a man committed to God, that he had been wronged and that the baronetcy had been stolen from him.

The Tichborne family appeared to harbour some guilt about Castro. They allowed Roger Tichborne's initials to be engraved on his coffin.

This fact, says the 'pro-Castro' author Edward Docker, seems to indicate that the Tichbornes knew all along that Castro had been genuinely entitled to the great fortune he fought so hard to secure. Docker, a noted historian, became interested in the case when he met the British writer Douglas Woodruff who in 1957 published a definitive book on the Tichborne controversy.

Woodruff was privately convinced that Castro was genuinely heir to the Tichborne estates.

He found it vastly improbable that any impostor, no matter how cunning, would have tried to pull off so massive a hoax. Roger had been missing for only 11 years when Castro came forward – hardly long enough to fade from memory. Lady Henrietta was in absolutely no doubt the ill-spoken 'Australian' was her son – and close associates of the family were equally convinced. To Woodruff it seemed 'inconceivable' that a Wagga butcher would expect to pass himself off as a titled aristocrat.

For his book *Furphies: Fact or Fantasy in Australian History*, Edward Docker built on Woodruff's research. He conducted what was probably the first detailed study of the mass of evidence against Castro – and concluded that much of it was fabricated.

The financial stakes, in the case of Tichborne versus Castro, were huge – as were the misunderstandings and mistaken interpretations. Castro, during his years Down Under, had acquired an Australian accent. This, when he arrived in England, was wrongly thought to be an East London accent – leading to his misidentification as Arthur Orton. The principal 'confirmation' that Orton was Castro's real name came from a man happy to change his testimony according to the bidding.

Records of the celebrated case show that Castro eventually began to speak in an upper-class English accent tinged with French – as if reverting to the speech patterns of his old life.

Was Thomas Castro really the 10th baronet? An exhumation in London's Paddington Cemetery, followed by a DNA test, would settle the matter.

And perhaps, one day, it will.

# What *Really* Happened to Harold Holt?

*He was one of Australia's most popular Prime Ministers. A photograph of him in the surf, wearing a wetsuit and flanked by three beautiful young women, was published worldwide – cementing Australia's reputation as a glamorous, sun-drenched sporting nation. Then, one Sunday morning he stepped into the sea – and disappeared. And despite all the theories and arguments and 'well-sourced' rumours, no-one could say for certain what became of him after that ...*

DESPITE HER ENGAGEMENT in the increasingly controversial Vietnam War, Australia in 1967 remained an easygoing, trusting country. And nothing exemplified the nation's relaxed approach to life more than the behaviour of the Prime Minister himself. Harold Holt, 59, handsome, sportsloving, reputedly a ladies' man, knew, better than most of his colleagues, how to enjoy himself. It's doubtful that the issue of personal security often entered his mind – or, for that matter, the minds of those around him.

Harold Holt had a reputation (albeit declining with age) as an ace in the water. After his presumed death, Norm Adams, then captain of Portsea Life Saving Club, remarked: 'Everybody at the club knew Harold. He was our patron and an excellent swimmer. He could dive down 20 feet [6 metres] with just a snorkel – and come up with a crayfish.'

It was Friday 15 December. For Australia's politicians the Christmas break would soon begin. At 11.30 a.m., when Harold Holt flew out of Canberra in an RAAF VIP jet, he was almost certainly thinking about his favourite swimming spot: Portsea's Cheviot Beach. On arrival in Melbourne he briefly visited his office, then, after telling his personal secretary, Pat De Lacy, it was a beautiful day, climbed into his red Pontiac Parisienne and set out for the Holt holiday house in Portsea.

En route he stopped off at the Sorrento fish shop, where he paid a bill for fish he had bought the previous weekend.

At the shop he happened to meet a neighbour, Marjorie Gillespie.

The Prime Minister reached his holiday house at around 3.00 p.m. – and reportedly spent the remainder of the afternoon and most of Saturday enjoying Portsea's summer relaxations: gardening, drinks, a barbecue, walks and tennis.

On the fateful morning of Sunday 17 December Harold Holt decided to watch the weekend's great event – the arrival in Port Phillip Bay of the English around-the-world solo yachtsman Alec Rose. It was a dazzlingly bright day and the water was already flowered with the sails of hundreds of yachts, gathered to greet Rose's nine-metre *Lively Lady* as she sailed through the Heads.

The Prime Minister was a gregarious man. With his wife Zara delayed in Canberra, he wanted company for the occasion, so he stopped by at the nearby holiday house of Winton and Marjorie Gillespie. A house-guest that weekend was 19 year-old Martin Simpson, a Monash University medical student. Years later, as a successful doctor in Sydney, he would recall, 'I was just a kid at uni – and the last thing I'd expected was to be meeting the Prime Minister. But that's how things were at Portsea – very informal. He dropped by and invited all of us down to Point Nepean, first to watch *Lively Lady* and afterwards to swim at what he looked on as his private beach.

'He was an incredibly friendly bloke. I was a young leftie at the time, so I'd never have voted for him – but I couldn't help liking the man.'

Harold Holt and Marjorie Gillespie led the way in the

Prime Minister's red Pontiac. The young people – the Gillespies' daughter Vyner and her boyfriend Martin, with Alan Stewart, former fiancé of the Gillespies' other daughter – followed in a white Holden station wagon.

After watching *Lively Lady* battle through the rip, the party drove on to Cheviot Beach and descended the scrub-bearded cliffs to the water's edge. Cheviot Bay is a wild place. Over the millennia, waves have gnawed away more than 200 metres of sandstone cliff to create a broad rock shelf, torn by rips and pocked by immense potholes. The beach itself is a small strip of sand protected by a jagged reef, incessantly attacked by huge ocean waves.

It was Harold Holt's favourite spot for swimming and spearfishing. Several months earlier he had described, to a newspaper reporter, his passion for skindiving ...

'It's both aesthetically and athletically satisfying. There's a new world to be seen under water. You hear about the marvels an astronaut encounters when he goes into space, but he doesn't see one-tenth of the beauty and wonder that any skindiver who roams around a bit will find.'

By the time the group reached the strip of beach the sky had darkened and a cold breeze was blowing. The other party members began to express reservations – but Holt was undaunted. 'I know this place like the back of my hand,' he shouted from behind a rock, as he changed into swimming trunks. Without looking back, he strode into the water and breaststroked toward a rockpool.

That was example enough for Alan Stewart. 'If the PM can take it, I guess I'd better go in too,' he announced.

Stewart waded in a short way – but not liking the feel of the water, decided to return to shore. It was 11.30 a.m.

Martin Simpson recalled: 'Vyner and I went for a walk along the sand. I'll never forget, when we got back, seeing Marjorie Gillespie standing like a statue on a rock, staring out to sea. I remember she was wearing a green chiffon thing over her swimsuit. The fabric was billowing in the wind.

'As we got nearer she said, "He's gone!"

'It took me a moment to understand what she meant – then I just couldn't believe it.'

While Martin Simpson and Marjorie and Vyner Gillespie waited on the sand, desperately hoping that Harold Holt would reappear, Alan Stewart scrambled up the cliffs and ran for help. To the watchers on the beach, it seemed an eternity before anyone came.

INSPECTOR LAWRIE NEWELL was an instructor at the Police Officers' College in South Yarra. He specialised in teaching young policemen how to conduct field and emergency operations. But as the college had closed for the Christmas recess, he had been rostered as duty officer at Russell Street police headquarters. On Sunday 17 December Lawrie Newell's shift was due to start at 2.00 p.m. At 12.45 p.m., he was taking a leisurely shower after a morning's gardening at his Moorabbin house when his wife summoned him urgently to the phone. He hurried into the kitchen and, dripping in a thin dressing gown, took the call. It was a colleague, Inspector Russell Hildebrand.

'Listen, Laurie,' Hildebrand said. 'We've just had news

to say the Prime Minister's gone missing in Bass Strait. You'll have to go down and search for him.' As Hildebrand was known in the force as a dry humorist, Newell's initial response was, 'Stop bulldusting.' But his friend quickly convinced him that the matter was deadly serious.

Ten minutes later a police car pulled up outside the house. Inspector Newell kissed his wife and said, 'See you tonight.' He was wrong. He would not return home for a week.

The search for Harold Holt would eventually involve 25 organizations and more than 300 people – becoming the biggest operation of its kind in Australian history.

The police car, siren wailing, soon struck problems. The beach road to Portsea was jammed with holiday traffic. Inspector Newell ordered the driver to divert to Moorabbin airport. He was in luck. Waiting on the tarmac was a helicopter that had been chartered to deliver six Santa Clauses to city emporiums. The pilot was more than willing to give the Prime Minister priority over Father Christmas.

In retirement, Lawrie Newell recalled: 'The bay was clear and still that afternoon – and I was confident that with a few passes by the helicopter we'd quickly find either Harold Holt or his body. But when we crossed over the peninsula and I saw the wild ocean on the other side, I was taken aback. I could scarcely believe that two bodies of water so close together could be so different.'

When the 'copter landed on the cricket field at an army officer cadet training school, members of the volunteer Sorrento fire brigade had already started searching. Shortly afterward the skies over Portsea were criss-crossed with

# HOLT'S DEATH FEARED

**634,130**
Average Daily Sale

BUREAU SAYS — CITY —Occasional light rain. Cool change developing. Expected top temperature: 78 deg. (Yesterday's top, 80).
• Weather details, P. 35

The Sun
NEWS-PICTORIAL
44 FLINDERS ST. 4c By Air, 5c PHONE 63-0211
14,107. Melbourne, Monday, December 18, 1967. 56 Pages.

↑ **THIS IS THE SPOT** where the Prime Minister, Mr Holt, dived off the rocks into the surf at Portsea yesterday.

In this picture, by staff photographer LLOYD BROWN, a skindiver is searching the water near the rocks while other searchers stand by.

Heavy kelp, which covered most of the area, hindered their search.



**Search scene— See Back Page**

## Vanishes in Portsea high surf

**THE Prime Minister, Mr Holt, 59, is feared to have drowned.**

**He disappeared after swimming far out in rough surf near Portsea yesterday.**

**A day and night search has failed to find any trace of him.**

**Inspector L. J. Newell**, in charge of the search said last night:—

**"I regret to say I do not hold out much hope for Mr Holt now."**

**Mr Holt went swimming with a friend, Mr Alan Stewart, 30, of Elm Grove, Armadale.**

**Mr Stewart found the surf difficult and left the water. He said Mr Holt appeared to be swimming strongly when he suddenly disappeared.**

If Mr Holt is dead, the Deputy Prime Minister, Mr McEwen, 67, will be sworn in as Prime Minister today or tomorrow.

**Mr McEwen would hold the post until the Government parties elect a new leader, probably next month.**

Cheviot Beach, which yesterday became Search Area L — is 500 yards of sand, protected by a jagged reef incessantly attacked by huge ocean waves.

It is near Mr Holt's holiday home.

Two platoons from the Army Apprentice School at Balcombe patrolled the beach last night.

**Mr Tony Eggleton**, Mr Holt's Press secretary, said in Portsea last night:—

**"It is a very slender hope, but I believe Mr Holt may have got ashore somewhere."**

Mr Eggleton said Mrs Holt was behaving very bravely.

Late last night police appealed to sightseers and "unauthorised persons" not to approach the Portsea search area.

police, army and air force helicopters. Soldiers patrolled the rugged coastline. Navy vessels and launches sailed up and down the peninsula, while divers probed the kelp-clogged shelves and rockpools.

One of those divers was police officer John Simon. 'I was watching *World of Sport* on telly when a newsflash came on saying a high-profile politician had disappeared at Portsea,' he recalled. 'It was easy to work out who that might be.

'I rang my superior and he told me to go by helicopter to the beach where the Prime Minister had disappeared. Two of our members had already dived, but the water was so rough it was decided we should come back next morning.

'At 5.00 a.m. Monday we gathered, in our wetsuits, at the Portsea army camp. It was cold and drizzling. Three Iroquois helicopters came out of the mist and lifted us down to Cheviot Beach. There were already navy clearance divers down there – and people trying to work out the currents, using buoys they'd floated out.

'A few people had the faint hope he might somehow be found alive – possibly by the soldiers patrolling the shores. But it was clear to us we were searching for a body – and in the end, we didn't even locate that.'

As coordinator of the massive search, Inspector Lawrie Newell followed every lead – conventional and otherwise. When a self-styled psychic drew a map showing where Harold Holt would allegedly be found, Newell's men routinely checked the information out – with zero result. Police were also advised to hunt down and open the body of a shark, which had escaped from nets at Clifton Springs.

There might be a human body part in its stomach, said the well-meaning informant. But visibility in the wild water was so poor that divers were forced to abandon their shark-chase.

While the world watched, the search for Harold Holt continued for a further three weeks. The Supreme Court subsequently ruled that he was 'presumed dead by drowning in Bass Strait'. The judges said they would be prepared to reopen the case if new information surfaced. Numerous people were convinced that Harold Holt had died in far stranger circumstances than the court believed – and that something other than drowning had occurred. But Lawrie Newell wasn't one of them.

'I've stayed open-minded over the years – but I've found nothing to convince me it wasn't an accident,' he said. 'Those photos of Harold Holt in his snorkel gear gave him, I think, the feeling he was a better swimmer than he really was. The media played up this aspect of him so much that he may have forgotten he was a man of 59. In other words, he placed too much trust in his own abilities in the water.'

Inspector Newell's theory was that the body had been washed from an underwater cliff metres from the beach – and into thick kelp where it was destroyed by such creatures as sea lice and crayfish. 'When I was a young constable in Brighton we'd have quite a few people disappear at sea,' he said. 'Often they'd be recovered next day – and even in that short time the sea lice would have eaten through their faces.'

The official explanation did not satisfy British author Anthony Grey, who in 1983 published a book *The Prime*

*Minister Was a Spy*. In it he made the bizarre claim that Holt had been an undercover agent for Communist China. According to Grey, Chinese frogmen had placed the cooperative Prime Minister in a plastic air bubble and propelled him from the waters off Cheviot Beach to a submarine waiting a kilometre offshore. Holt, said the writer, was alive and enjoying asylum in the People's Republic.

Another theory – which gained considerably more credence – was that Holt had suicided. According to *The Harold Holt Mystery*, a television documentary aired in 1985, the Prime Minister had been in a depressed mental state because of:

- The death of his brother;
- Moves to unseat him as Liberal leader;
- The disaster of Australia's involvement in Vietnam;
- His own burgeoning health problems.

In an interview conducted for the program, Marjorie Gillespie said Holt had 'put himself into a situation where he was almost certain to die'. She was simply expressing the opinion of many people shocked by the Prime Minister's recklessness in walking into a wild sea, with a powerful undertow. Proponents of the suicide theory often point out that Holt's briefcase, opened after his death, contained a stern letter from Liberal Party Whip Dudley Erwin, complaining that the government was slipping in the polls – and inferring that the Prime Minister's leadership might be a factor. The only problem with this argument is that Holt had not opened the envelope.

Holt's widow, Dame Zara, and his press secretary, Tony Eggleton, scorned the talk of suicide. He had been cheerful, with absolutely no sign of depression, Eggleton told reporters. Dame Zara was more succinct: 'Suicide? He was too selfish for that!'

To some commentators, Holt's death simply didn't make sense. Several speculated that he might have been assassinated by the CIA because he was planning to withdraw Australian troops from Vietnam. Others theorised that the disappearance was a political murder, somehow linked to the inexplicable deaths of Australian physicist Dr Gilbert Bogle and Mrs Margaret Chandler, four years earlier (see Chapter 1).

In 1987 two powerful (and contradictory) rumours swept Canberra. The first, seemingly supported by circumstantial evidence, was that Holt had never gone to Cheviot Beach – but had been killed in Portsea by drug bosses. The second rumour claimed that the former Prime Minister had not drowned or been murdered at all, but, for arcane personal reasons, had begun a new secret life in Brazil … dying in southern France in 1982.

Whatever did, in fact, happen to Holt, an innocent era had died with him. Never again would an Australian Prime Minister enjoy the freedom he had known: to drive, to swim, to visit friends without a cadre of security operatives lurking in the background.

IN 2005, AN INQUEST, held 38 years after the event, found that Harold Holt had accidentally drowned. But the drama may not yet be over. A retired Labor politician, who in his time was a very senior minister, has told more than one journalist that he has, in a hidden file, the stunning truth about Harold Holt's disappearance. So disturbing is the revelation the file contains, says the ex-minister, that he has specified in his will that it must not be published until after his death.

# What Crashed into Guyra Dam?

*In early December 1999 an unknown object slammed at colossal speed into the Guyra water supply reservoir in the Great Dividing Range of northern New South Wales. Police divers reported that the hurtling missile had drilled a tunnel 20 metres long into the dam floor – and seemed irretrievably to have embedded itself four metres deep into the granite below. Officials said it could only have been a meteorite. But a motorist reported that his skin had been burned …*

FILTRATION PLANT MANAGER Peter Starr was first to raise the alarm. Around noon on Wednesday 8 December 1999 he was conducting routine maintenance at Guyra Dam, nestled in the picturesque hills above the Gara River, when he noticed a strange pattern in the reed beds.

On the water surface, here at the dam's western edge, an area of reeds 15 metres long by 6 metres wide had been flattened. It seemed clear from the circular scar in the centre that something had crashed into the reservoir, skipping across the surface before continuing its downward trajectory. Starr's mind flashed back to the stories of plunging meteorites carried on radio newscasts over the past few days.

He reported his finding. The official reaction was swift and dramatic. Within hours the 2,200-population New South Wales town was aswarm with RAAF and army personnel, police investigators, officials from the Environment Protection Authority and hazardous materials experts from state and federal agencies. Television and radio crews also poured into Guyra, along with jostling crowds of sightseers who proved difficult to control.

On the visiting experts' advice, the town council shut off the water supply. An area two kilometres around the dam was declared a prohibited zone.

While police mounted roadblocks in an often-vain attempt to keep everyone but essential investigators out, divers with powerful lights plunged into the reservoir. Some took water samples that would later be checked for dangerous residues. Police divers concentrated on searching for the object itself. They didn't locate it – but they did find its footprint: a tunnel in the dam floor, 40 centimetres in diameter and 20 metres long. Police probes indicated that the object had kept going – embedding itself at least four metres deep into the granite bedrock.

The investigators brought in earthmoving equipment, hoping to wrench the object free. But if anything remained, after it crashed at an estimated 36,000 kilometres per hour, it was too deeply wedged into the rock to be moved.

The site of the mysterious splashdown was shown on television news services around the world. The little town had not received so much attention since the 1920s, when the infamous Guyra Ghost (described in newspapers as a vicious poltergeist) had allegedly driven members of a local family from their house.

Everyone in Guyra's main shopping street had a theory about the latest intruder. Some suggested to reporters that the RAAF – which had been conducting flight training in the area – might have lost a piece from one of its F-111s. The air force dismissed the idea, pointing out that a mere aircraft part could hardly have drilled a 20-metre tunnel. And besides, no F-111 was missing a component. Other popular explanations – that the plunging object had been space junk or a block of frozen urine from a passenger plane – were dismissed on similar grounds.

Most people believed that a lump of space rock had crashed into the dam. In the days preceding the splashdown, numerous witnesses had reported seeing what appeared to be meteors, blue and yellow in colour, plunging to earth. Coincidentally, Guyra had experienced two power blackouts at about the same time.

Dr Ron Barnett of Phenomena Research Australia flew from Melbourne to inspect the crash site. He reported that:

- The angle of the object's entry into the dam had been very shallow – about 45 degrees.
- He could find no-one in Guyra who could recall hearing an explosion or sonic boom.
- And the surface of the reeds had burn marks – 'unusual for a meteorite impact'.

On Thursday 9 December the Environment Protection Authority announced that the dam water showed no trace of toxins or radioactivity. Next day the council turned the town's water back on. Two consultant geologists from nearby Armidale then declared that the object had almost certainly been a meteorite – grapefruit-sized and weighing about 5 kilograms.

The media went away happy – unaware of the testimony of Brian R., which didn't seem to fit in anywhere …

Brian told an investigator from the research group UFOs Over Australia that between 2.00 and 3.00 a.m. on Monday 6 December he had been driving his Subaru station wagon past Guyra. He was en route to Queensland, to stay with his daughters over Christmas.

'I came to a section of road where there were hundreds of red and white reflectors,' he recalled. 'It looked like a busy traffic intersection. There were no vehicles other than myself and a trailer coming a long way behind me. He had his big lights on and they were worrying me. I had my lights on low beam.

'... There was all this frizzle of lights ahead of me. I thought, what the hell was it? [Then] I was struck by this red light. It lit everything up and everything went red ... I was blinded. I slowed down because I couldn't see. I could feel heat – and the light shone in the rear view mirror, hitting me in the eyes. With all those reflectors you'd have sworn you were coming in at Kingsford-Smith Aerodrome.

'I had the shakes all Monday and my sight was so affected I had to wear dark glasses.'

After Brian arrived in Ipswich, Queensland, he heard a radio report about the Guyra splashdown – and immediately rang Ipswich police. He wondered if his experiences on 6 December might somehow have been connected with the meteorite crash.

Brian's daughters were concerned about his physical state. The moment she saw him one of the girls asked, 'Gee Dad – what's wrong with your eyes?' Brian recalled: 'They were bloodshot – really bloodshot.' His skin also was affected. 'It's like I've got a mild sunburn.'

In October 2000 a fresh layer of complexity was introduced to the Guyra mystery, when a scientist opined that nothing had fallen into the dam.

Gary Kemlo, a former BHP metallurgist, told the *Newcastle Herald* that talk of a meteorite was – in the most literal sense – a load of hot air. In Mr Kemlo's opinion the flattened reeds and the long tunnel in the mud had been caused by methane gas.

The process would have begun with a layer of rotting vegetation, lying beneath the reservoir mud, forming a gas bubble. When the bubble burst it released methane at high velocity, blasting a hole into the mud and shattering the reeds.

'In the month preceding the hole's appearance there was nine inches [23 centimetres] of rainfall in the area,' Gary Kemlo said. 'I believe that fine silt blocked up the normal vent holes in the surface and everything went bang. About 10 to 15 cubic metres of gas would have come out of that hole at a velocity of around six metres per second.

'If you put a 10-tonne truck on a jack and raised it two metres in half a second, that would be the equivalent energy released.'

What really happened in Guyra in December 1999? The answer may lie forever buried in the bedrock at the bottom of the dam.

## Explorers Baffled by 'Eternal Fire'

Aborigines told many strange tales to the early settlers. One of these stories concerned a mountain that had been burning since the beginning of the world – spewing clouds of suffocating black smoke over anyone who dared to approach.

The Aborigines feared the mountain; thinking it was the home of *Bhaiani*, the Creator, whose voice could sometimes be heard in the smoke.

Europeans dismissed this account as just another legend – until a party of explorers stumbled upon the mountain their indigenous informants had so accurately described.

The 'fountain of eternal fire', as one contemporary called it, was eating at a peak in the Hunter Valley region of New South Wales, about 25 kilometres north of Scone. At first, geographers described it as a volcano – but closer inspection revealed the fire's seat: a seam of burning coal 180 metres below the surface.

Geologists surmised that centuries before the birth of Christ a tree, set ablaze by lightning, might have collapsed on the exposed coalface. For more than 2,000 years the burning coal had continued to smoulder along the seam.

A later theory was that the blaze was caused by sulphur pyrites oxidising and generating intense heat.

But no scientist can say confidently how the never-ending fire began. The burning mountain keeps its secret.

# Murders by Moonlight
# The Atrocity at Gatton

*Whether it was a madman's work*
*Or that of a fiend from Hell*
*Only the stark white ringbarked gums*
*And the silent moon can tell.*

*John Manifold's long-forgotten poem crystallises the horror colonial Australians felt when a multiple murder of unprecedented brutality was committed near the rural Queensland town of Gatton. Two sisters raped – and shot alongside their brother. The brains of all three dashed from their skulls with a timber club. One newspaper called it 'the most Satanic crime in our history'. And although theories and suspects abounded, the killers went unpunished.*

LOUISA THAUERKAUF WAS ABLE to pinpoint the time precisely. The antique, ever-reliable grandfather clock her family had shipped to Queensland from Europe several decades earlier had just finished striking ten. That prompted Louisa to put out the cats, their stomachs distended by two days of excessive feasting on Christmas scraps.

Just after she closed the front door of the lonely cottage on the outskirts of the tiny Queensland town of Gatton, she heard a 'great commotion'. First of all, she told policemen, there was a noise like a pistol shot. Then someone – a woman, she was reasonably sure – had cried out 'Father! Father!' After that, there was what sounded like another shot.

Louisa's first neighbourly impulse was to hurry out to see what was wrong. But she thought better of it. It was such a bright moonlit night she feared she might be noticed by whoever was out there – and possibly attacked. However, following the brief disturbance everything became peaceful and silent again. It wasn't long before she had talked herself into a more sensible frame of mind. Probably the noises were nothing serious at all. They'd most likely been made by young people, behaving foolishly on the way to that evening's town ball. Perhaps even firing guns into the air. It wasn't unknown in these parts for farmworkers to misbehave in that way.

But Louisa's first instinct had been correct. A paddock less than 100 metres away had become the scene of an atrocity that would shock the emerging nation of Australia.

It was 26 December 1898. The people of Gatton, west of Brisbane, were settling down for the night. The oil lamps had even been turned off in the Tarampa Divisional Board Hall, where the Boxing Day dance was to have been held. Too few young ladies had turned up, prompting the organisers to cancel the occasion.

Gatton's citizens slept – unaware that in a moon-silvered patch of scrub known as Moran's Paddock, off the Gatton-Tent Hill Road, a scene from a nightmare was spread out beneath the glittering stars. Three savagely mutilated corpses sprawled, bleeding, in the grass. Alongside the dead, their horse, its head half shot away, still harnessed into an overturned sulky.

The indignities to which the victims had been subjected, even after death, would next day strike fear into the people of Queensland. An unspeakably malignant butcher was at large.

IRISH-BORN DANIEL AND MARY MURPHY lived with their ten offspring in a ramshackle farmhouse at Tent Hill, eight kilometres from Gatton. On Boxing Day the couple's son Michael, 29, asked if he could borrow his father's old sulky to go to the town Ball with his sisters Norah, 27, and Ellen, 18.

Mr Murphy reluctantly agreed. Strict and pious, he shared his equally religious wife Mary's distaste for the irreverent young people with whom his children tended –

almost defiantly – to strike up relationships. He didn't much like the thought of his daughters going to a public dance. But he did very much want them to find life partners – and in secluded rural areas like Tent Hill, there were few other chances for young people to meet.

Daniel Murphy's son-in-law, William McNeil, didn't think the proposed trip was a good idea. The sulky, he pointed out, was in very poor condition and unfit to be driven on Tent Hill's rough roads at night. There might be an accident. Will's warnings were ignored. Everyone in the family knew he was a chronic worrier. The three young people, excited and dressed up for the dance, assured him they would be safe.

Michael and his sisters left the house at 8.00 p.m. and arrived in Gatton an hour later.

Next morning Daniel Murphy noticed that the three had not slept in their beds. He assumed that they must have spent the night in town.

But William, the worrier, was immediately alarmed. As he later revealed to a newspaper reporter he sensed very strongly that something untoward had happened. He mounted his horse and rode, as swiftly as the primitive road would allow, to Gatton.

As he approached the town McNeil caught sight of wheelmarks the sulky had left on the dirt road the previous night, as it headed back toward Tent Hill. Abruptly he reined his horse in. The tracks, clearly visible in the light of the low morning sun, suddenly veered to the left and through a sliprail into a paddock.

McNeil dismounted, tied up his horse, which seemed

twitchy and disturbed, and tramped into the field, following the twin trails of flattened grass. With every step his heart sank. He knew now that his instinct had been right. Something terrible had happened. But the gruesome spectacle he was about to witness would exceed his worst imaginings.

He came upon the little sulky first. It was on its side, one wheel broken off. The horse, still in harness, was dead, glistening blowflies buzzing around its shattered head. Beyond the cart lay the bodies of two people whom he knew must be Michael and Ellen. They lay back to back in the still-dewy grass with their hands tied behind them. Their skulls had been shattered – obviously by a heavy bloodstained bush club which lay discarded nearby. Norah's body was sprawled in knee-high grass a little further into the paddock. She was lying on a rug. Her hands, too, were tied behind her back. Her face, barely recognisable, had been smashed in.

Almost fainting and fighting for breath, William McNeil ran back to the road, un-tethered his horse from its ironbark post and galloped into town.

The investigation of what quickly became known as the Moonlight Murders was a fiasco from the beginning. As word of the killings flashed through Gatton, scores of townsfolk hurried to Moran's Paddock. When a district policeman and a doctor finally arrived, the killing field had been trampled flat – destroying any footprints or other evidence the murderer might have left behind.

The young sergeant, whose experience of crime was confined largely to cattle thefts and drunkenness, struggled to comprehend the complexity of the scene. His report simply recorded that the victims had been beaten to death with a wooden club – and that the two women had been shot, either before or after the savage beatings. It appeared that they had been raped. The local doctor – equally inexperienced in matters of murder – failed to find the bullet in Michael Murphy's head. This would only be retrieved months later, during a second postmortem.

Gatton is 90 kilometres west of Brisbane – but police investigators took 24 hours to reach the bloodied paddock. The special squad was headed by an Inspector Fred Urquhart, an ambitious investigator imbued with a strong personal aversion to criminals of all kinds – and a determination to see them receive maximum punishment. Colleagues called Urquhart 'the terrier' because of his tireless persistence. But there was a downside to his doggedness. As the old yellowing records of the Gatton atrocity reveal, he was a man who had difficulty letting go of an idea once it had taken hold. And almost from the beginning – ignoring a mountain of evidence to the contrary – he was sure he knew who the killer was.

After collecting what clues they could from the contaminated crime scene, the inspector and his subordinates interviewed a queue of Gatton residents who were convinced they could help. Several supported Louisa Thauerkauf's recollection, saying they too had heard a gunshot at around 10.00 p.m. on Boxing Day. But what interested Inspector Urquhart most was the testimony of no fewer than eight witnesses who told an identical story.

On the night of the killings, they revealed, they had

seen a sinister-looking man, silhouetted in the brilliant moonlight, standing near the entrance to Moran's Paddock. That was enough for Urquhart. In his mind there was no mystery about the identity of the man in the moonlight. The time he had spent loitering (at least two hours) and the savagery of the crime he eventually committed, pinpointed him as Richard Burgess, a violent rapist. Burgess had been released from the island prison of St Helena four weeks earlier – and witnesses had since seen him near Gatton. Urquhart issued an order for the suspect's immediate arrest.

Meanwhile the other squad members – rather less dogmatic than 'the terrier' – were engaged in quite different lines of investigation. Initially one of their principal suspects was William McNeil, the hapless brother-in-law who had discovered the three bodies. The detectives' suspicions were not idle. The police doctor, who accompanied the team from Brisbane, had found semen stains in Michael Murphy's trousers. The discovery prompted detectives to surmise that he might have been engaged in an incestuous relationship with his sisters. On discovering them engaged in sexual intercourse in the paddock, McNeil, accompanied by his outraged father-in-law, the patriarch Daniel Murphy, might have shot and clubbed them to death.

Both men insisted they were innocent – and the investigators soon conceded that logic supported the denials. The sisters' fingernails were broken and their thighs heavily bruised and scratched – evidence that they had resisted their attackers with all their strength.

Intercourse could not have been consensual.

The probable innocence of William McNeil and his father-in-law is further supported by modern forensic research. Scientists now recognise that semen is involuntarily ejaculated in 70 per cent of male deaths.

Inspector Urquhart enthusiastically dismissed his subordinates' incest theory. In a letter to Queensland's Commissioner of Police he wrote:

> *It is clear that if McNeil is connected with the crime it must be with the knowledge of at least the senior members of the Murphy family, who are shielding him and throwing dust in the eyes of the police. To my mind, such an assumption is little short of monstrous. Apart from the character of the family during an almost lifelong residence in the district, there is not one single fact that can be put forward as affording anything like reasonable grounds for it.*
>
> *In fact it seems to me that the McNeil theory has to be founded on strained inferences drawn from circumstances of which the more natural explanations have to be ignored in order to concoct a hideous tangle of incest, fratricide and unnatural barbarity which a short consideration in the light of common sense is sufficient to destroy.*

In his anxiety to prove Richard Burgess was the triple murderer, Urquhart worked hard to divert suspicion from anyone else. He described the Murphys as 'a peaceful, pious family', respected by everyone in the district. But in fact (as the subsequent inquest established), they were surrounded by enemies ...

- Three of the six Murphy sons had built sections of the fence around Moran's paddock, in which the massacre would later occur. They angrily claimed that they were never paid – prompting a years-long feud between their family and the farmer who hired them.
- The year before the murders, one of the Murphys' horses was found dead. It had been skinned.
- Polly Murphy, eldest of the couple's four daughters, testified at the inquest that her mother had given her a beating as punishment for keeping company with a local farmer, Tom Ryan. Mrs Murphy several times abused Ryan in the street.
- When Polly married William McNeil in a Protestant church, her commitedly Catholic mother interrupted the service, screaming that her daughter was a whore. She subsequently barged into the couple's house – accusing them of living in a sinful union.

The controversies swirling around the Murphys did nothing to shake Inspector Urquhart's belief that one man, the released rapist, had committed the crime. Urquhart's subordinates were unable to agree. It would have been impossible, they argued, for a lone gunman to manage the murders unaided.

The solo killer would have had to bail up the sulky at gunpoint, force Michael to tie his sisters' hands behind their backs, bind Michael, shoot the horse and rape the sisters. The young women's feet were not tied – and (the detectives argued) they would surely have tried to run away.

Urquhart consistently argued that lust had been the motive for the crime. His detectives were convinced that the killers – at least two, and possibly three – were driven by hatred. The two doctors who conducted the postmortems reported that the bush club beatings had been so brutal they broke every bone in the victims' skulls. The culprits, quite plainly, were bitter adversaries of the Murphy family.

One of those culprits, Urquhart's men believed, might be a young local, Tom Day, whom one witness identified as being 'that man in the moonlight'. A local police sergeant reported that he had seen blood on a blue jumper belonging to Day. And at the inquest, a constable, Robert Christie, testified that when he expressed a belief that Day was one of the killers, Inspector Urquhart had followed him along the street and warned, 'I don't want you speaking about this man, Day. If you do, I'll make it hot for you.'

Spared by this intervention, the suspect packed his belongings, left Gatton and was never heard from again. Historians in the late 20th century tried to check Tom Day's background – something no detective at the time had thought to do. They discovered evidence suggesting that he might have been related to influential friends of Queensland's Police Commissioner, W. Parry Okeden. To an ambitious police inspector this fact might have placed him above suspicion.

Urquhart's *bete noir*, the rapist Burgess was arrested on a vagrancy charge and questioned for two weeks about the Gatton murders. The police were not only unable to link him to the killings, but eventually established that he had an unbreakable alibi.

In its findings a Royal Commission into the Gatton Murders inferred that the killers had gone free because of police incompetence. 'Sufficiently exhaustive investigations were not made,' the Commissioner concluded.

It was a stinging rebuke to Inspector Fred Urquhart. Nevertheless he survived the embarrassment – and went on to become Queensland's Commissioner of Police.

But in a forgotten grave, somewhere, the Man in the Moonlight still mocks him.

# Outback 'Quake – or Nuclear Bomb?

*Experts still argue about the cause of a mysterious tremor that shook the Western Australian outback in May 1993. The Big Shake's 'signature' on seismographs differed from patterns typically created by an earthquake. Was this the test-firing of a nuclear weapon – by terrorists who had bought a uranium-rich sheep property nearby?*

AT 11.00 O'CLOCK ON THE NIGHT of 28 May 1993, a blazing object, described by truckdrivers as a whistling fireball, cruised above the Laverton–Leonora area, northwest of Perth.

Three minutes later a vast expanse of the state's goldfields was shaken by a 30-second earth tremor measuring 3.7 on the Richter scale. At first the disturbance was officially described as an earthquake – the first noted in that part of the outback since records began in 1900.

But then the objections began. Local Aborigines, whose tribes had inhabited the remote territory for thousands of years, said there was nothing in their verbal lore about previous tremblings of the earth. Truckdrivers and private motorists, who had been on the roads that night, also dismissed the seismologists' explanation. The fireball they'd seen not only belied the 'quake hypothesis – it hadn't behaved like a meteorite either.

Several theorists suggested that the tremor might have been caused by a mine explosion – but engineers promptly pointed out that it had been 170 times larger than the biggest mining blast ever recorded in Australia.

The controversy rated a headline or two – mainly in Perth newspapers – then it was forgotten. In 1995, however, a geologist, John Watts, revived interest in the mystery. While visiting a goldmine where the shockwaves had been felt, he discovered underground damage that puzzled him.

Watts on many occasions had been employed by insurance companies to assess 'quake damage – and he had seen nothing quite like this before. At the mine's 24-metre level, seven-centimetre steel pipes had been sheared in half – and a nearby shaft had collapsed.

To the surprised geologist this looked like instantaneous blast compression, of the kind caused by a major meteorite impact or a nuclear test.

Watts asked a professional colleague, Harry Mason, for a second opinion. Although he favoured the meteorite theory, Mason pointed out:

'Some of the descriptions of the flying object are not what you would expect of a meteorite. It was very slow, there was no sonic boom, and it had no luminous tail. It was accompanied by no unusual pulsing noise and it was followed by an enormous flash of light, a major explosion and a fireball rising vertically.

'On those descriptions it could have been a cruise missile with a one-kiloton nuclear warhead ... which causes an explosion roughly equivalent to 3.7 on the Richter scale – or some other kind of aircraft with an exotic high-energy weapon.

'Modern one-kiloton high-blast nuclear weapons are known to generate extremely low radioactive fallout, which would be very difficult for radiation detectors to pick up.'

In March 1995 the Japan-based terrorist cult Aum Shinrikyo (Supreme Truth) launched its deadly sarin attack on the Tokyo subway. Government investigators subsequently learned that in April 1993 the cult had bought a 202,342-hectare sheep farm (complete with a large uranium deposit) at Banjawarn, only a few kilometres north of the seismic shock zone.

The revised official belief was that an iron meteorite, 1.8 metres in diameter, had struck the earth at an oblique angle, triggering the tremor.

But there was a problem. A meteorite's impact would have gouged a 90-metre crater, easily visible from the air. Despite numerous flights over the shock-zone, neither Harry Mason nor others could find such a crater.

Had the Aum Shinrikyo cult tested some kind of nuclear or seismic weapon in Western Australia's boundless outback?

The verdict remains open.

# Missing – the Yacht with a Deadly Name

*When the luxury schooner Patanela disappeared off Sydney Heads in November 1988, rumours about her possible fate swept Australia. Federal Police investigated conflicting theories ranging from piracy and seizure by drug-runners to collision with a Russian spy-submarine. Seven years later, academic researchers, studying an old manuscript, learned that the name Patanela (innocently chosen by the yacht's original owner) had overtones of evil ...*

THE VOYAGE INTO NOWHERE BEGAN on 16 October 1988. The elegant steel-hulled yacht *Patanela*, 20 metres long and lavishly equipped, set out from Fremantle's blue sparkling harbour for Airlie Beach, Queensland. On board were the schooner's owner, wealthy businessman Alan Nicol, his skipper, the commercial pilot and Admiral's Cup sailor Ken Jones, Mrs Noreen Jones, daughter Ronnalee, and two young sailors, John Blissett and Michael Calvin.

The latter pair had so admired the magnificent boat moored in the harbour that they approached Nicol to ask if they could work aboard her. Nicol hired them as crew for the voyage to the Whitsunday Islands. Now they were simultaneously enjoying themselves and accumulating a generous block of sailing hours that would count toward their navigation certificates.

*Patanela* was fitted with enough safety devices to satisfy the nerviest of millionaires: radar, satellite navigation, watertight compartments, spacious lifeboats – and in the unlikely event of a dire emergency, an electronic radio beacon (ERB) that would signal her position for 48 hours.

The first leg of the pleasant summer journey ended at Esperance, where Alan Nicol disembarked. He had business to attend to in Perth. Ronnalee left the yacht at Port Eyre, South Australia. She was needed back at the office. With four people aboard, *Patanela* sailed on, regularly radioing her position along the way.

At 12.57 a.m. on 8 November, Keith McLennan, an Overseas Telecommunications Commission (OTC) radio operator, received the first of what would be three messages from *Patanela*. In a voice which, on the audiotape, sounds relaxed and calm, Ken Jones gave the yacht's callsign, Victor Mike Papa Tango, and reported that the schooner was 10 nautical miles east of Sydney's Botany Bay. Then he said:

'I believe we've run out of fuel ... we've hoisted our sails and we're tacking out to the east, tracking about zero-eight-zero ... our intention is to tack out for a couple of hours, then tack back in. We may need some assistance in the morning to get back into Sydney Harbour.'

The night was overcast, with a light north-east wind and a moderate swell which the powerful boat would easily have been able to ride. Keith McLennan subsequently testified that *Patanela*'s seemingly routine message set off no alarm bells. It was quite common for vessels to run out of fuel – and in calm weather like this, there appeared to be nothing to worry about. The yacht would have been within sight of the lights of Botany Bay.

Ken Jones made his second call at 1.58 a.m. This time he asked for a weather report, explaining that with the wind abating he didn't want to be caught too far out before sailing into the harbour. Puzzlingly he then requested directions to the New South Wales coastal town of Moruya. McLennan replied that the centre was about five hours away, cautioning that there was a strong wind warning in the area. Again, the radio operator recalled, he detected 'no sign of distress' in the skipper's voice.

Just after 2.00 a.m., OTC picked up the third call from *Patanela.* Ken Jones' voice faded and crackled. He could just be heard, saying: 'Three hundred kilometres south? Is it? South ...'

Then his words were drowned in static. No further message would be received from the schooner.

When Keith McLennan ended his shift at 3.40 a.m. he mentioned the three calls to the relief operator. No-one at this stage was concerned. It was not unknown for skippers to radio that they would be entering Sydney Heads, only to change their minds and sail elsewhere – without advising the shore station. No one expected that Ken Jones would necessarily contact Sydney OTC again.

Alan Nicol, *Patanela*'s owner, tended to share OTC's view. He was confident that Jones had made a late decision to bypass Sydney and proceed straight to Airlie Beach. However, as the days passed, Nicol, along with relatives and friends of the four people aboard, began to worry. Particularly concerned was Ken Jones' son Peter, who rang Perth police to say he had been unable to contact his father by ship-to-shore radio.

By 18 November, the date on which *Patanela* had been expected to arrive at Airlie Beach, there was a full alert. Families wanted the Federal Sea Safety and Surveillance Unit to mount a major search for the yacht – but it was too late. After ten days the vessel could have been anywhere. At least 100 aircraft would have been needed to scour 200,000 kilometres of Australian coastline and ocean – and even then, the rescuers could not have been sure they were looking in the right vicinity. *Patanela* might well have sailed straight out to sea, en route to any country on earth.

It would also have been impossible to search for a sunken vessel (if sunken the yacht was) off Sydney. The navy told Federal Police that the chances of finding anything, even in a narrowed eight-kilometre radius, would be less than one per cent. The water ten nautical miles beyond Sydney Heads is 140 metres deep – almost impossible for a minesweeper or divers to negotiate.

The parents of the two young crewmen, Blissett and Calvin, were understandably distressed by the authorities' inability to act. In media interviews, two eerie facts emerged:

- On the afternoon of 5 November – three days before the yacht vanished – Michael Calvin radioed his father in Taree. He uttered two words, ' G'day Dad', before the line went dead.
- By a remarkable coincidence Calvin had been employed as a set construction rigger on the Australian movie *Dead Calm*, which starred Nicole Kidman and Sam Neill. The film tells the story of a couple holidaying aboard a yacht in the Whitsundays, who are terrorised by a crazed stranger. Scenes from the movie, directed by Philip Noyce, were shot in June 1988 at Airlie Beach – the destination which, only five months later, *Patanela* would fail to reach.

Peter Jones suspected that something sinister had happened to his parents. His father's radio calls, he believed, could have been made under duress. 'It's certainly my father's voice on the tape,' he said. 'But it doesn't seem to be his words. I don't think he'd ever say he "believed" he'd run out of fuel. He's too experienced to be so vague. I think his radio contacts were veiled calls for help.' Peter agreed with Alan Nicol that *Patanela*, with her 2500-litre capacity tanks, was most unlikely to have run out of fuel – especially as she had been filled to capacity when she left Fremantle and had topped up with additional diesel en route to Sydney.

Searchers in the zone from which Ken Jones had said he was calling could find no sign of debris. Federal Police and the Sea Safety Unit checked all 48 vessels known to have been in the area during the early morning hours of 8 November. There was no evidence of a collision. And even if there had been, the yacht, with her four watertight compartments, would have been hard to sink. She had demonstrated her extreme toughness in 1958, when she struck a submerged rock off the Tasmanian coast. The collision tore a hole 1.5 metres long in the steel hull. The damage would have finished an average vessel – but *Patanela*, her bowsprit almost submerged, had managed to limp 200 kilometres to a port for repairs.

Police were sceptical about the yacht's three final messages. They speculated that she might have been hundreds of kilometres distant from Sydney Heads when they were transmitted. Possibly the broadcasts were a ruse, designed to confuse rescuers while the schooner's hijackers made their escape.

The first solid evidence of *Patanela*'s fate was discovered on 9 May 1989, seven months after she disappeared. A professional fisherman at Terrigal, 50 kilometres north of Sydney, hauled in a barnacle-encrusted lifebuoy. The man immediately saw that something was printed on the buoy's edge. Curious, he scraped away the barnacles to read it.

The lifebuoy bore the inscription: *Patanela*, Fremantle.

With the removal of the sea organisms, possibly valuable evidence had been destroyed. But Federal Police did their best with what remained. They engaged a marine biologist to examine the buoy's surface. He concluded that it could not have been in the ocean for more than four weeks. If this analysis was correct, *Patanela* was likely still to have been afloat six months after her 'final' radio transmission.

In the years following *Patanela*'s disappearance hundreds of sightings were reported from Australia's northern coastline, South America and south-east Asia. Many callers were adamant that they had recognized the yacht's distinctive profile.

Theories, some wild, some seriously considered by police, proliferated:

- A Russian submarine, on a spying mission outside Sydney Heads, had accidentally collided with the yacht, then sped away, lest its incursion be revealed.
- Arms dealers or drug-smugglers had seized control of the schooner and killed all aboard. They had then refitted and renamed the vessel, pressing it into service in seas far from Australia.
- The yacht had hit an uncharted reef or a half-submerged container, fallen from a freighter. It had sunk, entombing

the four voyagers. In the light of the vessel's extraordinary buoyancy, investigators found this supposition hard to sustain.

The inquest at Glebe Coroner's Court lasted four days. Federal Police witnesses said there was insufficient evidence to suggest the yacht had been hijacked, or was being used, somewhere on the planet, by drug-smugglers or arms dealers. The most likely conclusion was that she had sunk after colliding with a tanker or some other large vessel, which had hit and run.

The New South Wales deputy coroner, Derrick Hand, declared an open finding on *Patanela*'s fate. However, he said, he was satisfied that the yacht had indeed gone down on the morning of its skipper's final broadcast – and that everyone aboard had died.

THE STRANGE MATTER of the schooner's name did not come to public attention until 1995. Phil Waterworth, the yacht's original owner, had wanted her to sail with 'good vibes' – so he chose the name *Patanela*, which he understood to be an Aboriginal term describing a kind god who protects the tribe.

In 1964 a group of scientists chartered *Patanela* for an expedition to Heard Island. They researched the name for themselves and concluded that it actually meant 'Storm Spirit' – an apt sobriquet for a vessel capable of fighting through wild weather.

But the scientists and Phil Waterworth were mistaken.

The Danish explorer Jorgen Jorgenson got it right in

the 1830s when he published a definitive glossary of the language used by an Aboriginal tribe in northern Tasmania. In the late 20th century Lyall Wilson, a lecturer in Aboriginal Studies at the University of Tasmania validated at least one of Jorgenson's definitions.

He confirmed that *Patanela* was the tribal word for 'Devil'.

## Messages Scratched on Glass

On 2 September 1967 a fisherman, walking along a lonely beach at Parengarenga, New Zealand, stumbled across a large object partly buried in the sand. Shielding his eyes from the harsh sunlight the artefact reflected, he stooped and worked it free.

He recognized his find as a float fashioned from fibreglass. Obviously it had been lying here for several weeks after the tide had washed it up. The fisherman sat down to study the curious piece of flotsam more closely. On the glass were a series of scratches, which, with a jolt of surprise, he eventually recognized as messages in capital letters.

The inscriptions read 'Gone back to boat' and 'Caledonia due east'. There was a third message which he was unable to decipher. The fisherman immediately took the float to the police station at Houhora, near the northernmost tip of New Zealand.

Police studied the fibreglass with magnifiers – and after great difficulty managed to decipher the third line of capitals as: 'I'LL BE OK, GUSS'.

They also noted that the float had been deliberately removed from the main structure of the craft (plainly a trimaran) to which it had been attached. The beams were cut cleanly and sawmarks were clearly visible.

Within days police established the float's origin. It had come, not from a New Zealand craft, but from the Queensland yacht *Privateer* which was at the centre of one of Australia's deepest maritime mysteries.

Thirteen months earlier (16 August 1966) the 11.5 metre vessel had left Moreton Bay to sail to the United States. En route she was scheduled to call at Tahiti and Honolulu.

Aboard the yacht were skipper Hedley Nicol and his friends Emil Van Bommell and Gus Baldwin. They planned to exhibit *Privateer* (which Nicol had designed and built) at the Long Beach boat show. On 19 August Nicol radioed that they were 800 kilometres from Brisbane and that all was well. It was the last message ever received from *Privateer*.

When the yacht failed to make its planned visits to Tahiti and Honolulu, fears for the three sailors' safety began to grow. But the trio's families and friends considered it unlikely that anything would have gone wrong. *Privateer*, they told the media, was one of the safest yachts Brisbane had produced – and Nicol was a resourceful skipper. The yacht was carrying ample water and three months' provisions.

Possibly Nicol had changed his plans and was heading straight for the United States of America.

However, when the trimaran also missed her rendezvous with San Francisco the mood began to darken. In Brisbane, air-sea rescue experts plotted the craft's possible change of course. Theorists wondered via the media whether France might somehow be to blame for the disappearance. On 4 October officially-sanctioned French vandals had exploded an H-bomb on Mururoa Atoll, 1280 kilometres south of Tahiti. Had the little Queensland yacht blundered into the nuclear test zone?

If this had happened she might have gone undetected. *Privateer*, made of plywood and sheeted with fibreglass, was invisible to radar.

On 2 December, with the yacht now long overdue in San Francisco, the United States Coastguard conducted a broad but unproductive search of the Pacific between California and Hawaii. From Cleveland, the skipper's father, Hunter Nicol, surmised that the three men might have been wrecked on one of the hundreds of uncharted islands specked across the Pacific's coral reefs.

But surmise was all anyone had to go on – until the discovery of the fibreglass float. New Zealand and Brisbane police said the float had been upside-down when the messages were scratched on it – indicating the yacht had capsized, with at least one person, the writer of the cryptic messages, clinging to it. Detectives speculated that a crewman had laboriously managed to saw the float away, in an attempt to right the vessel. But why and how the yacht had capsized, no-one knew. And the tantalising question of whether any of the trio aboard might have survived remained unanswered.

The *Queensland Police Gazette* published the following report on 4 November 1967:

> *MISSING: Hedley Gordon Nicol, 40 years, 5 feet 11 inches, dark-brown hair, grey eyes, medium complexion and build; native of Queensland; boat designer and builder. Accompanied by Emil Van Bommell and Gustaf Baldwin. Left Manly Jetty, Queensland, on 16.8.66 in a trimaran named 'Privateer' with the intention of sailing to Los Angeles USA and anticipated to arrive there on or before 23.11.66. On 19.8.66 a radio message was received from the 'Privateer' stating, '300 miles out, all well, love to all at home, signed Hedley'. No further information was received from the trimaran, but on 2.9.67 a port float which has been definitely identified as part of the trimaran 'Privateer' was found at Houhora in Parengarenga Harbour, North Auckland, New Zealand; but no trace of any member of the crew was found. Inquirer, Hunter Nicol (father) corner Passage and Princess Streets, Cleveland, anxious as to whereabouts and safety.*

## Curse or Coincidence? Western Australia's Unlucky Shipwreck

When the American Liberty ship *Alkimos* smashed into a reef off Western Australia's coast, few seamen were surprised.

For two decades she had been known as the unluckiest vessel afloat. Hundreds of officers and men had refused to serve aboard her.

The evil reputation that dogged *Alkimos* dated back to 1943, at the height of World War II. The builders who laid her hull had a proud reputation for constructing Liberty ships in ten days or less. But the construction of *Alkimos* was plagued by so many accidents and injuries that the task took six weeks to complete.

When the seemingly jinxed vessel finally put to sea she became notorious for breaking down in the midst of Atlantic convoys, as they tried to avoid German U-boats. After World War II the mishaps continued. In 1963 she ran aground on Western Australia's Beagle Island. Torn and leaking, she struggled back to Fremantle for repairs. But when she managed at last to return to the ocean she was almost immediately overwhelmed by mountainous waves. The wild seas drove her toward the coast, hurling her onto a reef.

Over the ensuing years several attempts were made to salvage the ship. All failed. One salvage company owner died. Another was bankrupted. Convinced the wreckage was cursed, many locals stayed clear of the stretch of beach from which *Alkimos* could be most clearly seen. Diver and television documentary-presenter Jack Sue commented, 'It's probably just coincidence, but I can scarcely count the number of people who've driven down to photograph the wreck – then had their four-wheel drives break down, or their watches stop, or their cameras fail.'

In 1973 a crowd of onlookers watched, puzzled as smoke billowed from the ship's shattered funnels. Two journalists went aboard to investigate – and found that drums of tar had caught fire.

Perhaps the eeriest event in the unpleasant history of *Alkimos* had occurred in 1969, when the long-distance swimmer Herbert Voight disappeared. Voight had been trying to swim from Perth to Rottnest Island. His route had been nowhere near the *Alkimos* wreck. But years later, his skull was found lodged in the ship's hull.

# Lasseter's Deadly Gold – Fantasy or Fact?

*According to legend, the vast reef of gold, its specks shimmering under fierce desert sun, was at least 14 kilometres long. Harold Lasseter, the young prospector who had stumbled upon it, was in no doubt it would make him rich. But all that the mocking treasure-in-the-wilderness would bring him was a lifetime of disappointment and a slow, agonising death. Since Lasseter's distant day literally hundreds of expeditions have sought the fabled reef, at a cost of more than 50 lives. But the location of the lode (if, indeed, it ever existed) remains a puzzle, perhaps never to be solved ...*

## Lasseter: the Legend

LEWIS HAROLD BELL LASSETER (his friends called him 'Possum') hated the poverty in which he had spent the first 17 years of his life. In 1897 he quit a wretchedly-underpaid labouring job in Cloncurry, Queensland, and set out to make his fortune as a prospector in the gemstone fields of the McDonnell Ranges, north-east of Alice Springs.

When the pickings proved slim the tiny adventurer – only 157 centimetres tall – decided to search instead for gold, which had been found in large quantities around Kalgoorlie, Western Australia. Young Harold travelled with two horses via Alice Springs, then in an almost direct line toward the Kalgoorlie goldfields.

About 700 kilometres west of Alice he stumbled across an immense outcrop of quartz, its rich lode of gold flashing almost painfully to the eye. Confident that he was on the brink of becoming a rich man he filled a bag with samples, then continued his journey to Alice Springs. There he intended, by dint of cautious questioning, to find himself partners who would help him map, assay and lay claim to the reef.

But the searing heat came close to claiming Lasseter first. When his two horses died within hours of each other, he was able to carry only a fraction of the food and water from their packs. Hungry, hallucinating and thirst-crazed he began to wander in circles, hopelessly lost. He was lying unconscious when an Afghan camel driver found him and took him to a nearby surveyor's camp.

The surveyor, Joseph Harding, nursed Harold Lasseter back to health. It didn't take the young prospector long to decide that he liked and trusted the older man. He opened his bag and showed Harding the gold he had collected. Harding feigned surprise at the richness of the samples. He didn't mention that he had already assuaged his curiosity while Lasseter lay delirious.

The rescue sparked a friendship which, three years later, would lead to Harding and Lasseter becoming partners in an endeavour to rediscover the gold reef. After considerable difficulties they were successful. Harding took bearings of the location, something his relatively unskilled partner had not managed to do first time. He also conducted an assay which, not to his surprise, indicated that the reef would yield a spectacular 90 grams per tonne of ore.

Excited and armed with their survey map, the pair arrived back in Carnarvon, Western Australia, ready to find investors. Only then did they realise that they both had made a careless and infinitely costly mistake. Harding's watch was slow, as was Lasseter's. This meant that the bearings they had taken of the gold reef were hopelessly incorrect. However, they remained optimistic. Believing that they knew – within several thousand kilometres – the general area in which the reef could be found, they approached investors anyway. But none were willing to gamble on men with slow watches. Harding, who had accumulated cash enough for a comfortable retirement, shrugged and walked away from the project.

Lasseter decided to raise his own capital. Over the next decade he worked both as a prospector and miner in the gold rushes occurring across Western Australia. In that heady era, gold seemed to be oozing from the ground in inexhaustible quantities – and some prospectors were making fortunes. Lasseter, however, was not one of them. In 1916, as the gold bonanza began to peter out, he determined to try again to find the reef – using someone else's money. He approached the Western Australian government, whose tax revenues from gold were in steep decline.

The financially-strapped administration agreed, under profit-sharing terms that were weighted in its favour, to fund two expeditions to rediscover the lost treasure. Both failed – and several expedition members died.

It would be 14 years before Lasseter launched a new attempt to rediscover his reef.

## The Facts and the Theories

BY THE TIME the Great War, and all its horrors, ended in 1918, Australians had matured into a more seasoned and less romantic people. The exploding of comfortable old myths became a national sport – and in academic circles the legend of Lasseter's Reef was not spared.

Although they would publish very little of the truth during Lasseter's lifetime, sceptical historians began to explore the prospector's previously murky background. They learned that he had been born to a labourer and his wife at Bamgarnie, Victoria, in September 1880. In several letters applying for employment, Lasseter the man claimed that he had served in the Royal Navy from the ages of 17 to 21. Possibly this contradicted, or at least imposed a time-squeeze, on his story that, while working as a prospector, he discovered the 14-kilometre reef in 1897.

After his discharge from Britain's navy, Lasseter migrated to the United States, where he worked as a labourer and married an American woman in 1903. Records show that he returned to Australia in 1908 and began farming at Tabulam, New South Wales, occasionally writing letters to newspapers.

Lasseter's surviving writings and inventions demonstrate that he was a talented, insightful man whose interests extended far beyond prospecting for gold.

He invented speed bumps – and designed Sydney's first multi-storey carpark, at a time when A-model Fords had just begun to appear on the roads.

He was the first Australian to propose and design an arched bridge over Sydney Harbour.

He campaigned to have an industrial centre built at Welshpool on Victoria's Gippsland coast. No-one was interested at the time, but BHP acted on the idea 50 years later.

In letters to newspapers Lasseter accurately predicted that Japan, our ally in the Great War, would eventually turn against Australia.

And in 1926, he wrote that Australia should sever her ties with Britain and become independent. Prophetically he argued that Britain would be incapable of protecting her empire, Australia included, in the event of a second world war. In the 1940s this forecast came to fruition when

Prime Minister John Curtin turned to the United States for help in repulsing the Japanese.

By rediscovering Lasseter's long-forgotten letters and drawings, historians were able to build a picture of a self-educated and highly intelligent man. But most of these scholars tended also to believe that he had been a fantasist. They pointed to several novels that Harold might have read as a boy – such romantic adventures as Bill Wright's *The Mine with the Iron Door* and Conrad Sayce's *Golden Buckles*: books which described the discovery of immense gold-lodes in the Australian desert. Had these heady narratives inspired Lasseter to invent a reef of his own?

Perhaps – and perhaps not. It would never be easy to prove that the fabulous reef was not a fact – especially as Lasseter implicitly believed in its existence all his life. And would die trying to find it again.

In 1925 Harold Lasseter settled in Sydney with his second wife, Louise Lilywhite, and went to work as a construction labourer on Sydney's new, arched Harbour Bridge. But the reef was never far from his mind – and in October 1929 he glowingly described his exploits in a letter to the federal member for Kalgoorlie, the Rt. Honourable A.E. Green. In 1911, Lasseter alleged, he had found 'a vast goldbearing reef in central Australia'. As a prospector and qualified surveyor he would be prepared to survey a 1300-kilometre route from a proposed dam on the Gascoyne River to that reef.

The letter contained an inaccuracy and a contradiction. Lasseter was not a surveyor – and his original story had been that he stumbled upon the gold reef in 1897, not

1911. In any case, the federal member for Kalgoorlie was not interested – and Lasseter was obliged again to look elsewhere.

Lasseter's final chance to rediscover his El Dorado came in March 1930, when Australia was gripped by the Great Depression. He went to John Bailey, president of the Australian Workers' Union (AWU), and described how, 33 years earlier (1897 was again his favoured date) he had found an immense fortune in gold. The reef contained enough to make the AWU the richest union in the world, able to build cooperatives to employ its members and rescue them from poverty.

Bailey was impressed. It was a desperate era – and it didn't take him long to persuade his colleagues that the investment would be worthwhile. The union established the Central Australian Gold Exploration Company Limited, voting a budget of £5,000 to fund the great enterprise.

On 21 July 1930 the exploration party left Alice Springs and headed west. The leader was Fred Blakeley, an experienced bushman. He was a strange choice for the job because, from the beginning, he openly doubted that Lasseter was telling the truth. Lasseter was the guide; George Sutherland the prospector; Phil Taylor the driver-engineer and Errol Coote the pilot of the accompanying plane. Tagging along (to the republican Lasseter's disgust) was a Captain Blakeston-Houston, aide to the Governor-General. For want of a more useful title he had been dubbed 'explorer'.

The party took two trucks. The plan was that everyone, including the pilot, would travel together until they reached a suitable place to build a landing strip. Pilot Coote would then drive back to Alice Springs to collect his plane.

After nine days of relatively easy travel, the explorers reached Taylor's Creek, about 500 kilometres west of Alice Springs. They built a simple airstrip, then waited while Coote returned for the aircraft.

As Blakeley revealed in his subsequently published book, *Dream Millions*, the long wait by the creek quickly degenerated into ill-feeling and suspicion. Lasseter was 'a man of jumbled moods'. When other expedition members sought his opinions about the directions they might take as the expedition progressed he seemed angry and evasive. Blakeley feared that the expedition would end in disaster. And when the long trek resumed, others began increasingly to share his concern.

As the expedition struggled further into the interior, it was plagued by food and water shortages and treacherous weather. But the worst mishap occurred when the plane's engine stalled. *The Golden Quest*, as it had optimistically been named, spun down from the sky, overturning on impact and badly injuring pilot Errol Coote. He was taken back to Alice Springs, and thence to an Adelaide hospital, for treatment. The expedition's financiers promptly provided a fresh plane and pilot – but the explorers' will was almost exhausted. As they continued west – hoping that Lasseter would recognise landmarks pointing to the reef – they encountered an exhaustingly unfriendly terrain. The remaining truck became repeatedly bogged. Often it had to be dug out by hand, only to be trapped again after moving several metres.

When the sand dunes became impassable, the explorers were forced to turn back – finally arriving at Ilbilba, where they were greeted by an Aboriginal tribe whose members seemed suspicious and menacingly defensive. In 1930, many 'wild' tribes, which had experienced little or no contact with Europeans, still roamed remote areas of Australia. The Aborigines at Ilbilba knew little of white men – and when the replacement aircraft arrived, fled from it in terror.

The following day, the new plane, with Lasseter aboard, flew west, in the hope he would recognize landmarks. When Lasseter announced excitedly that he could see topography he knew, the expedition seemed to be back in business. Aided by the maps Lasseter had drawn from his aerial vantage point, the ground party headed south-west. But, as had happened two weeks earlier, the grim landscape eventually became impassable. The goldseekers had no alternative but to return to Ilbilba and seek instructions from the Central Australian Gold Exploration Company's steering committee.

Harold Lasseter was too impatient to spend weeks awaiting the whim of a distant board of directors. When he and his colleagues arrived back at Ilbilba, a dingo-trapper, Paul Johns, happened to be passing through with five camels. Lasseter told Johns about his reef – and, as had happened dozens of times before, the story worked its magic. Harold Lasseter and his eager new friend set out together to find the reef.

The camels made all the difference. Quite effortlessly they negotiated terrain which the truck drivers had found impossible. Within two days the two men were close to the distinctively-shaped mountains Lasseter had seen from the air. And then, if Paul Johns' account is to be believed, they came upon the reef itself. Delighted, the two men returned to Ilbilba. Blakeley, having assured Paul Johns that he would receive a share of the treasure, despatched him to Alice Springs with the news. Meanwhile the impatient Lasseter headed back to the site to peg the expedition's claim.

When he was several days into this ill-advised solo journey, his two camels took fright for some reason and bolted – leaving him in the desert without water or food. Several private pilots, aided by three planes from the Royal Australian Air Force, searched for him unsuccessfully. The exploration company then engaged Bob Buck, owner of Tempe Downs Station, to take up the search. Buck, an expert bushman with intimate knowledge of the area, risked his own life by scouring the desert for 11 weeks, seeking tracks that would lead to Lasseter.

Eventually he found his quarry – too late. A local Aboriginal tribe had rescued the reckless prospector, but weakened by days in the relentless heat, he had died at their camp. Harold Lasseter was buried near Alice Springs. The reef's secret was buried with him. No-one was ever able to find the map which he had drawn in the plane and which he took with him as a guide on his final journey. All he left was a smudged note reading:

> *... one old woman ... feed of ripe figs ... as I'm done for ... I am paying the penalty with my life. May this be lesson to others.*

Lasseter was neither the first nor the last explorer to die in search of his legendary reef. In the half-century following his burial, hundreds of expeditions scoured the desert in which he had walked his last steps. In these hopeless forays the lives of more than 50 explorers were lost. The opinions of sceptics, who doubted whether the reef existed at all, were heard by few. Australians preferred to believe the stirring prose of author Ion Idriess, whose book *Lasseter's Last Ride* prompted more reef-seeking expeditions than all other books on the subject combined.

Even his supporters would concede that Harold Lasseter had a tendency to bend the truth. He would change his story according to the person to whom he was talking – claiming, for example, that he was a surveyor and had discovered the reef on dates as distant from each other as 1897 and 1911. But there is no report that suggests that he was delusional. He believed so strongly that he would rediscover his 14 kilometres of gold that he eventually perished in the attempt.

Is the reef real? Might it eventually be found again, either by a prospector as persistent as Lasseter, or by someone simply lucky?

When all the arguments, pro and con, have been weighed, there is only one possible answer:

Perhaps.

## Australia's Lost Treasures

WHERE IS THE BANK BOOTY BURIED?

The loot from Australia's first-ever bank robbery may still safely be hidden – somewhere. For decades after the money's disappearance it was rumoured to have been buried on Sydney's foreshore – but hundreds of hopeful diggers, working at night to avoid official detection, abandoned the search unrewarded.

The raid, conducted in 1828 on the Bank of Australia, was greeted with great amusement in the lawless colony. The culprits were escaped convict Charles Dingle, his safecracking friend Will Blackstone, a fence, Tom Woodward – and a dishonest bricklayer Tom Turner, who had helped build the bank in the first place.

Dingle and his associates crawled through a drain to gain access to the building's foundations on George Street. For almost a week they patiently chipped a tunnel into the strongroom, from which they filched more than £12,000 – a fortune in old Australia. The criminal colleagues buried their booty mere hours before they were arrested. They had been careless enough to leave tools and empty rum bottles at the crime scene.

A newspaper of the time, the *Sydney Monitor*, could scarcely disguise its glee. The bank's wealthy directors, the paper observed, were so generally unpopular that it was hard to feel sympathy for them. News of the robbery had been greeted in the colony with 'secret, and in many cases open satisfaction'.

Safecracker Blackstone was the only culprit willing to talk. He offered to tell the authorities where the fortune was hidden – on condition that he be released immediately from his hellish jail cell on Norfolk Island. His offer was not taken up. In the end, no-one appears to have benefited from the bank treasure, which is believed still to be buried, either in a Sydney garden or under the foundations of a suburban house.

### THE HORSE'S SKELETON TREASURE

For more than a century, bushmen in what is now the Northern Territory have kept watch for the skeleton of a horse which, they believe, might make them rich. Overture to the drama was played out in February 1880 when prospector Patrick Murphy and his three partners reportedly struck a rich vein of gold. They worked desperately to cram as much of the treasure as they could into the saddlepacks of one of their horses, before the wet season swamped them.

At the end of a week the colleagues had their steeds saddled and ready to leave – with a fortune in gold in one of the animals' saddlepacks. The men, by mutual agreement, had not touched drink while they were working – but now, at last, it seemed the right moment to reward themselves. They opened bottle after bottle, to celebrate their good luck – and before long their carousing degenerated into a violent fight.

The noise frightened the horses away – including the one carrying the gold. The partners searched for months, but could find no sign of a vanished treasure that had literally galloped away from them.

BLOODY SAGA OF THE SILVER REEF

Prospectors in Western Australia swear that this story is true – but they don't like being asked for proof ...

Two centuries before Europeans colonised Australia a Malay merchant, Hadji Ibrahim, reputedly discovered a rich lode of silver in the King Sound region of the continent's north. He collected as much silver as he could carry to his ship and subsequently sold it for a large profit in Macassar. Ibrahim promptly returned for more, only to be shipwrecked and drowned en route. But he had kept a journal of his voyages, in which he recorded all the details of his reef. All, that is, except for its precise location.

Ibrahim's silver mountain – just as Lasseter's gold reef would do in the 20th century – fired the imaginations of generations of explorers, none of whom managed to locate it. Then, in the 1850s, a young prospector, Jack Fletcher announced to drinking companions that he had found the lode and was in the process of staking a claim. Several days later, Fletcher's body was found in a rented room, the head split open by a sharp instrument. In a corner was a kerosene tin filled with silver ore.

Several years later (so the storytellers claim) an employee of one of Ibrahim's descendants mounted several expeditions in search of the reef. He failed to find it, went mad – and according to author Bill Beatty, in his *Treasury of Australian Folk Tales and Traditions* (1968), 'was last seen travelling with a tribe of wild natives in the Kimberley country'.

The tale of Ibrahim's fabulous reef with an ocean view should probably be taken with a grain (or even sackful) of salt. But many other Australian treasures are real and waiting to be found ...

SEARCHING FOR BUSHRANGERS' GOLD

In the lawless Australian colonies of the 18th century, many young men who were either work-shy or unemployable took up bushranging as a career. Those who carried their loot around with them risked either being arrested or robbed in their turn. The most sensible thing to do with the proceeds of a large robbery was to bury it, then return to unearth it secretly, later. In many cases, however, bushrangers were either killed or seized by police before they could revisit their caches.

Historians estimate that scores of never-retrieved chests and canvas bags crammed with bushrangers' booty may be buried in bushland (and under the spread of suburban concrete) across Australia. Examples:

- *When Captain Melville, otherwise known as the Bushranging Dandy, was captured he boasted to police that he had buried 'an enormous fortune, somewhere between Melbourne and Ballarat'.*

*Melville predicted that the loot would 'never be found in a hundred years'. Novelist Marcus Clarke became obsessed by the idea that the fortune was hidden in Victoria's Grampians – and spent fruitless months searching for it.*

- *In 1862 the notorious bushranger Frank Gardiner, aided by Ben Hall, masterminded the celebrated Eugowra Rocks gold robbery. Part of the large cache was never recovered – and fortune-seekers have been trying unsuccessfully to locate it for almost a century-and-a-half.*
- *Ben Hall's gold haul is believed to be hidden in a cave complex about 40 kilometres from Goulburn, New South Wales.*
- *Frederick Ward, alias Captain Thunderbolt, hid his ill-gotten nuggets somewhere in the Mudgee Ranges of New South Wales. In 1870, weeks after he buried them, he was shot dead.*

Gold experts, working with old police records, estimate that the bushrangers' hidden gold would be worth tens of millions of dollars by 21st century standards.

But first it has to be found.

# What Formed the 'Forgotten Footprints?'

*The Queensland farmer could scarcely believe what he had found. While clearing his property for cropping he had unearthed what resembled an immense footprint, almost six metres long. It seemed to have been left by a creature of unimaginable size and weight. Within days he discovered more of the inexplicable 'prints'. The Bundaberg Craters, as they came to be known, have been puzzling the world's scientists ever since ...*

OWEN AND AILEEN MURREN owned a mixed-crop farm 20 kilometres from Bundaberg. In the winter of 1971 they decided to clear a motley assortment of grass tussocks, trees and stumps to create an area in which they could grow zucchinis, a vegetable that was becoming increasingly popular in Queensland's produce markets.

The terrain was harsh and difficult to tame. In the midst of one dense tangle of bushes and stands of trees, Owen found his path blocked by an enormous boulder. He used his tractor to dislodge it – and discovered, underneath, something that would transform his life.

Imprinted deeply into the bedrock was what appeared to be a huge footprint, almost six metres long – and so deep that when he stepped into it some parts of the rim came up to his knees. His first thought was that some enormous prehistoric creature must have left its mark here. The Murrens were curious, but they still had a farm to run. In the days that followed they continued to clear the property. But before long it became impossible to continue. They kept finding 'footprints'. In the end there were 27. A subsequent professional excavation would reveal that the total was 35.

Owen and Aileen showed their discovery to friends and anyone else willing to look. Before long local newspapers picked up the story – and geologists and other scientists began to arrive at the farm.

Every new expert advanced a theory about the depressions in the rock – but no-one had the faintest idea of what they might actually be. However, an initial geological dig (the first of several over two decades) revealed several indisputable facts. The site was at least 25 million years old. The rock was an extremely puzzling mixture of sandstone and red ochre – a combination not found naturally anywhere else on earth. (Red ochre is the material Aborigines mix with water for their paintings.) The two types of rock were evenly mixed, as though they had been churned and boiled in a gigantic cauldron.

Embedded in the craters' walls are thousands of minute marine creatures, suggesting the rock might once have been battered by the waves of some long-receded ocean. Also found were relics possibly from a later era: large pieces of petrified wood, threaded with fossilised worms.

Particularly puzzling are the remarkable features on the sides of some craters – parallel trails resembling a gigantic representation of fingermarks in drying cement.

Whenever there is a heavy downpour the craters 'behave' in an intriguing way. The uphill depressions brim with water, while those below quickly empty: a phenomenon which seems topsy-turvy to many observers.

Several of the craters resemble matched left and right footprints. But at least one marine biologist who studied the site thought it unlikely that feet were involved at all. She opined that the craters might have been excavated in prehistoric times by crablike sea creatures. When the ancient seas rolled back, their sand holes hardened into rock.

Since Owen Murren discovered that first 'footprint' more than three decades ago, at least 200 international scholars have visited his old farm to excavate, photograph and theorise. All they can agree on is that the Bundaberg craters are unique in the world – and that they were not formed by a volcano or an earthquake.

In scientific papers, published in many languages, experts have suggested that the craters might be:

- The roof of a subterranean lake.
- A distortion of the rock caused by pressure from an underground oil deposit.
- An unidentified animal's fossilised trail.

But these are theories only.

Research into the craters continues. But (at the time of writing) they remain, to borrow Churchill's phrase, 'a mystery wrapped in an enigma'.

# Enigma of the Vanishing Editor
# The Juanita Nielsen Story

*In the months before she disappeared without trace, crusading Sydney newspaper editor Juanita Nielsen had campaigned against the ugly redevelopment of her tree-lined street. Is her body buried in the foundations of one of the building complexes she opposed?*

JUANITA NIELSEN – ONE OF THE BRAVEST journalists Australia has produced – lived in an old handsome terrace house at 202 Victoria Street, Kings Cross. Her home was part of a grand avenue, lined with overarching plane trees, often described as Sydney's Montmartre. The street commands stunning views of the Harbour and of Hyde Park and St Mary's Cathedral. All this, paradoxically, within a few blocks of the seething Kings Cross red light district.

With idyllic Victoria Street as her springboard, Juanita, heiress to the Mark Foy retail fortune, could have enjoyed a pleasant, work-free existence filled with social engagements and overseas holidays. But she was an idealist. She chose instead to use her journalistic talent to write exposes of the official corruption, gambling and vice that stained Sydney. Eventually these courageous campaigns would cost Juanita Nielsen her life.

From a home office Juanita produced her own weekly newspaper, *Now*. This journal, letterboxed around Kings Cross and environs, was unlike most other suburban giveaways. Its news stories and editorials ruthlessly outed and attacked greedy public officials, corrupt police and cynical state governments. Juanita received numerous death threats from the powerful people she had offended. She ignored the warnings. Ugly things were happening in her city. She saw it as her responsibility to investigate and lay blame where it belonged.

At about 10.30 a.m. on 4 July 1975, Juanita Nielsen left her house to keep an appointment with the manager of a Sydney nightclub. She was never seen again.

No-one at the subsequent coronial and parliamentary enquiries expressed the slightest doubt that Juanita had been murdered. The question that would haunt Australia ever afterward was: who did it? The problem was that she had so many enemies ... so many people with compelling reasons for wanting her dead.

To place the abduction and killing of Juanita Nielsen in context, it is essential to understand the bitter struggle that was consuming Sydney's inner suburbs during the 1960s and '70s. State governments and local councils, greedy for property taxes and the rate revenues that denser settlement would bring, were gung-ho to allow property developers to have their way. Residents of the threatened inner suburbs, many of whose streets and houses were of irreplaceable heritage value, were trying to fight back ... but with limited success. Despite the efforts of residents' action groups, vast swathes of such areas as the Rocks and Redfern fell to the wrecker's ball.

It was an era when Victorian-era terraces (so prized and highly-priced today) were officially regarded as 'slums' – to be knocked down and replaced by high-rise tower blocks. These ugly warrens were blatant copies of the 'super-buildings' which increasingly were blighting many American and European cities – and which, today are being progressively demolished.

Juanita Nielsen entered the fight when a government-approved building company announced that it would redevelop her own, beautiful Victoria Street, Kings Cross. The investors' plan was to smash the avenue's rows of historic terrace houses, rip out the plane trees and fill the resultant crater with a multi-apartment housing complex comprising three massive towers. Each tower was to be 45 storeys high. Victoria Street's residents, Juanita included, were outraged – and pledged at public meetings never to sell their houses to the developers. They pointed out that the proposed building would cast a gigantic shadow over the area, destroying its character forever.

But the homeowners were struggling against seemingly invincible forces. They no longer had a council to protect them. The state's pro-development Liberal government (only slightly more venal than its Labor predecessor) had earlier dismissed the Sydney City Council, appointing a tribunal of commissioners in its place. And tame government agencies were fast-tracking demolition applications throughout the city.

Some Victoria Street owners caved in to the pressure and sold. But a solid core were determined to stay put – even when gangs of hoodlums tried to intimidate them by breaking up their meetings. The battle became increasingly grim. One resident, merchant seaman Mick Fowler, returned from a voyage to find his house had been stripped of furniture and possessions. Fowler, a leader of the anti-development campaign, fought a long court battle to keep his property. The strain led to his premature death at 50, from cardiac arrest.

Buoyed by the inspirational articles in Juanita Nielsen's newspaper, the people of the besieged avenue fought on.

To their delight they received an offer of help from a powerful sympathiser: the New South Wales branch of the Builders Labourers Federation (BLF) led by Jack Mundey. Appalled by the officially-condoned destruction in such areas as the Rocks and Woolloomooloo, Mundey and his members had announced their intention to do nothing less than 'save Sydney from vandalisation'.

Although he was widely-condemned at the time as a politically motivated troublemaker, Mundey is recognized today as a visionary who fought (with considerable success) to preserve the beauty of inner-suburban Sydney. The union imposed the first of its Green Bans in 1971, when it prevented building companies from chainsawing the last large tract of uncleared bushland on the Parramatta River. The union's intervention in the battle of Victoria Street, Kings Cross, was crucial in preserving the avenue's beauty – in part, at least.

The residents' exhausting struggle for Victoria Street was reaching its climax. Although the BLF had succeeded for five years in stalling the demolition crews, the state government was determined to exert all its powers to ensure that the work went ahead. In 1975 the Federal BLF deposed Jack Mundey and his supporters. The new BLF leadership immediately lifted the Green Ban on Victoria Street.

Juanita Nielsen and her neighbours were now fighting alone. Juanita's newspaper was the only voice of opposition to the 45-storey towers. The position seemed impossible – and the 38-year-old heiress had begun to fear daily for her life. On 30 June – four days before her disappearance – two men came to the house. They seemed surprised and disappointed when Juanita's friend David Farrell answered the door. While Juanita listened in an adjoining room the pair claimed that the nightclub that employed them wanted to buy advertising in *Now*. Both Farrell and Juanita Nielsen knew this was a lie. The newspaper did not accept ads of that kind.

Two years later, on 6 November 1977, one of the men confirmed that the advertising query had been a hastily-concocted excuse – and that they had planned to kidnap Juanita and 'take her to people who wanted to talk to her'.

He added: 'We just intended to grab her arms and stop her calling out. No rough stuff, no gangster stuff. We thought that just two guys telling her to come would be enough to make her think that if she didn't, she might get hurt.'

Two and a half years after Juanita disappeared, the men were arrested and charged with conspiring to abduct her. They were jailed for three and two years respectively. But their conviction did nothing to solve the mystery of who had killed the heiress, or where her body had been hidden.

All that was ever discovered (on 12 July 1975) was her black handbag. It had been abandoned on a freeway in western Sydney.

LONG BEFORE SHE VANISHED Juanita Nielsen had known that she was living on a blade's-edge. A series of death-threatening letters and telephone calls, climaxed by the sinister doorknock of 30 June, had convinced her that one or more dangerous people were determined to silence her. Frightened, but determined to continue her campaigning, she told David Farrell and her boyfriend John Glebe that she would keep them informed of her movements – and would be more than usually careful from that time on. But she seemed to abandon her newfound caution on 4 July 1975 – possibly, the last day of her life. Puzzlingly, she accepted an invitation to visit the same nightclub whose two employees had so badly frightened her four days earlier. According to her final phone message she left the house at about 10.30 a.m.

Although police were satisfied that Juanita Nielsen had been murdered, they could find no culprit. The number of corrupt officials and career criminals who would have wanted her dead was considerable. At the 1983 coronial enquiry John Glebe gave evidence that her activism had extended far beyond the preservation of Victoria Street. She had been carrying cassette tapes in her handbag which, she told him, could 'blow the top off' an issue she was investigating. Journalists subsequently speculated that she had amassed documents, photographs and even some phone taps implicating several prominent and 'respectable' Sydney businessmen embroiled in organized crime.

Hours after the disappearance John Glebe received a threat from an anonymous phone caller. The man said: 'Juanita has been killed ... it was an accident. Back off, or accidents can happen to other people.'

It was well-known in Sydney's underworld that Juanita Nielsen had been investigating the networks that funnelled drugs into Kings Cross. She had also been planning an article about the white-slaving pimps who 'tamed' their prostitutes by keeping them in heroin-addicted misery.

The murder – and the issues of corruption and crime surrounding it – created a political storm in New South Wales. In 1976 the journalists Tony Reeves and Barry Ward wrote a media release alleging that their investigation of the case had revealed a cover-up. They asked the government to establish a Royal Commission. Their plea was ignored. But public concern about the sinister forces that had brought about Juanita Nielsen's death refused to abate.

In 1994 the federal government established a joint parliamentary committee (unprecedented of its kind) to enquire into the murder. It concluded: 'The adequacy of the police investigation can be questioned, as can the (police) conclusion that there were no further leads to be followed up.'

Despite years of investigations – and thousands of pages of testimony by scores of witnesses at two inquiries – nothing is known of how Juanita died, who killed her, or where her body is hidden. In the weeks following her disappearance, while police fruitlessly searched dams and rivers, numerous rumours swept Sydney: She had been buried beneath the third runway at Sydney Airport; her remains had been ground up, taken to a farm on the city's outskirts, and fed to pigs; her body had been cremated and the ashes scattered in Sydney Harbour. And – the most persistent report of all – she had been buried in the foundations of one of the residential buildings her newspaper had opposed.

In 1998 a woman approached police with new information. She claimed that a flatmate had told her he was Juanita's killer. Police flew to London to interview the man. At the time of writing they have laid no charges.

Juanita Nielsen's extraordinary courage in defying the dark lords of Sydney's underworld has inspired numerous books and two feature films. In *The Killing of Angel Street*, director Donald Crombie explored a young woman's crusade against official corruption in a property development – misdeeds which resulted in kidnap and murder. In the Phillip Noyce production *Heatwave*, Judy Davis portrayed a character clearly based on Juanita, as she campaigned to save a low-income inner-city street from destruction.

Countless tributes have been paid to Juanita Nielsen. But a visitor to Kings Cross need only walk a few hundred metres to experience her most enduring legacy. Thanks to her sacrifice, many of Victoria Street's shady plane trees and beautiful terrace houses still stand.

# Bizarre Beach Blob that Bewildered Scientists

*In 1960 an unidentified sea creature of immense size was washed up on a remote Tasmanian beach. Eyeless, freakishly tufted with white fur and equipped with what seemed to be tusk-like sensors, the beast bore no resemblance to any fish or animal known to science. For years marine experts argued about what the creature might be – until, gradually, memories faded. But then, in January 1998, a second white-furred monster, uncannily like the first, was washed ashore on the same stretch of coastline. And the controversy began all over again ...*

THE TWO YOUNG DROVERS ran barefoot down to the ocean for a swim, racing each other to be first in the water. Suddenly one of them pulled up short and grimaced in disgust. The big toe of his left foot had squelched into something. Something soft, jelly-like and cold.

He disengaged himself and called out to his companion. He could see now that he had blundered into the carcass of a sea creature of some kind. Obviously it had been lying on this seldom-visited beach for some time because it was partly buried in sand. But even so he could see that it was huge – breathtakingly so. Its body, as he would later describe it, seemed to spread on and on …

Trying to ignore the sewer-like stench the friends crouched in the damp sand and tried to make sense of what they had found. They couldn't. The creature was unlike anything they had seen or read about before. It was covered with clumps of stiff white fur. It had no eyes – or none that they could find, anyway. And near what appeared to be the mouth were soft, tusk-like protuberances of unknown purpose.

The bizarre, blob-like creature, which would prompt an international outpouring of scientific speculation, was found on the west coast of Tasmania between the Pieman River and Sandy Cape. The drovers told friends about their discovery. Before long, local farmers and a trickle of tourists had begun to visit the beach to inspect the rotting remains.

No-one seemed to think it necessary to report the creature's existence to the 'authorities'. It was two years before a newspaper picked up the story – prompting a Commonwealth Scientific and Industrial Research Organization (CSIRO) scientist to mount an expedition to study the carcass.

Results of the scientist's investigation were published around the world. He was able to report that the creature, although considerably decomposed by this time, was six metres long and almost equally as wide (5.5 metres.) Its body was 1.5 metres thick – and it weighed an estimated eight to ten tonnes. The carcass had a spine and six long fleshy lobes, purpose unknown. This was an animal that conformed to no known species. It seemed to promise a new era in zoological research.

Photographs of the multi-tufted blob (which one columnist nicknamed 'Sea Santa') appeared in hundreds of newspapers and scientific journals. Some marine experts theorised that it was a giant squid – although they couldn't explain the white fur. Others believed it might be a creature which somehow had managed to migrate from the sunless depths of the ocean floor.

One marine biologist of the time pointed out that the world's oceans can be graded into clearly-defined 'life-support zones'. These range from the densely-populated inshore shallows, with their rich seaweed gardens and tidal pools, to the cold deeps, whose inhabitants are obliged either to feed on each other or on vegetable matter that drifts down from the surface. Many of these dwellers in darkness have greatly enlarged eyes, sensitive to the dimmest flicker of light. Others supply their own ghostly illumination. Countless species spawned in the abyss, ranging from fish to worms, glow luminescently through rows of 'lamps' along their sides. Others even carry 'torches', which they dangle in front of their mouths, perhaps as a lure for prey.

The Tasmanian beach blob, the biologist speculated, might well belong to a third variety of abyssal animals – those which had no eyes at all, and relied on sensors (the blob's unexplained fleshy lobes?) to find their food. It was a popular theory. The remoteness of the ocean floors had long led scientists to surmise that they might be a home for living fossils from ancient eons of terrestrial time.

This belief had been strengthened in 1952 with the discovery of a living coelacanth. Found as fossils in the rocks of the Devonian period 300 million years BC, this fish had been presumed extinct. When fishermen caught a coelacanth that had been swimming in deep water off the coast of Madagascar, a cherished scientific belief was exploded. Many biologists were convinced that the Tasmanian monster would prove to be a discovery of even greater importance.

But as the years – and then the decades – passed, no-one seemed able precisely to solve the puzzle of the Blob's provenance. Its nature remained an enigma, much argued-over at first, but then, in the manner of many mysteries, gradually forgotten.

Thirty-eight years later, however, on New Year's Eve 1998, the Blob (or its cousin) made international headlines again. Ricky Eaves, a Tasmanian photo-journalist, was about to go surfing when his nostrils were assailed by what he described as a vile stench. Following his nose he discovered a remarkable creature – immense, white-furred and extremely dead – suppurating in the dunes under a fierce sun.

Ricky Eaves had not heard about the 1960 beaching – but he reported his find and scientists were soon at the site, Four Mile Beach, only a few kilometres from where the original Blob had appeared. The new remains were almost identical to those shown in the photographs taken 38 years earlier. Barry Bruce, a CSIRO fisheries biologist, commented, 'We have another big smelly monster from the deep – it's a mystery.' He did not rule out the possibility that the Blob could be a member of a species new to science. A number of marine creatures had remained unidentified until they were stranded on beaches, he said. One example was the plankton-eating mega-mouth shark. But he tended to believe this was something more mundane, like shark tissue or whale blubber.

Monster Mark 2 was not quite as massive as its predecessor. But it was, nevertheless, a respectable five metres long and two metres wide, with an estimated weight of four or five tonnes. When photographs of the carcass were published, a fisherman recalled having seen it before Christmas, floating in the ocean several kilometres from land. He said he had mistaken it at first for an overturned boat.

Experts resumed their familiar arguments about what the Blob might be. After studying the pictures, Tim Kingston, curator of zoology at the Queen Victoria Museum in Launceston, said he had never seen anything like it. But his guess, on the photographic evidence, was that it was either an uncommonly large squid or a slab of blubber from a dead whale. He was at pains to add that nothing had been scientifically established. And lack of scientific proof was the problem. The carcass was so big that great effort and ingenuity would be needed to move it from its resting place. Scientists, despite the fact that they were struggling with small budgets, were anxious to do just that. Typical was Parks and Wildlife Service biologist Irynej Skara who said the preliminary step should be to dig the carcass out of its sand-drift. 'It has no head and no tail,' he said. 'It will take a lot of time to identify something like this.'

Within a week CSIRO had come to the rescue. Genetic testing at the organisation's Hobart laboratories established that the remains were, indeed, blubber from a whale. 'It would have died at sea and decayed before washing ashore,' marine biologist Barry Bruce said.

And the mysterious clumps of white fur? They were, simply, the gigantic mammal's sun-dried sinews.

The mystery of the celebrated Beach Blob had baffled mankind for almost 40 years. In the end it had been solved with the aid of a spade and a DNA test.

## Strange Case of the Stampeding Cattle

Darling Downs (Queensland) graziers John and Zora Poulsen were mystified by the strange behaviour of their cows.

Through June and July 1999, between 5.30 and 6.00 a.m. daily, about 1,000 head of the Poulsens' Hereford-Brahmans would suddenly stampede toward the west. After charging about erratically for five to ten minutes, the palpably distressed animals would crowd together or hide under trees.

The Poulsens initially assumed their cattle were running from emus or dingoes. But there was no evidence of either.

The enigma intensified when they learned the bovine panic attacks were not unique to their property. Cattlebreeders from Chinchilla and Jandowie to Nanango and Mt Perry had begun to report the same phenomenon.

In every case, the cattle stampeded only in the morning – and only toward the west. And curiously, the problem seemed confined to cows. Horses, dogs and other farm animals remained calm.

What was haunting the cows of Queensland? No-one had an answer, but theories were plentiful. Attempted explanations ranged from earth tremors and lunar changes to secret army exercises and soundwaves inaudible to humans. A Sunshine Coast clairvoyant even laid blame at the invisible feet of Aboriginal spirits.

Eventually the haunted cows calmed down – but the malady lingered. Sporadic stampedes are still being reported.

# Who Was the 'Respectable Rapist'?

*When a 12 year-old girl was found raped and strangled in a Melbourne alley, newspapers placed intense pressure on police to find the killer. Detectives hastily arrested and charged an innocent saloonkeeper – withholding evidence to ensure he was convicted. On execution eve the condemned man's solicitors received an emotional anonymous letter from someone thought today to be the real murderer. Who was he? Time may yet tell …*

HE WAS A RICH, RESPECTED member of Melbourne society. A man who, in his own flowery words, was 'honoured and fawned upon'. His mother idolised him. To his sisters and brothers he was a model to be emulated. And yet, unknown to them all, there was a cold, secret underside to his nature.

This pillar of the establishment was a ruthless paedophile who rented enslaved children for his pleasure – and, when the mood took him, attacked others unfortunate enough to stray across his path. Often, it can now be assumed, he was close to the brink of murderous insanity. On one terrible afternoon he snapped (perhaps not for the first time) – and in a black frenzy stripped, raped and strangled a girl of 12.

He was never punished for the crime – not in this life, anyway. But he did have conscience enough to be consumed by guilt and self-disgust. His remorse was merely self-indulgent, however, because he allowed another man – a completely innocent man – to be hanged for the killing.

THE SINISTER SAGA that culminated in one of Australia's worst miscarriages of justice began at about 3.30 p.m. on the afternoon of Friday 30 December 1921. Joseph Graham, a Melbourne cabdriver, was waiting for a customer in Collins Street when he heard a series of 'heart-rending screams' emerging from the coyly named Adam and Eve

Lodging House, diagonally opposite. Graham told police that he and another man across the street tensed and listened – but when the screams abruptly ceased, both men went about their business. It had seemed hard to believe, said Joseph Graham, that anything particularly untoward could really be happening in the calm and orderly city of Melbourne in broad daylight.

The police gave the cabdriver's testimony far less attention than it deserved. By the time he approached them they had another agenda altogether ...

At about 2 o'clock on that fateful afternoon, 12 year-old Hawthorn schoolgirl Alma Tirtschke's aunt sent her on an errand. She was to collect a parcel of meat from her uncle's Swanston Street butcher's shop and take it to a customer in Collins Street. This minor task should not have taken more than 15 minutes, but the aunt knew Alma well. She was a girl who loved to dream and dawdle and window-shop. Only when she had not returned after several hours did her alarmed family contact the police. Alma was a good, well-behaved girl, they said. It was completely out of character for her to worry her loved ones in this way.

A desperate night ensued, with no sign of the missing girl. But then, in the early hours of the following morning, a bottle collector was shocked to find the naked body of a young female in Gun Alley, a laneway off the Eastern Market's Little Collins Street. She had been raped and strangled. The grieving family identified her as Alma.

The brutal crime enraged conservative Melbourne. Newspapers demanded in front page editorials that the police use every possible resource to hunt down the murderer. When the government offered a £250 reward, it was immediately castigated for its meanness. The premier responded by quadrupling the bounty to £1,000 – a sum to which the Melbourne *Herald* added a further £250. It was one of the biggest rewards ever offered in Australia: enough, in 1922, to buy several houses and set up the recipient for life.

The police force assigned two renowned detectives, John Brophy and Frederick Piggott, to lead the investigation. From the first day both men were keenly aware of the need for speed – driven by the overwhelming public (and press) expectation that they find the 'Gun Alley fiend' as quickly as possible. They appealed for witnesses. Alma, it transpired, had last been seen alive between 2.30 and 3.00 p.m. at the corner of Alfred Place and Little Collins Street.

Brophy, Piggott and their subordinates immediately doorknocked every dwelling and business in the area. Among the scores of people they interviewed was 28 year-old Colin Ross, the knockabout manager of a wine saloon. The police disliked Ross. Weeks earlier they had taken him to court on a charge that he had produced a pistol at his premises. They were irked when the magistrate threw the case out. However, rough and rebellious though he was, Ross was no different in his attitudes from other members of the public. He wanted to help in any way he could to see the murderer caught. He readily told detectives that he had seen a girl answering Alma's description walking past his saloon on the day of her disappearance. This matched the testimony of other witnesses. Police questioned Ross closely, but he insisted he knew nothing else about the killing. Colin Ross's record consisted of petty offences only – usually associated with fisticuffs. He had never been convicted of – or even questioned about – a sexual crime.

But the police had decided that Ross was their man, anyway. On 5 January 1922, six days after Alma Tirtschke's death, they took him in for eight hours of questioning. Ross repeatedly denied any knowledge of the murder. He was able to name numerous witnesses who could testify that they had bought drinks from him in his busy saloon right through the afternoon of Friday 30 December. Other witnesses had seen him travelling home on the tram at the time he was supposedly killing the girl. His girlfriend and his brothers offered further supporting alibis – all to no avail.

On 12 January, amid a welter of triumphant newspaper headlines and photographs, Detectives Piggott and Brophy went to Ross's Maidstone house and arrested him for the rape and murder of Alma Tirtschke.

The hysterical press and public were satisfied. Overnight, Colin Ross became the most hated man in Australia. But he knew he was innocent – and as he sat in the remand section of the Melbourne Gaol in Russell Street he remained optimistic and strong. He would be vindicated, he told the lawyers and friends who visited him, because he simply had not committed the murder. He could not have brought himself, in a million years, to perpetrate such an abominable crime. The defence lawyers tended from the start to believe Ross – not only because he was open and sincere but because the police had no evidence of any substance against him. Friends and family believed him also. They knew at first-hand that Colin Ross had been elsewhere when Alma died – and importantly, too, they had long known him as a rough, roistering but essentially decent bloke. None of Ross's prison visitors could have guessed that within three months he would be swinging dead from the gallows after 40 minutes of agonising strangulation.

The trial of Colin Ross began on 20 February 1922. The quiet, ordered judicial proceedings were dramatically at odds with the atmosphere in the surrounding city. The courtroom resembled the eye of a tornado. Beyond its leathered and mahoganied hush, Melbourne at large was seething with the frenzy of the lynch mob. The prosecution led with evidence from two principal witnesses. The first was John Harding, a proven perjurer and multiply-convicted thief who had reoffended so often that he was under threat of being imprisoned 'at the Governor's pleasure'. Harding, who had a great deal to gain by helping his natural enemies, the police, claimed Colin Ross had confessed to him in jail that he was the murderer.

A similar story was trotted out by the second major witness, a prostitute named Ivy Matthews. A fortune-teller, Julia Gibson, who worked under the name Madam Gurkha, also gave damning evidence. For her pains she was later paid part of the £1,250 reward money.

The prosecution so far had built a case based on the dubious claims of a prostitute, a crystal ball-reading charlatan and a perjurer from a prison cell. But its *piece de resistance*, the confused and self-contradictory forensic evidence, was yet to come. A policeman testified that on 3

January, just before Alma Tirtschke was buried at Brighton Cemetery, he had visited her aunt's house in Hawthorn and, with permission, cut a lock of her dark auburn hair. Detective Frederick Piggott told the court that on 12 January, the day of the accused man's arrest, he had noticed a 'sheen of golden hairs' on a blanket in the hall of the Ross house in Maidstone. He had taken this and another blanket away for scientific evaluation.

The state government analyst, Charles Price, was called to the witness box. He testified that he had removed 27 hairs from the two blankets found at Ross's house and compared them under the microscope with hairs taken from Alma's head. Price, a chemist by training, had no expert knowledge of hair analysis. But in those forensically primitive times – when identification seldom went beyond fingerprinting – he was prepared to give it a go. The conclusions he presented to the court were confused and criminally contradictory.

Price said that the blanket hairs 'were not identical in colour' to the hairs cut from Alma's head but were in fact 'a light auburn colour', compared with the darker red of Alma's hair. Moreover, the blanket hairs were 'a different diameter' from Alma's hair – and did not appear to have been 'dragged direct from the scalp', but were probably cast off in the ordinary process of nature.

Analysis of Price's long, rambling testimony suggests that he believed the hairs (which didn't match Alma's anyway) were shed by someone who had slept on the blanket, rather than having been torn out by a rapist.

But astoundingly – and unchallenged by the judge –

Price, many thousands of words later, ultimately reached the utterly contradictory conclusion that the hair samples, although unmatched either in colour or diameter, 'were derived from the scalp of one and the same person'.

It was these words – more than any others – that sent Colin Ross to the gallows. The accused man's defence counsel was outraged. Barrister Thomas Brennan averred: 'Mr Price might, on the facts he deposed to, have been called as a powerful witness for the defence.'

The saloonkeeper's lawyers sought the judge's permission to call their own analyst to compare Alma's hairs with those on the blankets. They were confident, they said, that the blanket hairs would be shown to have come from the head of Ross's girlfriend. The judge refused permission – on the bizarre grounds that a second analyst might damage the exhibits.

Convinced by the testimony of false witnesses and the garbled confusion of what passed as forensic science, the jury found Colin Ross guilty. The judge sentenced him to death by hanging. From the dock, Ross asserted angrily that his life had been 'sworn away by desperate people'. In the dark atmosphere of mass hysteria that prevailed in the city, there were some observers, especially those with knowledge of the law, who realised that an appalling injustice was being done. But the few cool voices of reason were drowned by the screams of the mob. As one lawyer of the time put it: 'Public feeling is as inflamed as it has not been inflamed within the memory of this generation.'

Ross's legal representatives sought permission to appeal. The judge refused. Colin Ross's manifest guilt had been 'proved' beyond further argument. Thomas Brennan, who had not the smallest doubt his client was innocent, then went beyond the court, to seek leave to appeal to the Privy Council in England. The Attorney-General of the State of Victoria refused the application.

On 24 April 1922 Colin Ross was executed in the Melbourne Gaol. For the first time, an experimental four-strand rope was used. The subsequent report from the prison hospital was headed: 'Important. Never use it again.' It had taken Ross 40 minutes to strangle, slowly, to death.

Thomas Brennan was shattered by his failure to save his client. But he saw it as his God-given duty to try to restore Colin Ross's good name – posthumously, at least. Immediately after his final appeal attempt failed he sat down to write a book, *The Gun Alley Tragedy* – a detailed and damning indictment of a trial that had been little better than a legalised lynching. Brennan's introduction reads:

> *On the early morning of the last day of the year 1921 the dead body of a little girl of twelve, named Alma Tirtschke, was found by a bottle-gatherer in an L-shaped right of way off Little Collins Street. She had been violated and strangled, and her nude body had been placed in Gun Alley. On the morning of Saturday February 25th 1922, Colin Campbell Ross, a young man of twenty-eight, was found guilty of her murder, and on the morning of April 24th he was executed in the Melbourne Gaol. Face to face with his Maker, as he himself put it, he asserted his innocence on the scaffold in terms of such peculiar solemnity as to intensify the*

*feeling, already widely prevalent, that an innocent man had been done to death ...*

SEVENTY-ONE YEARS LATER, something extraordinary happened.

As one observer expressed it: 'You could be forgiven for believing that Colin Ross stretched out his hand from the grave to tap a man of goodwill on the shoulder – and ask that man to prove him innocent of a long-ago outrage. Innocent, so that his soul could find rest at last.'

It began with an exhibition of paintings by the Australian artist Charles Blackman, mounted by the National Gallery of Victoria. Blackman, born seven years after Alma Tirtschke's death, had been darkly fascinated by the murder from the first time he read about it. The brutal killing moved him so deeply that he spent eight years creating a long series of 'schoolgirl paintings' – bleak cityscapes in which young girls with huge, frightened eyes, wandered lost. Especially powerful were the backgrounds – views of what the artist called 'the mad wedding cake' of gothic architecture and labyrinths of wrought iron that characterised the now-demolished Eastern Market.

It was apparent to all who saw these paintings that the dead girl's plight had gripped Blackman's imagination like no other subject.

In July 1993, a 37 year-old former schoolteacher began to share the artist's obsession. Kevin Morgan had been appointed to a student librarianship at the gallery. Coincidentally he was there at the same time the Blackman pictures were on display. Every morning, as he approached his workplace, Morgan's steps would slow. He could scarcely tear his eyes from the stark images of frail and terrified children in mushroom hats, passing through deserted streets shadowed by menacing chimneystacks.

Morgan hadn't the faintest idea what, if anything, had inspired the paintings – but he was curious. He read a catalogue and learned that Blackman had based his series on 'the infamous murder of a schoolgirl in 1921'.

The trainee librarian felt an inexplicable compulsion to discover all he could about the case. He began with the newspapers of the time, moving on to the writings of Thomas Brennan and others. It wasn't long before he concluded, like others before him, that there was something deeply suspicious about the arrest, trial and hanging of Colin Ross. He set himself to research the tragedy ever more deeply – finding documents along the way that convinced him Ross had been an innocent man, framed by police.

Particularly compelling were the notes in Ross's Bible, which one of his relatives had discovered in a dusty box in a backyard shed. This was the Bible the condemned man had had with him in the condemned cell. In its pages, he privately expresses despair and anger at the cruel wrong that has been done him. In Verse 11 of Psalm 35, for example, he underlines the words 'false witness' – writing, in the margin, 'against Colin'. Prophetically he adds, 'Time will tell.'

In Verse 10 of Psalm 26 he underlines the phrase 'full of bribes' – scrawling beside it, 'This is our police force, which our people think so much of.' In Verse 11 of Psalm

31 he underscores 'slander of many' ... and 'take away my life'.

Kevin Morgan was deeply affected by what he read in the old Bible's pages. He found it impossible to believe that these could be the annotations of a guilty man.

Even more telling were the thousands of pages of documentation associated with the trial:

- The testimonies of six independent witnesses, providing Ross with an unshakeable alibi, had simply been ignored.
- Cabdriver Joseph Graham, who reported hearing a girl's screams coming from a building in Collins Street at a time when Ross was serving customers in his saloon, was given short shrift by investigating police and was not asked to give evidence at the inquest. He was so distressed when Ross was found guilty that he went to a solicitor and repeated his story but he was not allowed to tell it to the jury.
- The court proceedings were a melange of contradictions and anomalies. The Crown successfully based its case on the testimonies, among others, of a convict seeking a shortening of his sentence, a prostitute who disliked Ross, a former wine saloon employee whom Ross had sacked, and a fortune-teller who subsequently received a share of the reward.
- The rambling, muddled evidence regarding the hair samples, presented by someone self-admittedly ignorant in the field, should never have been accepted as 'proof'

> of the defendant's guilt. It suggested, rather, that he was innocent.

Colin Campbell Ross died on the gallows 34 years before Kevin Morgan was born. But to the trainee librarian the miscarriage of justice transcended the old, foxed documents in which it was chronicled. Ross seemed to be crying out for his name to be cleared. With his wife's agreement, Morgan resigned his job, cashed his superannuation and devoted seven years to conducting research into Alma Tirtschke's death and the guilt or otherwise of her alleged killer.

In 1995 he made a remarkable discovery. In an archive box at the Office of Public Prosecutions library, he found an envelope bearing the words 'On His Majesty's Service'. Inside were three cards, containing hair samples from Alma Tirtschke, Ross's girlfriend and the blankets removed from Ross's house. Morgan proceeded to fight a long bureaucratic and legal battle to have the three sets of hair DNA-tested. It took him three years to win permission to remove one strand from each card for evaluation.

The effort paid off. In 1998 Dr Bentley Atchison of the Victorian Institute of Forensic Medicine declared that the hairs did NOT come from the same scalp. The evidence given 76 years earlier by State Government Analyst Charles Price – evidence which helped to hang Colin Ross – was simply wrong. Dr Atchison's tests were later confirmed by Dr James Robertson of the Federal Police forensic unit.

Kevin Morgan will publish a book which he believes will conclusively prove the innocence of the long-dead Ross.

BUT THE LAST WORD must come from the person who, in all likelihood, was the real killer. On the eve of the execution an anonymous letter addressed to Colin Ross arrived at his solicitor's office. Convinced that it was genuine, Thomas Brennan subsequently reproduced it in his book, *The Gun Alley Tragedy*. From the shadows, the monster who would sacrifice another man's life to preserve his own wrote:

> *You have been condemned for a crime which you never committed, and are to suffer for another's fault. Since your conviction you have, no doubt, wondered what manner of man the real murderer is who could not only encompass the girl's death, but allow you to suffer in his stead.*
>
> *My dear Ross, if it is any satisfaction for you to know it, believe me that you will die but once, but he will continue to die for the rest of his life.*
>
> *Honoured and fawned upon by those who know him, the smile upon his lips but hides the canker eating into his soul. Day and night his life is a hell without the hope of reprieve. Gladly would he take your place on Monday next if he had himself alone to consider. His reason, then, briefly stated, is this: A devoted and loving mother is ill – a shock would be fatal. Three loving married sisters, whose whole life would be wrecked, to say nothing of brothers who have been accustomed to take him as a pattern. He cannot sacrifice these. Himself he will sacrifice when his mother passes away. He will do it by his own hand.*
>
> *It is too painful for him to go into the details of the crime. It is simply a Jekyll and Hyde existence. By a*

*freak of nature he was not made as other men. This girl was not the first. With a procuress all things are possible. In this case there was no intention of murder. The victim unexpectedly collapsed.*

*May it be some satisfaction to yourself, your devoted mother, and the members of your family to know that at least one of the legions of the damned, who is the cause of your death, is suffering the pangs of hell. He may not ask your forgiveness or sympathy, but he asks for your understanding.*

The author of this chilling letter would, by now, be dead – possibly, as he promised, by his 'own hand'. Kevin Morgan believes he knows who the self-pitying child-killer was. He will reveal the fiend's name when his researches are complete.

# Dilemma of the Disappearing Ad Man

*In March 2001, David Eason, a London advertising executive, took a day trip to Queensland's wildly beautiful Fraser Island. While his companions went on ahead to explore, Eason lay back against a sand dune and smoked a cigarette. He was never seen again. And despite intensive air and ground searches, no clue to his disappearance was ever found. Police describe the case as one of Australia's most perplexing mysteries ...*

MORE THAN 600,000 TOURISTS visit Queensland's lavishly tropical Fraser Island every year. But the world's biggest sand island, covering 184,000 square kilometres, seldom seems crowded. With its white sweeping beaches, towering dunes framing freshwater lakes, and horizons of coloured sand, the island is infused, even today, with the primal hush that stilled the lips of the earliest white settlers.

Named after Eliza Fraser, whose ship *Stirling Castle* foundered on the Great Barrier Reef in 1836, the island has long been characterised by poets and novelists as a place of mystery. And perhaps the greatest mystery of all has been the sudden and inexplicable disappearance of an English tourist, David Eason. Police, who conducted massive and prolonged searches for the missing man, described the total absence of possessions, clothing or other clues as 'bizarre' and 'beyond belief'.

Eason, aged 46, was art director of a British advertising company specialising in pharmaceutical products. On 29 March 2001 he visited Fraser Island as a member of a four-wheel drive tour group. Around lunchtime, following several hours of sightseeing, the group's coordinator announced that everyone should head now for Lake Wabby, two kilometres inland. From there they would proceed to Kingfisher Bay on the other side of the island, where they would board a tour bus at 3.00 p.m.

David Eason hadn't yet experienced enough of the island. Fresh from a grey London winter, he was entranced by the wild crashing surf, the endless stretches of dazzling beach, the kauri pines and gigantic ferns whose roots were anchored in pure sand, the sting of the tropical sun. He told his companions he would sunbathe for half an hour before following them on foot to the lake.

When police interviewed them singly next day, the other members of the party shared much the same recollection. As they departed, Eason, who was wearing a green singlet, dark shorts and sandals, had lain back, smiling, against a dune and placed a cigarette in his mouth. He had seemed relaxed and carefree. Beside him on the sand lay a leather bag containing his expensive camera gear.

It was 1.00 p.m.

The tour group waited an extra hour at Lake Wabby carpark – then decided to return without David Eason. At 6.00 p.m., when there was still no sign of him, the tour's organisers alerted police and park rangers. That night, dozens of officers and volunteers searched the island, using spotlights and torches. Next day helicopters and light planes scanned the island from the air – the first of many searches over the following days and weeks.

Particularly puzzling were the results (or lack of them) obtained by 80 State Emergency Service workers who picked painstakingly over an area of two square kilometres surrounding the spot where the advertising man was last seen. They found nothing: no tracks, no scrap of clothing, no cigarette butts and no camera bag.

David Eason and his possessions had vanished from

the face of Fraser Island.

Police printed flyers and posters, asking for information from the Easter crowds. No-one could help. The missing man's sister, Janice Eames, and her husband Harvey flew to Queensland from Britain. They told reporters they were 'dumbfounded' by David's disappearance – and dismissed suggestions that he might have suicided or drowned as 'just not on'.

'He was an experienced sailor with a healthy respect for the water and all its dangers,' said Janice. 'Besides, he'd never have gone into the sea from here. He had a lifelong fear of sharks.' She repeated what she had told police. David had been financially secure and in a happy relationship with his girlfriend Jo. There was absolutely no reason why he would have harmed himself – and if he had done so on land, there would be evidence.

Detective Sergeant Bruce Hodgins summed up the bafflement experienced by his colleagues. 'People have gone missing – but usually there is some sort of trace,' he said.

One month after the disappearance, a nine year-old boy, Clinton Gage, was mauled to death by dingoes on the island. Could David Eason have suffered a similar fate? According to police, it was extremely unlikely. Dingoes would have left traces: body parts, bloodied clothing. And they would have been incapable of consuming a camera bag and its contents.

After debating and exhausting a broad range of explanations, David Eason's family was left with only one theory – that he had been murdered. Why, by whom, and for what reason they could not begin to imagine. They asked police, nevertheless, to treat the case as a homicide enquiry. But with no body, no belongings, no tracks and not the faintest indication of the missing man's movements, it was a difficult request.

As Senior Detective Hodgins put it: 'Where do you begin?'

POSTSCRIPT: As this volume went to press, Queensland police announced that 'skeletal remains' had been found near Lake Wabby. Forensic scientists identified the bones as belonging to David Eason.

# Glowing Globes of the Outback

# The Enigma Nobody Can Explain

*Min-Min lights – the eerie luminous spheres that startle stockmen and cheekily tailgate cars on outback roads – have been intriguing Australian scientists for decades. Experts regularly attempt to explain what Min-Mins might be. But so far no-one has produced a sustainable theory. Most perplexing of all are the statements by numerous witnesses that these baffling balls of light have behaved in a seemingly intelligent and purposeful way.*

THE CHILDHOOD MEMORY would haunt Queenslander Helen McBride all her life. Even half a century after the event she was able to describe its elements to me in stark and vivid detail:

'As a ten year-old girl in the 1940s I holidayed with my grandparents in Toowoomba. One evening I went out to pick some wildflowers and was surprised to see they were casting long shadows, although the sun had set. At that moment grandpa's dog began barking. I looked up and saw a ball of light, the size of a large balloon, hovering about a foot above his head. The ball was as brilliant as a small sun and it hurt my eyes.

'The dog seemed very scared and was backing away, snarling defensively with the light following him. It was dancing about, in a pattern that seemed to react to the dog's panicky movements. I got the powerful impression the light was teasing him. At that moment my grandma came out to see what the fuss was about. When the back door creaked open the globe vanished – just like a large lamp being switched off.

'My grandfather said I'd seen a 'ball of electricity' of a type which often appeared around that area. In recent years I've looked back with my mind's eye and I feel grandpa was wrong. The thing might well have been electrical. But it had a mind of its own – and it was taunting that dog.'

Helen had been privileged to observe the inexplicable Min-Min light – a phenomenon witnessed by Aborigines over thousands of years and entrenched in tribal legend across the Australian continent. The lights were remarked upon also by the earliest European settlers.

Min-Mins are not unique to Australia. In Europe they are known as will-o'-the-wisps, Jack-o'-Lanterns, earthlights and spooklights. Some African tribes call them *aku* (devils). In Malaysia they are *penangal* – the ghostly heads of women who died in childbirth. Wherever they appear these earthlights share a common characteristic: they defy explanation, inspiring a maze of theories which never succeed in explaining and encompassing all aspects of their behaviour and physical nature.

Another Min-Min witness whom I interviewed was Ted Baynes of Yelarbon in Queensland. He recalled sheltering under a tree after a pulsing globe of brilliant light chased him along a rural road.

'It was a dark wet night. I was near Warwick, walking along the main highway, when I felt a car had caught me in its headlights. I turned around, ready to jump out of the way and saw a bright yellow ball hovering several feet above the road, approaching me at quite high speed.

'The thing was so strange and uncomfortable-feeling that I didn't wait around. I took shelter under a bushy tree, from where I watched the ball. It was just across the road from me, moving around and radiating light. Curiosity finally got the better of me and I walked over to get a better look. But as I approached, the sphere vanished – and the night was pitch-black again.'

Ted Baynes and his wife saw a similar Min-Min light in the 1950s, when he was working at Gurley Station, south of Moree, New South Wales.

'This one seemed to move incredibly fast – hovering in one spot for up to a minute, then whizzing off somewhere else. Frankly I found it very frightening, but the overseer insisted there was nothing to worry about. He said it was known as a Paddy's Lantern in those parts. It had been seen around the district as far back as anyone could remember.'

In 1992–93 the investigator Fred Silcock chronicled more than 500 first-hand accounts of Min-Min activity. Particularly intriguing was the experience of the Lanahan family, owners of a Queensland cattle property. Every winter during the 1950s, a gigantic Min-Min roughly five metres in diameter would fly in circles above the cattle yard, terrifying the animals. One year, when a family member fired a shot at the sphere, it collapsed into a tiny red 'coal'. Minutes later, however, it puffed out to its full size again. After about an hour, during which the hovering shape filled the yard with a brilliant red light, it vanished – briefly reappearing over a distant paddock before it zoomed out of sight.

Although Min-Mins had always been locally reported they decisively entered the consciousness of the general Australian public in the early 20th century – when they began to appear near the old Min-Min Hotel, 73 kilometres east of Boulia in central-west Queensland. The inn, which was to give Min-Min lights their English name, burned down in 1918. In the same year a regional newspaper

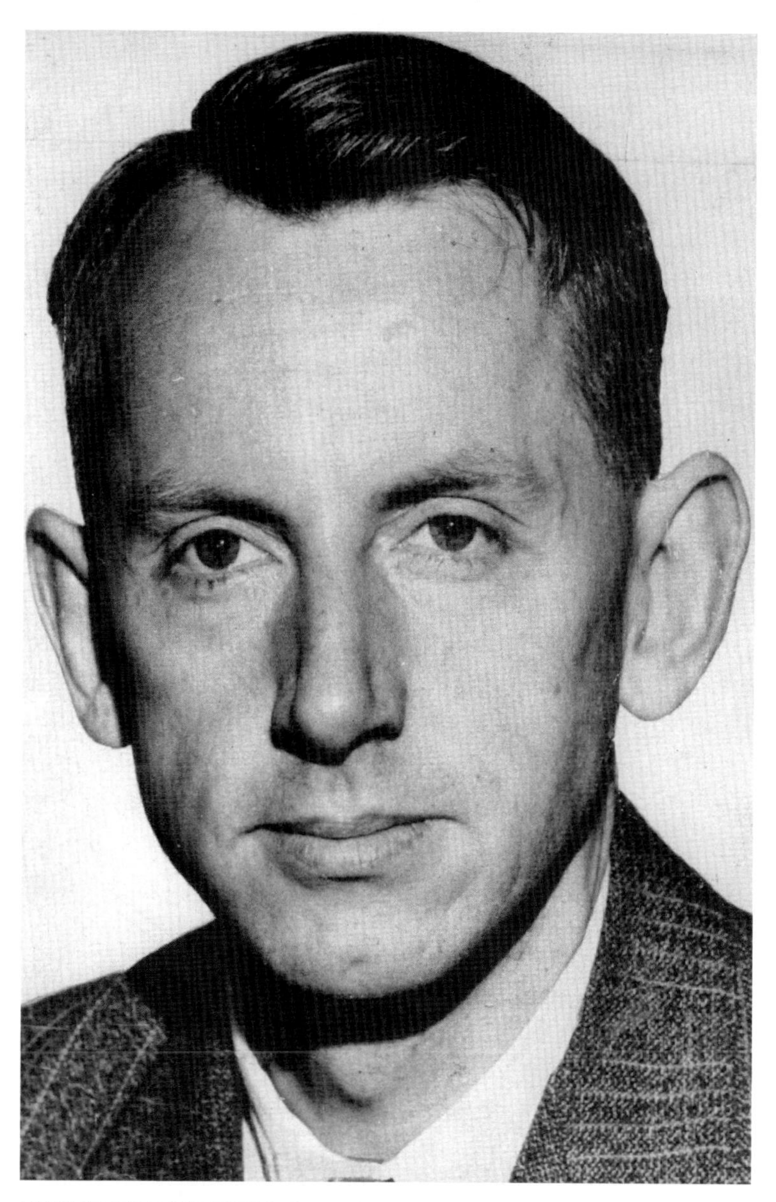

NEW YEAR'S DAY DEATHS On the morning of 1 January 1963 the corpses of laser-beam physicist Dr Gilbert Bogle (above) and Mrs Margaret Chandler, the wife of a colleague, were found part-naked, beside Sydney's Lane Cove River. Despite forensic investigations that would span years, police were unable to determine what had caused the couple's deaths. America's FBI also probed the murders.
*Courtesy Newspix*

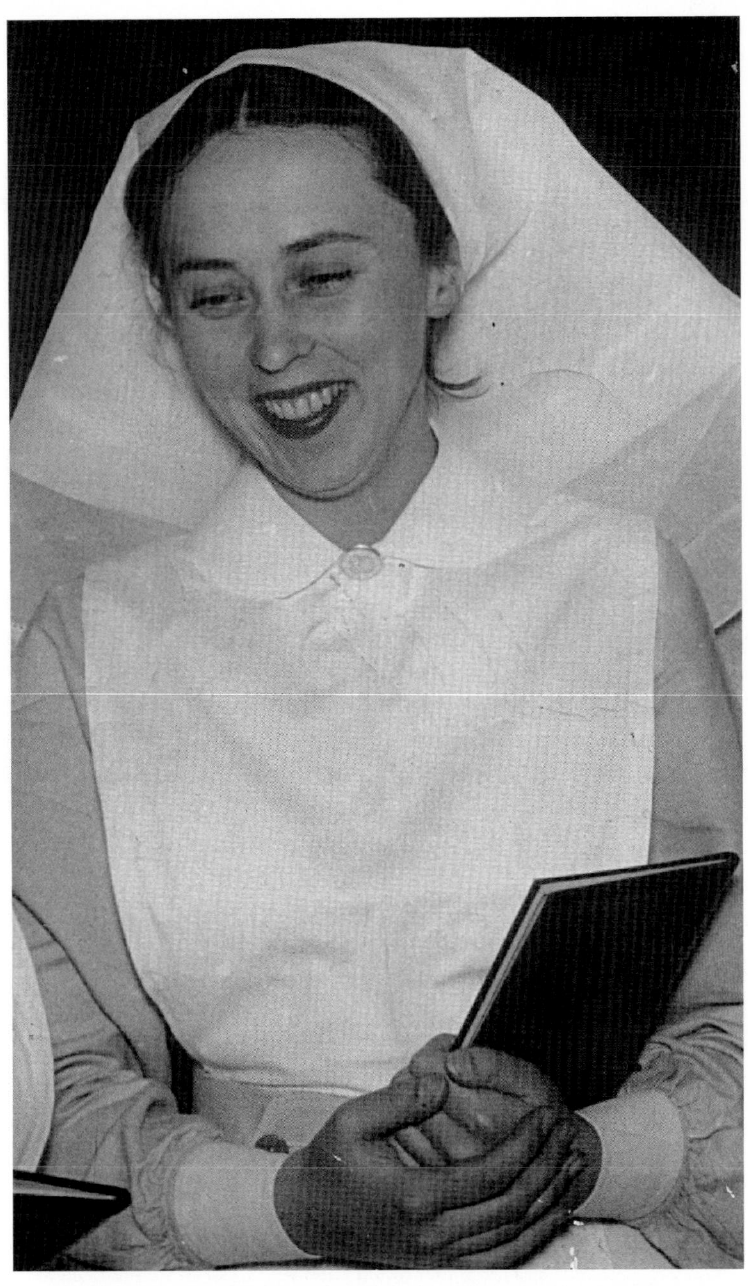

PARTNER IN MYSTERY Mrs Chandler was 29 years old at the time of her perplexing death. She worked as a nurse before her marriage. *Courtesy Newspix*

RIVERBANK RIDDLE Detectives in Lane Cove National Park search the scene of the Bogle/Chandler deaths for clues – without success. *Courtesy Newspix*

MONSTER, OR TRICK OF LIGHT? This photograph of what appears to be a gigantic fur-covered hominid streaking through remote bushland, was taken by a Canberra businessman.
*Courtesy 'Tim the Yowie Man'*

HE SAW 'MONSTERS'
While living for 32 years with an Aboriginal tribe, escaped convict William Buckley (right) regularly saw 'Bunyips' swimming in lakes and rivers. In his 1852 biography he described the creatures as 'very extraordinary amphibious animals' which the aborigines feared. 'When alone,' writes Buckley, 'I several times attempted to spear a Bunyip; but had the natives seen me do so … my life would have paid forfeit – they considering the animal as something supernatural.'

PANTHER WITNESS  Wildlife artist Jahne Hope-Williams sketches the large panther-like creature she watched from the safety of her car at Mount Macedon, Victoria.
*Courtesy Herald & Weekly Times Photographic Collection*

'MIRACLE' MAP This near-perfect space-eye-view of Australia was imprinted by sheer chance on a rock slab roughly 500 million years ago. The heat-seared image lay in siltstone darkness until 1967, when stoneworker Jack Martin (pictured) helped split the rock open while dynamiting a quarry near Bacchus Marsh, Victoria. *Courtesy Matthew Bouwmeester, The Age*

TRAGIC SEARCH In February 1966 South Australian police and volunteers scour sand dunes in a fruitless hunt for the bodies of the missing Beaumont children, Jane, Arnna and Grant. What happened to the children is still a mystery. The fiend who abducted them was never found. *Courtesy The Advertiser*

DID PM DROWN? On 17 December 1967 Prime Minister Harold Holt vanished into the ocean off Portsea's Cheviot Beach. The disappearance sparked the biggest air-sea search in Australian history – and inspired international controversy. Some imaginative theorists asserted that Holt had simply staged the drowning and was still alive.
*Courtesy The Herald & Weekly Times Photographic Collection*

DOOMED YACHT MYSTERY When Queensland trimaran *Privateer* went missing en route to Honolulu, maritime experts advanced theories as diverse as a collision at sea to deadly contamination by a French nuclear test. But no solid evidence appeared until September 1967, when a New Zealand fisherman stumbled upon a fibreglass float buried in sand. The mystery only deepened when it was found that the float had been sawn from the missing craft – and that strange messages had been scratched on it. *Courtesy Courier Mail*

VANISHED On 21 October 1978, while flying over Bass Strait to King Island, young pilot Frederick Valentich (above and on facing page) radioed that he was being 'orbited' by a 'long shape' shining a 'green light.' Abruptly, the transmission ceased. Neither Valentich, nor any fragment of his Cessna (constructed from floatable modular units) was ever found. Frederick Valentich had become the 18th person since 1934 to mysteriously disappear without trace, while flying over the Strait.
*Courtesy The Herald & Weekly Times Photographic Collection*

BARONET OR BUTCHER? Tubby butcher Tom Castro (facing page) was jailed for fraud after asserting that he was the long-lost Sir Roger Tichborne (above), heir to vast English estates. But today, some historians believe the portly pretender from Wagga, NSW, was telling the truth. *Courtesy Newspix*

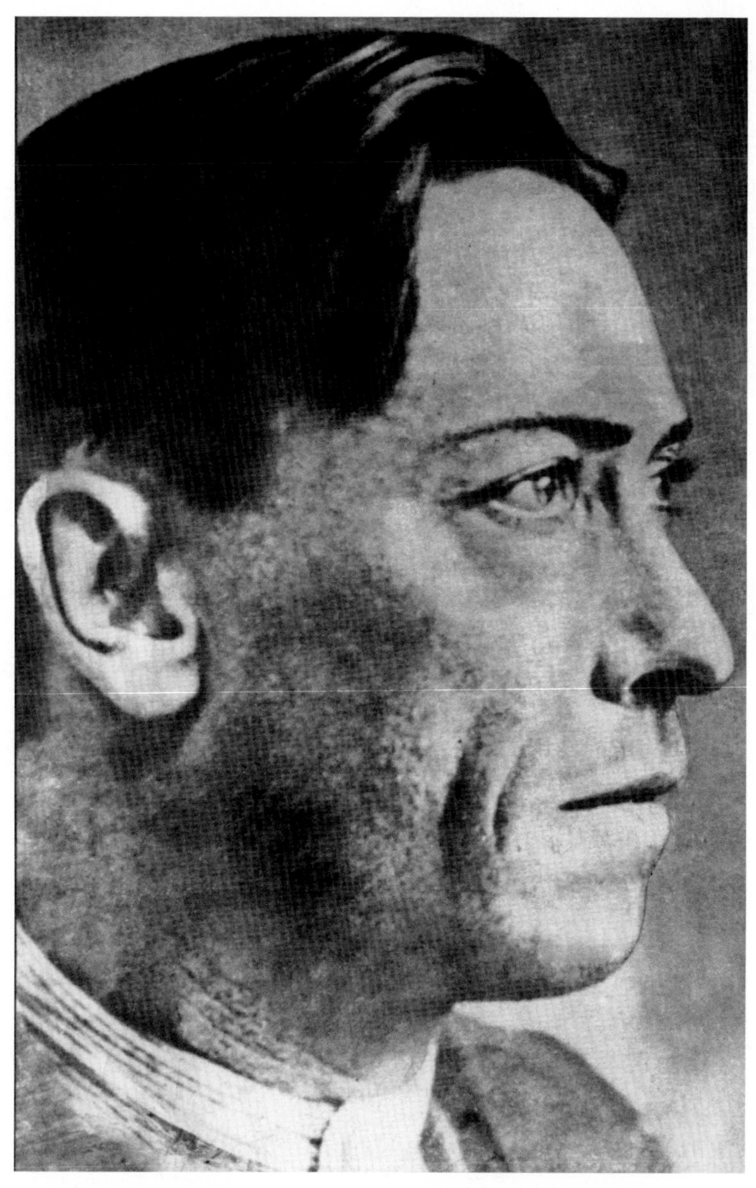

HANGED IN ERROR In February 1922 saloonkeeper Colin Ross, 28, was hanged in Melbourne Gaol for the rape-murder of a 12 year-old schoolgirl. Modern forensic research proves Ross guiltless – the victim of a prejudiced judge and police impatient for results. But who was the real killer? Recent research led to a series of fascinating discoveries.
*Courtesy The Herald & Weekly Times Photographic Collection*

MURDERED JOURNALIST Courageous editor Juanita Nielsen used her newspaper, *Now,* to expose corruption at the highest levels of Sydney society. Dozens of powerful people wanted her dead – and in July 1975 they got their wish.
*Courtesy Newspix*

MONSTER'S TRAIL? In 1971 a Bundaberg farmer, clearing land for zucchinis, stumbled upon a series of deep 'footprints', which seemed to have been created by a creature of stupendous size. The discovery would soon attract scientists from around the globe. No one knows with certainty what the 'forgotten footprints' are.

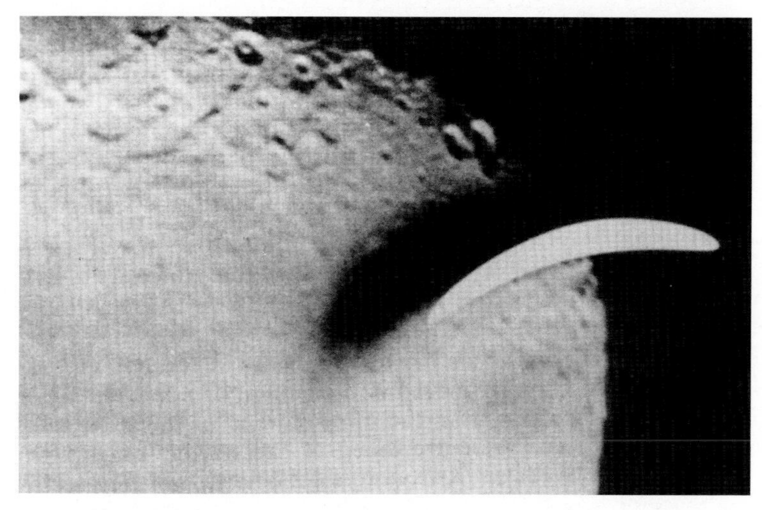

MOON MYSTERY On 4 June 1969 – 46 days before Neil Armstrong became the first man to walk on the Moon – two Ballarat astronomers independently took extraordinary photographs. Their pictures show an immense boomerang-shaped object looming above the lunar surface, casting a shadow kilometres in length.

reported that a stockman, headed toward Boulia, had been 'followed by a large, strange light, oval in shape and of an unknown nature'. The stockman first saw the brilliantly glowing intruder hovering above the cemetery behind the burned-out hotel. It proceeded to pursue him relentlessly as he rode, at increasing speed, across the open downs country. After keeping pace with him for several kilometres it vanished abruptly into the darkness. Throughout the century, so many additional witnesses claimed to have seen the Boulia light that it became a subject of speculation in scientific magazines. Typical is an essay by Pam Shilton for *The Journal of Meteorology, UK* (8: 248, 1983). She writes:

> *Around Boulia and Winton there appears from time to time an unmistakable light – a luminous fluorescent shape that fades and brightens, recedes and advances across the flat never-ending plain. It has mystified men for centuries. It fascinates. It begs you to follow. And it can be eerie and frightening on that lonely dark plain at night.*

Most investigators tend to believe that the Min-Min is a phenomenon completely distinct from that other profound enigma, the UFO. Many witnesses have described the light as being a seemingly natural element of the Australian landscape. There is little about it that seems alien, or out-of-place. But native though it may be, the phenomenon continues to generate considerable fear and superstition. Visitors to the outback are often warned never to chase a

Min-Min. People reckless enough to do so have vanished, never to return – or so the doomsayers claim.

For decades motorists on the vast Hay plain in New South Wales have reported being followed by the local 'ghost light' – a sphere of blindingly white brilliance, brighter than the moon. Repeatedly witnesses have commented on the light's seemingly intelligent behaviour as it circles and hovers above their cars – moving in, apparently to get a closer look, and retreating like a shy animal when threatened.

A classic example of seemingly deliberative action by a Min-Min was described to me in 1993 by Glenda Morris. From Home Hill, Queensland, she wrote:

> *My small daughter and I were driving on a bush road toward Ravenshoe. We were passing through basalt country, peppered with sparsely-grown bluegum, bloodwood and ironbark trees.*
>
> *As we approached the area known as Green Swamp, my daughter cried out with delight. She said she could see a pretty balloon following us. I looked back and was amazed to see it was true. The balloon seemed to be bouncing along with our car – slowing when I slowed and catching up when I accelerated.*
>
> *All the time it playfully zigzagged in and around the trees, sometimes bouncing almost to treetop height.*
>
> *I was raised in the bush and I am well aware that the moon can appear to be following a car, although it stays in one spot. But this was no moon. It lost and regained speed in a most peculiar way and constantly*

*changed its position. It kept us company for some time. But when we reached what is now the Millstream Estate, it suddenly vanished.*

*I reckon we must have got a glimpse of a Min-Min light.*

Country people whose jobs entail long periods outdoors are obviously likelier to participate in the rare experience of meeting a Min-Min than are citydwellers sitting sceptically behind their desks. A particularly thought-provoking rural encounter is recalled by Bruce McDougall, a contractor with the Royal Automobile Club of Queensland (RACQ).

Bruce met his Min-Min in 1999, ten kilometres from his hometown of Miles in western Queensland. One Tuesday night at around 9 o'clock he was called out to retrieve a four-wheel drive with broken fanbelts. En route to the stranded vehicle he noticed a light in his rearview mirror. He assumed it was a motorbike, which he judged to be about a kilometre behind him. It stayed at that distance for the next seven kilometres. But abruptly, as he reached the bottom of a slope, he realised that the light was almost on top of him. Nothing on the road could travel at that speed!

For the next two kilometres the light stayed about ten metres behind his service vehicle. Eventually he pulled off the road to park in front of the stranded four-wheel drive:

'When I got out I saw that the light had stopped about 20 metres back on the side of the road. I still thought it was a motorcycle, until I realised it was too big a light for a bike. Also, there was nobody behind it. The light (pale yellow and extremely bright) was about one foot [30 centimetres] in diameter and illuminated all the surrounding trees.

'The people in the four-wheel drive couldn't see the light because I was parked in front of them. I asked them to come round to the other side and take a look at the Min-Min light. They were shocked and scared and asked, "What is it?" I told them (again) it was a Min-Min, although I'd never previously seen one.

'It was a husband and wife. They'd never heard of Min-Mins before and were totally freaked out.

'After they started looking, the light slowly sank down onto the road. It hovered there for 10-15 seconds, then rose up to its previous height of three or four feet [90–120 centimetres]. I was completely awestruck. It was fascinating to see. The light hovered for about another 20 seconds, then shot away at incredible speed – I estimated 500 kilometres per hour. It lit both sides of the road as it retreated.

'I can't explain what the light was. It couldn't have been anything man-made. It had looked as though it was checking us out. I felt it strange that it would follow me for ten kilometres, stop and sit – then take off in the direction it came. I'm grateful to have seen this strange light and to have been so close ...'

Bruce McDougall's sense of wonder has been shared by thousands of earthlight-encounterers around the world. In every country these luminous globes seem to have their own particular modes of 'behaviour'. Attempts to rationalise them away as marsh gas, traffic light reflections or sub-atomic particle reactions fail to take into account the witnesses' near-universal testimony that the globes follow, watch and evade.

An example of this widely-observed international phenomenon has been reported from the two old graveyards at the base of Clinch Mountain in Belfast, Virginia. Visitors describe a beachball-sized sphere of light which hovers above the gravestones, then, 'at will', pursues passing cars at great speed. The globe, which varies in colour from red to blue, usually retreats at the moment a car stops, then hovers above the road several metres away, until the chase begins again.

The graveyard connection would not be lost on Australia's Aborigines, who have long been convinced that Min-Mins are spirits of the dead – in particular, the victims of white man's genocide. Some tribes regard the lights as being manifestations of tortured spirits which are not always friendly and are accordingly characterised as *debil-debils.*

A classic Australian earthlight encounter was described by the bushman and naturalist Henry G. Lamond. In a letter to the April 1937 edition of *Walkabout* magazine, Lamond recalled that in 1912 he was manager of Warenda, the biggest station in Queensland. At 2.00 o'clock on a black, wintry June morning he set out for an associated property at Slasher's Creek, where he planned to start the lamb-marking.

In that era, there were relatively few cars in western Queensland. Lamond was mildly surprised therefore when he saw what seemed to be a headlight approaching him through the darkness. He estimated the light's strength 'by the way it picked out individual hairs in the mare's mane'. But as it got closer he realised that it couldn't be a vehicle light.

> *It remained in one bulbous ball, instead of dividing into the two headlights, as it should have done. It was too greeny-glary for an acetylene light. It floated too high for any car. There was something eerie about it.*

The mare pulled up short, pricked her ears and 'snorted her challenge to the unknown'. Lamond remained in the saddle, watching the light slowly advance, 'airily as a bubble', about three metres above the ground. Then he got the mare moving again – and he and the light passed each other, moving in opposite directions. Curious, he turned to watch it, just as it began to melt away.

> *It did not go out with a snap. Its vanishing was more like the gradual fading of wires in an electric bulb. The mare acknowledged the dousing by another snorting whistle.*

Henry Lamond subsequently decided that the luminous globe must have been gas rising from a mud spring. He could not have guessed that almost a century later, sensible people just like him would still be trying to find rational explanations for the playful and elusive Min-Min.

Countless witnesses, separated by generations, have told similar stories. Sixty-four years after Henry Lamond's encounter, Bega's *District News* (17 September 1976) published the testimony of a local farmer who was accosted by a Min-Min while repairing a fence on his property. Just as he was finishing the job he heard an extremely high-pitched noise, 'a bit like air escaping from a high-pressure tractor feed':

> *I tried to locate the source of the sound, but as the light had almost gone it was difficult to see anything.*

The noise grew steadily louder. The farmer looked about him in the gloom – and finally realised that the cacophony was coming from a large rock in the middle of the paddock. From behind the boulder a brilliant light was shining.

> *My first thought was that it was a fire, but the light was too constant. As I got closer, the noise got louder. I got level with the rock and poked my head around the corner, and my heavens, did I get a shock ... There on the ground was a bright globe of 'something', about the size of a football.*
>
> *It ... was a very bright yellow, which then changed to a bright orange and then yellow again, the cycle taking about five seconds each time ... It was about six inches [15 centimetres] off the ground. There was no sense of heat, but when I tried to get closer I could feel my skin tighten and all the hair on my body stand up ... It was like trying to walk into a very strong wind.*

The farmer picked up a fallen branch and poked it at the globe.

*... But I couldn't get too close at all. It just seemed to slip away, like two magnets opposing each other. Then it went a vivid green and started to fade away ... finally there was nothing there. At this time the noise was unbearable, but as it faded, so did the noise. I did notice a sweet sickly smell, but that faded quickly, too.*

N.W. Bauer, the retired Queensland Commissioner for Police, took Min-Mins seriously, as did many of his officers. In an article published by the *Royal Geographical Society of Australia Bulletin*, Mr Bauer described what he regarded as 'the best-authenticated recording of this remarkable phenomenon'. He quoted a statement made to him by a subordinate, detective Sergeant Lyall Booth of the Stock Investigation Squad at Cloncurry.

Booth experienced his brush with the bizarre on the night of Saturday 2 May 1981. Following six days of mustering, he had established a camp by the Bulla Bulla waterhole, about 60 kilometres east of Boulia. The night was clear and cool – and he went to sleep early, at around 9 o'clock.

'I woke at about 11 (I don't know why) and saw a light, which I first took to be a car headlight, approximately 1500-2000 metres north-east from me. I thought it was a vehicle on the main road, but [then] I realised that the main road was further to the north ...The light appeared to be just to the west of the Hamilton River channels and appeared to be moving, but it did not seem to get any closer. (I know that's hard to grasp, but that is how it appeared.)

'The light was at treetop height. Its intensity seemed to

fluctuate a little and this may have given the impression of movement. It was a single light and white in colour, similar to the light thrown by a quartz headlight. After watching it for three or four minutes I realised that it was probably the Min-Min light.

'I kept it under observation for about half an hour and its position remained about the same (I can't say the same for my pulse rate). I went to sleep with some difficulty about midnight and awoke again at about 1.00 a.m. and saw the light again, just to the north of where the cook was camped.' (The cook, an Aboriginal woman, was the only other person at the camp.)

'... That means that if it was the same light, it had moved about 1,000 metres to the southwest from its original position. It was not as bright ... and had a slightly yellow colour ... about the colour of a gas light which is turned down very low ... but it was of much greater intensity.

'It appeared to be slightly bigger than the gas light used in the cook's camp. It seemed to be three to six feet [1–2 metres] from the ground. It illuminated the ground around it, but I was too far away to see any detail. I could, however, see the cook's camp.

'I watched the light for five to six minutes and then it suddenly dived toward the ground and went out ... I did not see it again.'

The following day Det. Sgt Booth described his experience to the cook. She had seen nothing. He then searched the area, but could find no clue suggesting a physical cause for what he had witnessed. He concluded:

'I am at a loss to explain in physical terms the lights that I saw. My enquiries lead me to believe that they were not caused by man.'

ON 27 JUNE 2002 Victoria's *Herald Sun* newspaper published an extraordinary report describing 'pulsing lights' which were striking awe into the inhabitants of a rural community near Stawell. For 12 months locals had been watching and videotaping up to 30 luminous globes (which, in my view, may or may not be earthlights) swarming around a remote Grampians valley.

Reporter Mark Dunn and photographer Paul Trezise watched the display through binoculars and a high-powered camera lens – and returned with photographs which their paper ran next day. 'The lights,' wrote Dunn, 'mostly white, but some red or yellow, float through the uninhabited valley and silently congregate above the plains.' He interviewed a Stawell man, Stephen Swanwick, who said he had visited the site almost nightly for the past year, watching the lights glow, then pulse in concert. Swanwick, who had shot 'reams of video footage', said he had watched two large egg-shaped lights floating above the gorge. 'You can see their core,' he said. 'They can turn orange, a strong pale yellow, or red.'

The weather bureau does not use balloons in the area. The lights are too low to be stars and too large to radiate from insects or animals.

The two newspapermen watched and snapped for almost two hours as the lights moved across the sky and hovered above the tree line of the ranges.

Dunn concluded his report: 'We left the Grampians with no understanding of what we had seen.'

Scientific attempts to explain encounters of this kind are almost as numerous as the earthlights themselves. Michael Persinger, a geologist at Canada's Laurentian University, believes they may be created by 'fields of force' that naturally occur in such potentially unstable environments as ore deposits, faultlines and rock outcrops. With fellow scientist Gyslaine Lafreniere, Persinger published the Tectonic Strain Theory (TST) – observing, 'The existence of man upon a thin shell beneath which mammoth forces constantly operate cannot be overemphasised.'

In 1986 the theory was vindicated (but only partially) when a light display astonished inhabitants of the Yakima Indian Reservation in Washington State. Fire wardens photographed immense globes of orange luminosity floating above boulders, while glowing 'ping-pong balls' bounced along ridges. The area is criss-crossed with faultlines.

In October 1995 the respected investigator Paul Devereux led an expedition to Western Australia's remote Kimberley region, to evaluate further reports of unexplained lights. Accompanied by colleague Erling Strand and a television producer with a Hi-8 video camera, he established an observation post commanding a deserted valley. Low-intensity blue-white lights appeared sporadically throughout the first night. But the patient observers received their greatest reward at another location five nights later, when they photographed a bright light emerging, seemingly, from a small hill. To the watchers, the light was 'vividly noticeable' in wild terrain that was devoid of artificial illumination. The outback darkness was so deep, in fact, that Devereux recalls seeing the 'glowing coal' of a meteorite hurtling across the night sky, even after its bright trail had dissolved.

The appearance of the large Kimberley Min-Min coincided with a sudden wild jump on the read-out of the team's magnetomoter – a result that seemed to bear out Persinger's prediction that earthlights will be accompanied by changes in the geomagnetic field.

Experiments of this kind help us to understand the physical effects that Min-Min lights create. But their essential mystery remains.

*Why* do they pursue travellers in remote places?

*What* is the explanation for their seemingly intelligent and curiosity-driven behaviour?

*Why* do farm animals and domestic pets panic when they appear?

*Why* do Min-Mins seem consistently to tease and harass the animals with which they come into contact?

But last – and most importantly – the question that no one has comprehensively succeeded in answering:

*What on earth* could Min-Mins be?

# Did Breaker Morant Survive the Firing Squad?

*The rumour has circulated for almost a century. And in every new generation of Australians there are some who believe it might be true. Put simply, the proposition is this: Breaker Morant – sentenced to death for murdering Boer prisoners – did not die in a hail of British bullets. Instead, his death was faked, the corpse of another military prisoner was quietly substituted for his – and he was spirited away to live a secret life in Australia's remote north, where he died of old age. Fantasy? Probably. But before you pass judgment, read on.*

THE LIFE STORY OF BREAKER MORANT has inspired an internationally successful Australian film, a play, a dozen books and uncountable articles. The following facts are those that historians and writers are generally agreed upon ...

Harold Harbord Murrant (his original surname) was born in Devon, England in December 1865. Toward the end of his life he would claim that he was the son of Admiral Digby Morant, changing the spelling of his name to fit the story. Historians have found Murrant-Morant's early years too shadowy to penetrate, but they accept that he was reasonably well educated, as his published poems attest. And he was a brilliant horseman.

At age 19 Harry Morant was abruptly obliged to quit his native England, possibly because he was the central figure in a scandal involving a married woman's 'honour'. With money thought to have been provided by his family he paid his passage to Australia, where his first recorded appearance was in the back country of Charters Towers, Queensland. He left – again in haste – after one of his cheques bounced.

After drifting for several months Morant found a job as storeman-bookkeeper at Esmeralda Station in northern Queensland. He hated this 'clerk's work', as he described it. Before long he was wandering again, working for an assortment of employers as a drover and horsebreaker –

and imbibing large quantities of alcohol whenever he got the chance. So expert was he at training station stock and hunting down and crushing the will of wild brumbies that admiring associates began to call him 'The Breaker'. This was the sobriquet he used on poems he published in newspapers and magazines (notably the *Bulletin.*)

Morant's bush ballads earned him little money – but they were popular in his time, and their originality of form is believed to have inspired such celebrated verse as *The Man from Snowy River*, *Jim Carew* and *The Geebung Polo Club*.

Horsebreaking was a perilous task. His skill notwithstanding, Morant broke bones on numerous occasions. He once boasted that he had been treated at every hospital and fallen down drunk at every hotel in outback New South Wales. He was also envied for his ability on horseback, prompting a friend to write: 'He and his steed are as one, in a partnership that is less horsemanship than a display of the sheerest art.'

In 1886 an event occurred in South Africa that would have fateful repercussions for Harry Morant. An Australian miner, William Harrison, discovered a rich seam of gold at the Rand in the Transvaal. Within a decade more than 50,000 British miners had flocked to the region. The Boer government treated the fortuneseekers badly, denying them legal protection and allowing permanent settlers to victimise them. By August 1899 Britain's Foreign Secretary, Joseph Chamberlain, had had enough. He announced that it was time 'to bring the Boers to heel and establish [who] is the paramount power in South Africa'.

The conflict that would become known as the Boer War began on 11 October 1899. The Australian colonies, more loyal perhaps than the British themselves, pledged men to the Imperial government. Harry Morant, sensing an adventure ahead, was among the first to enlist. He was assigned to the second contingent of the South Australian Rifles. Within a fortnight his skill with horses won him a corporal's stripes. By the time he reached South Africa in 1900 he was a sergeant.

The Boer War became notorious for the savagery displayed by both sides. As a colonial combatant under British command, Sergeant, then Lieutenant Morant, won renown for his courage – and ruthlessness. When Lord Kitchener, commander-in-chief of colonial forces, quietly ordered his underlings to take no prisoners, Harry Morant had no qualms about obeying. Two years of bitter fighting, during which he had seen friends slaughtered, had left him violent and vengeful. Morant's problem, however, would always be that Kitchener's order to kill prisoners was unofficial. This meant that if the British were ever embarrassed by a military murder, they could po-facedly punish the soldiers involved.

Lieutenant Morant committed his first transgression after the castrated corpse of Captain Hunt, his senior officer and close friend, was found. The well-liked officer had been tortured and horrifically mutilated. Several days later the grieving Morant came across a Boer prisoner wearing Hunt's uniform. Enraged, he shot him. The British Army forgave what commanders privately described as an 'understandable' killing.

Shortly after receiving his unofficial pardon Morant was appointed senior officer of an irregular army unit known as the Bushveldt Carabineers. While operating in the northern Transvaal, he ordered the summary execution of Boer prisoners he believed to have been responsible for Captain Hunt's death.

The incident created near panic in Britain's military leadership. Lord Kitchener knew that newspapers would eventually learn of the executions – the Boers would see to that. To forestall a scandal he had Morant, his farrier Peter Handcock, and two other soldiers, Whitten and Summers, charged with murder.

For good measure, he also ordered that Morant be charged with the politically embarrassing killing of a German missionary. Morant vehemently insisted that he was innocent on all counts. By killing the Boer prisoners he had done no more than follow Kitchener's orders – orders which the slippery peer now denied having given. And his only contact with the missionary, Morant claimed, had been when he warned him not to travel into dangerous Boer territory. The embattled lieutenant was probably telling the truth – but the British by this time needed scapegoats. Germany's Kaiser was demanding not only reparations but the deaths of the people who had killed his countryman.

Morant and his three companions were duly charged with the killings. The court martial, consisting entirely of British officers, was a farce. The defence counsel, the inexperienced Major J.F. Thomas, fudged and fumbled throughout the trial, showing too much 'respect' to Lord Kitchener to make capital of his 'take-no-prisoners' orders.

His evidence that other British units had also killed Boer prisoners was discounted by the presiding officers. The court-martial found all four men guilty.

Summers was cashiered. Whitten got life imprisonment (later reduced to three years, following intervention by Winston Churchill). Morant and Handcock were sentenced to death by firing squad.

The court's decision caused outrage in Australia – almost resulting in the withdrawal of Australian troops from the Boer War. Breaker Morant's last words, spoken as he faced the firing squad on 27 February 1902, became famous across the newly-federated nation. When asked if he had a last request he replied: '*Yes – shoot straight you bastards, and don't make a mess of it.*'

Jurist Isaac Isaacs, who was to become the first Australian-born Governor-General, summated the national mood. 'This matter,' he said, 'has agitated the minds of the people of this country to an unprecedented degree.'

As the smoke from the rifle volley cleared, Australians tried to reach an understanding of what had happened. In the face of silence from conservative elements of the army and from politicians still subservient to Britain, the nation reached a popular consensus on several broad points:

- Morant and Handcock had been shot to placate the Kaiser – and to reduce the threat of a war with Germany, for which Britain was unprepared.
- The men's deaths had been a political sweetener, designed to win favour with the Boers and shorten a costly conflict.

- No soldier should have faced punishment for shooting Boer prisoners. Morally repugnant though the murders were, they were sanctioned by explicit orders from the slippery Lord Kitchener.
- Members of British units had also murdered Boer POWs – but had gone unpunished. 'Better a colonial should die than one of our own.'
- It was time, thought many citizens, that Australia reconsidered her blind loyalty to Britain – a loyalty which did not appear to be reciprocated.

THE FLAME OF ANGER ignited by the executions was still burning strongly 100 years later. In 2002 the former Deputy Prime Minister, Tim Fischer, led a broadly-supported campaign to have the evidence reviewed and Morant and his co-accused posthumously pardoned. The government vetoed the idea.

*But* – had Australia's century of soul-searching been based on an official lie, anyway? Had Morant and Handcock in fact escaped the firing squad? This, certainly, was what some people (possibly fantasists, but purporting to be first-hand witnesses) claimed during the first decade of the 20th century. They said they had seen Morant, even spoken to him, in the years following his alleged execution. Modern historians may dismiss these stories as prototypical versions of Elvis sightings – and they're probably right. But the reports-cum-rumours are circumstantial enough to merit a degree of consideration.

According to the gossips a man, unmistakably Harry Morant, was working under an assumed name in

Australia's remote north. The man was an expert horsebreaker and an unusually skilled rider. He was plainly well-educated, but markedly reserved and unwilling to answer questions about his background. Despite this apparent shyness, however, he enjoyed reciting poems to his workmates during tea and tucker breaks: poems which he admitted to having written himself.

As the 20th century progressed, details – or embellishments – were added to the pseudonymous Morant's secret saga. He found work with a pastoral company, acquitting himself so well that he was promoted to supervisor. Unlike his roughly-garbed contemporaries in the Northern Territory he was always smartly dressed – and even kept a servant to wash and iron his clothes. According to the rumour-spreaders, he presented himself at all times like a polished army officer.

This mysterious figure was so good-natured and performed so many kindnesses that he became one of the Territory's best-loved characters. He died during the 1940s, never having revealed his true identity to anyone.

If this legendary poet and horsebreaker actually existed – and really was Lieutenant Harry Morant – how had he managed to cheat the firing squad? The storytellers explain it thus:

The announcement that Morant and his three companions were to be court-martialled created immediate and unprecedented tension between Great Britain and the newly-federated nation of Australia. In secret diplomatic talks the Australians warned that if Morant were made a political scapegoat, relations between the two countries could be soured for many years. Britain was trapped in a dilemma. To avoid war with the Kaiser's Germany, she had to execute the officer (allegedly Morant) who had murdered the Lutheran missionary. But if she did so, an enraged Australia might withdraw her military support – an action which could have grave repercussions in other Empire nations and colonies.

The British diplomats negotiated a compromise. If the court-martial found Morant and company guilty (a foregone conclusion) their deaths would be staged – thus appeasing the Kaiser and the Boers. And that – according to the legend – is precisely what happened. On the eve of the execution an Australian officer spoke to the doomed Morant and Handcock and promised them their lives on condition they keep their reprieve secret 'for all time'. Obviously neither Britain nor Australia could afford the diplomatic embarrassment of the deception ever becoming known. Both men happily agreed to the condition – Morant (so the rumour goes) averring that he'd rather his lips were sealed by diplomacy than by death.

The execution squad used blanks. Morant and Handcock fell to the ground, as arranged, and were carried away on stretchers. At the funeral, the bodies of two dead military prisoners were buried in the condemned men's uniforms.

When proponents of this alternate history are asked for proof, they usually cite a single dramatic example: In 1910, during his visit to Bathurst, New South Wales, Lord Kitchener was asked to unveil a memorial to Australian soldiers killed in the Boer War. He refused – unless Peter Handcock's name was removed from the list. The reason, in the rumour-believers' view, was that Kitchener knew Handcock was still alive – and hesitated to commit the sacrilege of honouring him in company with the dead.

But of course it's equally possible that the lying lord was loath to pay tribute to a soldier who had been executed for murder.

Were Britain's scapegoats slaughtered by the firing squad – or did they live on secretly for decades after a concocted execution? We may never know.

... Unless someone measures the skulls of the two men buried on 27 February 1902 – and compares the results with contemporary photographs of the unhappy Handcock and Morant.

# The Lady Vanishes
# Television Beauty's Unknown Fate

*In April 1992 Jacqueline Ramchen, former hostess of the television game show The Price is Right, vanished without trace after dropping her children at school. Police eventually charged her husband, Slavic Ramchen, with murder, but the case was thrown out of court. Ten years after his wife's disappearance Slavic Ramchen died. Whatever happened to Jacqueline may forever remain a mystery.*

JACQUELINE MERTENS WAS BORN in Holland in 1949. She spent the first three years of her life there, before accompanying her parents to Australia. Jacqueline's father Jos found work as a builder. Her mother Hennie became a catering specialist who ended up running the Highwood Inn restaurant in Belgrave, Victoria.

Jackie enjoyed an idyllic Australian childhood. One of her abiding interests as a little girl was fashion: a preoccupation that would benefit her in later years. Soon after her 21st birthday she was offered a job at the Mount Buller ski resort. It was here that fate smiled on her particularly kindly. A vacationing television executive, struck by her exceptional beauty, invited her to audition at his network's Melbourne studios. Within a month she was on-air, working with compere Garry Meadows as hostess of the nationally televised quiz *The Price is Right.*

Jackie found the role exciting, for a while. But she had larger ambitions. In the early 1970s she resigned from the network and moved to Hong Kong, where she began working as a model. During the same period she established her own fashion label, Jackie Leonard.

Many men, during those years, were attracted to Jacqueline Mertens. But the suitor who pursued her most assiduously was Slavic 'Vic' Ramchen, a charming Russian-born civil engineer, eight years her senior. He persuaded her to become his wife.

To acquaintances in Australia the Ramchens' marriage appeared stable and successful. The couple produced three children, Lev, Bobbi and Kim, of whom they seemed exceedingly fond. And their financial situation kept getting better. By the late 1980s they were living in a luxurious house in fashionable Domain Road, South Yarra, and also owned a 100-hectare rural property at Woodend. Slavic now was a millionaire, several times over.

Jacqueline seemed to be the woman with everything – admired and envied by those who failed to see beyond the smiling façade she presented to the world. But friends in whom she confided heard a different story. She insisted, to these close confidantes, that she was desperately unhappy.

On the morning of Friday 10 April 1992, the 43 year-old mother packed the children into her blue BMW sedan and ferried them to Christ Church Grammar School in Punt Road, South Yarra. She kissed them goodbye and drove off. She was not seen again.

That afternoon Slavic Ramchen collected the children from school and took them away for the weekend. The four returned to their South Yarra house on Sunday. Three weeks later Mrs Hennie Mertens went to the police. She said she had been trying for days to contact her daughter – with no success. When she had spoken at last to Jacqueline's husband he told her she had left him. Mr Ramchen later gave the same account to detectives.

Members of the Homicide Squad immediately began an intensive investigation. They established that none of Jacqueline's clothes were missing and that no money had been withdrawn from her bank accounts. Family members said it was completely out of character for her simply to have gone away – and especially uncharacteristic that she had made no contact with her children or parents.

More than 50 motorcycle and horseback police spent several days doorknocking and searching the Woodend district. They also searched around Werribee, where the couple, in happier times, had enjoyed birdwatching. Other officers dragged the nine dams on the Ramchens' rural property. They minutely combed the South Yarra and Woodend houses. But they could find no trace of Jacqueline Ramchen, or any clue to what might have befallen her.

In August 2001, coroner Phillip Byrne said Mrs Ramchen was likely to have been the victim of foul play. More than nine years after the disappearance, police charged Slavic Ramchen, then 60, with the murder of his wife. The committal hearing in Melbourne Magistrates' Court was bitterly contested. The prosecutor, Robert Johnstone, said that – notwithstanding a lack of forensic clues – he would present evidence that Jacqueline Ramchen was no longer alive. He asserted that no other conclusion was possible. Despite her widely-attested reputation as a devoted mother, Mrs Ramchen had never tried to contact her children. She had not left the country, worked, or taken money from the bank – all of which conclusively pointed to her being dead.

The prosecutor referred to the couple's marital problems – and the fact that Slavic Ramchen had neither shown concern nor reported that his wife was missing. Mr Ramchen, he said, had had the motive, the opportunity and the desire to kill her.

From the beginning, however, Slavic Ramchen had sternly defended himself. In an earlier affidavit he had said he would 'always defend' his innocence in the matter.

Robert Richter QC, appearing for Mr Ramchen, argued that the hearing was an abuse of process. Police had collected no clues in 1992 – and witnesses, separated from the events by ten years, could not be expected to give accurate evidence. He insisted that Jacqueline Ramchen was alive and had fled Melbourne of her own volition.

After considering the evidence of witnesses, including a Catholic nun in whom Jacqueline had confided her unhappiness, the presiding judge threw out the charges. His principal grounds were that no body had been found – and therefore, as Mr Richter had argued, Mrs Ramchen could not be presumed dead.

In October 2002, only months after the hearing, Slavic Ramchen died of cancer. Whatever (if anything) he knew about his wife's tantalisingly mysterious disappearance, he took to the grave.

# The Five Missing Men of Bermagui

*For more than half a century, the mystery regularly returned to newspaper front pages. Over the years dozens of police and amateur detectives believed they had solved it – but always their theories were proved wrong. The elements of the case were starkly simple: a fishing boat carried across sharp rocks – and abandoned 67 metres from the sea. The men who had been aboard the craft gone, never to be seen again. And in the sand, no trace of footprints ...*

A YOUNG FARM WORKER, William Johnston made the discovery. Late in the afternoon of Sunday 10 October 1880 he was riding his horse at Mutton Fish Point, near Bermagui New South Wales, when he noticed something 'shining' on the rocks. He dismounted, tied the horse to a honeysuckle tree and walked closer. He could see now what the shining object was: a fishing boat, painted green, with its mast and sail lashed to the thwarts.

In his subsequent statutory declaration Johnston wrote:

> *I went over to the boat and judged from her position that she had been wrecked. I did not touch or in any way interfere with anything ... I returned to my horse and only noticed my own tracks going out to the boat.*
>
> *I mounted my horse and rode away. After going about 100 yards [90 metres] it struck me to look at my watch, saying to myself, 'as this is likely to have been a drowning match they will want to know the time I found the boat'. I saw that it was about 4.20 p.m.*

Johnston galloped to a nearby property owned by dairy farmer Albert Read. The two men returned to the boat and inspected it more closely. It was obvious to them that the vessel had been deliberately damaged. Someone had dumped a pile of boulders, along with pillows, blankets and piles of clothing into the stern. Read reached down and retrieved a book. It was a geology text. Written in copperplate on the flyleaf was the name 'Lamont Young'.

TALL, BEARDED LAMONT HENRY YOUNG was a 29 year-old geological surveyor with the New South Wales Department of Mines. He was highly thought of by his colleagues, both for his considerable expertise and his modest demeanour. The latter was modified to some extent by the military bearing and air of quiet authority he had inherited from his father, Major-General C.B. Young of the Royal Engineers.

In October 1880 Lamont's superiors instructed him to survey the newly-discovered goldfields north of Bermagui. He took with him a 23 year-old field assistant, Maximilan Schneider, recently arrived from Germany. Lamont had almost missed out on the assignment. Several days earlier he had been struck down by an undiagnosed illness, characterised by acute back pain, vomiting and the spitting up of blood. But he seemed completely recovered when he boarded the steamer *Truganini* for the goldfields.

Young and Schneider reached their destination on Friday 8 October. After pitching a tent at Bermagui Heads they walked to the diggings, where they introduced themselves to Senior Constable John Berry, officer in charge of the police camp. The three men lunched together. Schneider then excused himself and said he was returning to the tent.

He was never seen again.

Young spent several hours familiarising himself with the goldfields. The policeman took a liking to him and suggested that they go fishing the following day. Young accepted the invitation, then set out on the long walk back to his camp. Shortly before darkness fell, Peter Egstrom, owner of a sly-grog shanty, noticed the young geologist near the local lagoon, walking toward Bermagui Heads. A second witness – a miner named Henderson – spotted him again, shortly afterward. That would be the last time anyone was known to have seen Lamont Young, alive or dead.

ON THE MORNING of Monday 11 October, Senior Constable Berry, accompanied by goldfields warden Henry Keightley and the dairy farmer Albert Read, rode to Mutton Fish Point to assess the abandoned fishing boat. Berry was disturbed that a book bearing his new friend Lamont's signature had been found in the stern. And now, lying amid the fishing lines, bag of potatoes and soiled clothes, here was a second book, also signed by the geologist. The three men had difficulty imagining what might have happened here. Why had Lamont been aboard the vessel? Who were his companions? And more to the point, where were all of them now?

While picking through the mess, Keightley noticed that someone had vomited copiously in the stern. Repelled, he abandoned the search and ordered the policeman to take over. The meticulous Berry prepared a minutely detailed inventory of the vessel's contents. His list included scores of items ranging from a pocket compass to several sacks of potatoes and a Meerschaum pipe and velvet-collared coat belonging to Lamont's assistant Maximilian Schneider.

Other clues enabled police to ascertain the name of the boat's owner: Thomas Towers. Two days earlier Towers had set sail from his home at Bateman's Bay, approximately 100 kilometres up the coast. He and his companions

William Lloyd and Daniel Casey, had intended to fish off Bermagui, then sell their catch, along with the sacks of potatoes, to the goldminers.

In a report to his superiors, Henry Keightley said there was 'nothing which indicated that anything of an unusual nature had taken place on board'. He noted that there were no blood marks and no sign of a struggle. He added that although a bullet had been 'found in the boat by some person' it could not have been an instrument of murder. 'The bullet could never have been fired from a firearm,' he said. 'The position in which it was found in the crack in the paint was such as to show that it had been placed there by some person who had made it a sinker for a fishing line.'

Senior Constable Berry was unable to continue the investigation. Shortly after returning to the police camp he fell ill with a fever and vomiting. When he returned to duty nine days later he was told that the remains of a campfire and a meal had been found close to the wrecked boat.

Henry Keightley offered a £10 reward for the recovery of Lamont Young's body. He seemed uninterested in the geologist's lowly-born companions: an attitude mirrored in a subsequent advertisement by London's Metropolitan Police, who offered a £300 reward for information regarding 'Mr Lamont Young and Mr Maximilian Schneider, Government Geologists and three boatmen, Casey, Towers and Lloyd'.

Police, Mines Department staff and hundreds of volunteers conducted a days-long sea and land search for the five missing men. They probed the sand with boring rods, dynamited rocks and caves, dredged 'likely' stretches of the sea floor – and found nothing. Mining Registrar Thomas Binny, a close friend of Lamont Young, played a leading role in the search. In a report on 28 October he concluded that the multiple disappearance was 'impossible to explain'. Bemusedly he pointed out that the country inland had been thoroughly scoured and was inhabited by settlers from Bermagui to Wodonga. No-one landing on the coast could possibly be lost, as there was fencing all along it, running back for miles.

On 10 November the New South Wales Premier Henry Parkes, in the *Government Gazette*, added to the multiplicity of rewards by offering £50 to anyone who could 'account for the disappearance of the five persons and afford proof of their fate'. If the men had been murdered, the government would pay a further £50 for information leading to the killers' conviction.

A journalist writing in the *Sydney Morning Herald* described the entire affair as 'a puzzle enshrouded in an enigma' – adding, 'I cannot conceive of any motive to account for the horrible suspicion that they were murdered ... but how could the murderers (assuming they existed) have known where the men were to land – unless they were murdered by the first party they met? ... The idea is so dreadful and the motive so unintelligible that I cannot yet entertain it.'

'Unintelligible' began to seem an increasingly apt description of the mystery. Lamont Young's father, Major General C.B. Young, was so dismayed by the New South

Wales police force's lack of progress that he asked the London Metropolitan Police to take charge. In a sympathetic but firm letter the police chief refused, saying he had every faith in the skills of his colonial counterparts. However, he did undertake to offer a £200 reward, to which Major General Young added a further hundred.

The Major General continued to fight. On 31 December, in a long letter to the New South Wales Under-Secretary for Mines, he wrote: 'The universal conclusion of all parties in this country *is that the five men could not have drowned or been murdered without leaving some trace behind.* Now I earnestly beg of you, my dear sir ... to take up this line, to see what the Governments, Imperial and local, have done in this direction, to look [for bodies].'

The old soldier seemed unaware that the state authorities had searched, at enormous length – and were continuing to investigate every scrap of evidence they could find. More pertinent, however, was the Major General's suspicion of his son's assistant: 'What sort of person and of what character was Mr Schneider? Where does he come from in Germany and to whom was he known in England?' Before long, the Schneider connection would provide newspapers with a series of sensational articles.

Lamont's mother, Mrs Emma Young, was also active in the case. In a long and passionate petition to Queen Victoria, she pleaded that a new search party be despatched to find her 'most excellent and noble son'. She referred to her husband's loyal service in India, for which he had earned five medals – and even recalled that her grandfather, Dr James Lind, had acted as physician to the Queen's grandfather, George III. The Queen's reply, via her private secretary Sir Henry Ponsonby, was icy: 'General Sir Henry F. Ponsonby, is commanded to express the Queen's regret that the request referred to in Mrs Young's letter cannot be complied with, as it refers to a matter which can only be brought under Her Majesty's notice through the Secretary of State for the Colonies.'

Australians tried to be a little more helpful. Among the numerous people who wrote to police and newspapers asserting that they could solve the case was an Alexander Gray. With a companion he devotedly spent three unpaid months examining cliffs, ravines, beaches and caves around the area where the boat still lay. The friends set fire to tracts of dense scrub, in the hope of finding clues buried by swiftly-growing vegetation. They did make several possibly significant discoveries: a theodolite and trousers which might (or might not) have belonged to the missing Young or Schneider, and two 2.4-metre poles, one of which seemed to bear bloody fingermarks. Police concluded that any of these items might have come from a passing ship. In an era long before DNA evidence was gathered, they had no way of ascertaining whose blood was on the poles – and why it was there in any case.

Police files bulged with public input. It seemed that almost everyone had a theory or suggestion. One man, William Tait of Little River, even visited police headquarters in Sydney with the news that he had had a long conversation with Lamont Young on 13 November – more than a month after the disappearance. Tait was a self-styled spiritualist. The dead geologist, he asserted, had appeared to him as a ghost, to reveal that he and his companions were murdered by three men who asked them for matches to light their pipes. After beating their five victims to death with oars, the killers buried the bodies in a deep hole near a black stump, about 50 metres above high water mark.

# Metropolitan Police.

# £300 Reward.

## *AUSTRALIA.*

Disappeared on 9th October, 1880, five persons:—

**MR. LAMONT YOUNG,**

Government Geologist.

**MR. MAX SCHNEIDER**

and three boatmen named

**CASEY, TOWERS, and LLOYD.**

They embarked in a boat at BERMAGUI, COAST OF NEW SOUTH WALES, 180 MILES SOUTH OF SYDNEY; the boat has been found jammed on the rocks at CORUNNA POINT, ten miles to the Northward; bullet marks were in the boat, but there was no trace of any struggle or foul play.

IT IS BELIEVED THE PARTY were kidnapped, and taken AWAY IN SOME VESSEL.

The sum of £100 will be paid by Major-General Young to any person giving the earliest information leading to the discovery of Mr. Lamont Young, and the Government of New South Wales will pay the Reward of £200 for such information as shall lead to the conviction of any person or persons who have been guilty of violence. Information to the COMMISSIONER OF POLICE, GREAT SCOTLAND YARD, LONDON.

They then covered the makeshift grave with boulders. Police by this time were open-minded enough to check any information. But they found no black stump and no cairn of boulders.

More promising to the detectives was a small blue bottle, filled with a mysterious liquid, recovered from a saddlebag found in the fishing boat. For several days, investigators – and journalists – speculated that the bottle's contents might be an exotic poison of some kind. However, the Government Analyst found otherwise, reporting that the liquid was the harmless balm, oil of copaiva. This finding did nothing to scotch the poison rumours that continued to circulate for decades afterward.

Purported solutions to the Bermagui Boat Mystery kept coming:

On 11 March 1885 the Melbourne *Argus* reported that Lamont Young's coat, bloodstained and rent with bullet holes, had been found near Bermagui. Buried nearby was a revolver with several spent cartridges – along, in the newspaper's words, 'with other indications that he and his companions were murdered'. Melbourne police investigated the report – and found it was a practical joke, perpetrated by a young tinsmith. The *Argus*, which should have checked, published a blushing retraction.

On 22 August 1888 the *Bega Gazette* announced that it had uncovered vital new evidence: 'Though the police authorities have kept the matter a secret, it has transpired that during the past two months the police have had under surveillance a person suspected of complicity in the Bermagui murder, but that he has escaped their clutches.

*A* Sydney Morning Herald *journalist describes the search for the five missing men. Sketched at Bermagui goldfields, 1880.*

It appears that some time ago a man who is said to have lived with a woman near the scene of the alleged murder, came to Sydney and married a barmaid employed in one of the leading hotels in Sydney. Shortly after their marriage, he gave way to drink and on several occasions uttered remarks which led his wife to believe he was concerned in the murder of Lamont Young and his companions. The detective police got wind of the affair and kept the suspect person under surveillance for several days. All at once, however, he disappeared ... The barmaid has since returned to her situation in the hotel from which she was married and expresses herself as willing to aid the authorities in bringing the supposed murderer to the police.' Bega police checked with their colleagues in Sydney. There was no barmaid. Nor was there a drunken husband who had conveniently confessed to murder. All that remained was an imaginative journalist.

The hoaxes, urban myths and misreports continued long after Lamont Young and his companions would have been old men, or dead from natural causes. Perhaps the grossest sensationalism was perpetrated in August 1891. It appeared after Australian newspapers gave considerable space to a cable story about a German man, Schneider, in whose house and its surrounding woods the bodies of several servant girls were found. Schneider and his wife were arrested and charged with kidnapping and killing the young women. These events inspired the *Sydney Evening News* (24 August 1891) to publish an extraordinary editorial:

> *... There is little in a name, and Schneider is one of the commonest Teutonic names, even more so than its Anglican equivalent, Taylor. But it is impossible to forget that the name Schneider is associated with one of the foulest and most mysterious murders in this country. We refer to those at Bermagui – the butchery of Mr Lamont Young and three [sic] others. A man named Schneider was Mr Young's assistant. That Mr Young and the others were foully murdered, there is not the*

*slightest doubt. What was almost equally certain was that Schneider was the murderer. To be sure, the probability of the Vienna Schneider being identical with the Bermagui murderer is remote; but the similarity in names is enough to recall a crime that will not easily be forgotten ...*

Excesses of this kind, accompanied by urban myths, misconceptions and untenable theories, characterised the case from the beginning. But none of the vast effort expended by police, scientific analysts and well-meaning amateurs made a scintilla of difference. The disappearance of the Bermagui Five remains as completely mysterious today as it was on the morning their abandoned boat was found.

*Where are you now, you five lost souls?*
*Only the sea winds know.*
*Did you rise far above, or sink deep below?*
*Only the foam-caps know.*
*Did spirits seize you and bear you away*
*In the sunset's amber glow?*
*Only the seawinds, only the waves, only the deep skies know.*

## Ghost Ship Perplexes Police

More than a century after the Bermagui boatmen vanished, a bizarrely similar maritime mystery gripped Australia's imagination.

On 4 January 2003 a Taiwanese ship, *High Aim 6*, was found adrift off the Western Australian coast. Australian naval officers boarded the vessel – and were immediately puzzled. Clearly the ship had been abandoned for some reason. There were no lifeboats or rafts; no sign of a struggle.

The only indications that there once had been life aboard were seven toothbrushes and large stores of canned food. From the hold a nauseating stench emerged. It was created by three tonnes of tuna and mackerel which (as subsequent tests indicated) had been rotting for up to two weeks. Although the boat's fuel tanks were half-full, the freezer had failed when the engines stopped.

Navy personnel promptly nicknamed the vessel *Marie Celeste* – and towed her to a quarantine bay off Broome. There, Federal Police took up the investigation. Officers, directed by operations coordinator Bill Graham, spent two days conducting tests on the 20-metre, 150-tonne vessel. They found 'no plausible reason' for the absence of the captain, Chen Tai-chen, his chief engineer, Lee Ah-Duey, and the ten Indonesian crew. A search by coastwatch planes and a PC-3 Orion failed to find any trace of the missing men.

*High Aim 6* had sailed from Taiwan on 30 October 2002. She was last heard from on 13 December when Captain Tai-chen called the owners from the Marshall Islands. Several weeks of silence followed. After repeated attempts to re-contact the captain, the owners reported the vessel missing.

The seemingly complete lack of evidence left Federal Police in a quandary. 'We can't say if the boat was hijacked ...whether it was steered toward Australia by a second crew ... or whether it was on autopilot,' said Bill Graham.

Stefan Frodsham, chief executive of the Port of Broome, told ABC radio that the ship had probably been attacked by pirates. 'It's becoming a very common problem,' he said.

But the police were keeping an open mind. One valuable indicator, they believed, was a series of 87 local calls made in Bali with a mobile phone belonging to the chief engineer. The engineer's daughter told a Taipei newspaper that she had rung her father's mobile many times between 27 December and 15 January. On three of those occasions she had heard the strains of karaoke emerging from the receiving end.

As this book went to press the fate of *High Aim 6*'s captain, engineer and crew remained unknown.

## Swallowed up, by the Hungry Mountain

Aborigines believe a hungry ghost haunts Black Mountain, a massive outcrop of granite slabs rearing from dense bush southwest of Cooktown (Queensland).

Tradition dictates that tribal members must stay clear of the area – but Europeans have been less cautious.

Old police files show that at least four people have mysteriously disappeared on the monolith.

The mountain's first recorded victim was farmer Charles Graynor, who in 1872 vanished, with his horse, while searching for stray bullocks. A two-day search by police, blacktrackers and volunteers uncovered no clues.

Ten years later two young bushmen, Jacob Owens and Thomas Hawkins, went missing while seeking runaway horses. No trace of them was ever found.

Shortly afterwards, a gold prospector, James Wren, was incautious enough to climb the mountain. He never returned.

The fate of the four men was no mystery to tribal elders, who had long warned settlers to avoid the mountain if they valued their lives. The monolith, they said, was the lair of a '*debil-debil*' which devoured human souls.

# Horror of the Bending Headlights
# UFOs Over Australia

*When a young mechanic was fatally injured after his car ran off a rural road, Victorian police treated it as just another regrettable accident. But then an eyewitness came forward to describe an inexplicable and terrifying event at the same spot three days earlier. Detectives searched the paddock where the mechanic had died – and found a circular depression that suggested something had landed there. In the days preceding the death dozens of locals had reported seeing UFOs over the area. A new chapter of Australia's profoundest mystery was being written.*

IT WAS A PARTICULARLY well-documented UFO case. A credible eyewitness attested to the central facts. He was supported by dozens of secondary witnesses. The powerful physical evidence was analysed by scientists and assessed by police. A major newspaper photographed the evidence and reported the incidents surrounding it.

The story began on Victoria's Bendigo–St Arnaud Road on 7 April 1966. Gary Taylor, a 19 year-old motor mechanic, died when his car ran off the road near Bealiba. Police took a blood test which showed he had not been drinking. Police at Maryborough, Bealiba, Newstead and Castlemaine told the Melbourne *Herald* (which published the interviews on 11 April) that they all had heard numerous reports of UFOs seen in the area.

A steel construction contractor, Ronald Sullivan of Maryborough, came on the scene. He approached police with a report about his chilling experience in the same spot, three nights before Gary died. Mr Sullivan said *the headlights on his new Ford Falcon had suddenly bent to the right* for no apparent reason. If he had followed them, he said, he would have run off the road. But he managed to stop before he crashed. Then, in a paddock nearby, he saw a display of gaseous lights 'in all colours of the spectrum'. It was as though they were in five centimetre-diameter tubes, running into a bright phosphorous glow on the ground. The lights stretched up into the night sky until they disappeared.

Ronald Sullivan said that he drove on to Wycheproof and had his headlights checked. They were in perfect condition. He returned with police to the paddock and there they found evidence that – something – had made a depression in the ground. In the ploughed earth there was a perfect circle, 1.2 metres in diameter and 15 centimetres deep. The farm's owner had no idea who, or what, had made the ring. But it proved to be very durable.

In February 1978 members of the Victorian UFO Research Society went back to the paddock and photographed the 12 year-old indentation. It was still barren – a bare ring where nothing grew. Many so-called saucer circles remain sterile thus. The phenomena which create them seem to be as debilitating to vegetation as to people and animals.

Most purportedly UFO-related events, no matter how singular they may seem, usually prove to be part of a pattern – and the Bendigo–St Arnaud Road case is no exception. Six years later – on 30 November 1972 – another motorist complained of bizarre headlight behaviour moments before he saw a startlingly strange object in a nearby paddock. The 7 December edition of the *Murray Valley Standard* reported that a young local man (also, coincidentally, a motor mechanic) experienced disturbing problems while driving. The article, headed 'UFO "Killed" his Car', reads:

*Neville Maxwell, an apprentice mechanic for Rothall Motors, had quite a shock in store for him last Thursday evening, after deciding to take his overhauled Holden for a trial run along old Rocky Gully Road.*

*The engine suddenly began revving and the lights flashing high and low as he reached the crest of a hill. When he stopped to check for suspected engine trouble he caught sight of an object, about the size of two cars, with flashing green and purple lights at its base. Neville says he was scared stiff, and his first move was to make sure all the car doors were locked.*

*He was unable to get any of the mechanical or electrical parts of the car to operate. All he could get from the radio was peculiar noises. The engine was dead and even the air horns were out of commission. Neville was stranded for about 40 minutes. After the first 10 minutes he relaxed a little and had a good look round – still from the safety of the car.*

*The object was in a nearby paddock, and when it took off it made a whirring noise. This was the only sound he heard. It lifted about 20 feet [6 metres] then headed toward Adelaide. The car started without any trouble after the object had gone, and Neville made a slow and shaky departure for home.*

*The car was given a thorough 'going over' the next day, by others in the Rothall Motors workshop, and all parts were in perfect running order.*

The sheer continuing volume of incidents of this kind – usually described in obscure country newspapers around Australia and the world – stagger the mind. Wise sceptics, who have neither conducted a first-hand UFO investigation, nor even know about the mass of rural reports, have no inhibitions about smilingly dismissing the 'flying saucer' phenomenon. Before commenting further, however, they should get out from behind their desks and actually study the data.

The syndrome of 'obscure' UFO reportage – stories which never reach the city dailies – was incisively dealt with by the late atmospheric physicist Professor James McDonald. In an address to the American Society of Newspaper Editors he said:

> *You editors probably think you know what is going on and that you are aware of the occasional UFO report from here and there. My reply is simple. If you read only what comes over your wires you would never guess what is really happening. The only way to get a glimpse of the situation is to receive ... packets of current Australian clippings about sightings on outback sheep stations and the like ... and to subscribe to a service that is clipping stories from the* Excelsior Springs Daily Standard, *the* Eagle Valley Enterprise, *the* Marion Weekly Leader *and so on.*
>
> *Only one or two per cent of locally reported UFO sightings are read beyond the circulation area of the nearest small-town paper. This is part of the reason why the problem is being ignored. If each day's paper in each major city carried an adequate account of all the UFO reports for the preceding 24 hours, the citizenry would be up in arms – demanding that the Congress find out what is going on.*

The enigmatic aerial phenomena watched, photographed and videoed by thousands of Australians produce a host of commonly reported side-effects. These include everything from the searing headaches in human witnesses and the fear evinced by farm animals to the disappearance of water, vegetables and fruit. But most intriguing of all are the so-called 'landing rings' which, over the decades, have been found in large numbers in every state and territory.

In December 1989 a farmer, Nancee Jolly, approached me with a particularly dramatic set of photographs. Nancee, with her husband Max and son Stuart, ran a 9,000-hectare wheat property, West Park, in Victoria's Mallee region. She and her family were convinced that a gigantic craft of some kind had landed on the farm.

The previous week two neighbours of the Jollys, Brian Finch and Austin Grace, had found something incomprehensible in the wheatfields. The two men made their discovery when they brought an International Combine Harvester onto the property to strip the crop.

Sitting in an elevated cabin about five metres from the ground, they spotted what everyone else had missed – two large, swirled circles of wheat, about three metres in diameter, surrounded by three smaller circles, each about one metre in diameter.

The Jollys could only conclude that 'something exerting colossal force' had left its imprint in the wheat. Outside the circles it was possible to scratch up dirt with the fingers. But inside the ground was compressed to cement-hardness. The wheat stalks were unbroken and swirled anticlockwise. 'The whole thing appears to be woven, almost like a straw basket,' Nancee commented. 'Amazingly the stalks seem to be undamaged, with the grain fully matured in the heads.'

Discovery of the circles climaxed two years of mystery and fear for the Jolly family.

In November 1987, following a series of sightings of strange lights over the property, Nancee found that the farmhouse's 4,000-litre water tank had been completely drained overnight. 'We haven't a clue what happened,' she told me. 'All we know is that someone – or something – took every drop of our water.' (Numerous farmers in Victoria and Queensland have reported similar series of events to me: sightings of unidentified flying objects, followed by the disappearance of water from dams or tanks, and the discovery of circles on the property.)

In December 1988, Stuart Jolly was startled from sleep by a shattering noise outside his bedroom window. 'I thought the racket would puncture my eardrums,' he recalled. 'It was like the scream of jet engines revving up and down, with the shrilling of thousands of cicadas mixed in. Normally my dog would have been on the spot and barking – but he seemed to have shot through. I ran outside but there was nothing to see. The noise seemed to be coming from an empty sky.'

In August 1989 the pandemonium struck the farm again. 'About 9 o'clock one night I heard a commotion and went out to see what was happening,' Stuart recalled. 'The trouble was centred on the sheep paddock. Our 700 ewes and lambs had gone berserk. They were dashing about and bleating in total panic. Then I saw why. Hovering above the paddock was a yellow light that seemed to be pulsating. At first I thought someone was spotlighting the sheep, but then I realised the light was too big for that. Also, it was making a high-pitched noise, like the blades of a helicopter with its engine off and slowing. I'd never seen sheep go wild like that before. If a dog had been threatening them they'd simply have huddled together, reasonably calm and disciplined. But this mob were stumbling all over the paddock. I could see it was the light and noise that were driving them crazy. And it was happening to Brian Finch's wethers, too. They were scrambling over the fence on the next block, trying to get away. After a few more minutes of this, the light began to move. Foolishly, perhaps, I got into the car to chase it. But before I could start up it vanished behind the pine trees.'

When Max and Nancee Jolly arrived home from a meeting an hour later, the sheep were still bleating in distress. 'And they weren't the only victims,' Nancee said. 'We went out with our torches – and came across a wedgetailed eagle, with a wingspan of about two metres, stumbling around the paddock, seemingly in shock. I've never seen a wedgetail walking around on the grass like that. They like to perch up high. But this one seemed totally disoriented. Although it kept slowly flapping its wings it seemed incapable of lifting off. Something seemed to have destroyed its sense of balance. But happily, the effect must have worn off, because the bird was gone next morning.'

FARMERS IN THE MALLEE wheatbelt are accustomed to uncanny intrusions of this kind. Within days of the aerial display over the Jollys' farm a mysterious light hovered above the dam of a neighbour, Mrs Aileen Casey.

Shortly after the Jollys' crop circles appeared, pilot John Auchetl (who had encountered a UFO himself, over Essendon Airport) asked the family's permission to investigate. John, then a scientific analyst with Victoria's UFO Research Society, flew over the farm and took photographs. He quickly learned that there were not five perfect, swirled circles, but hundreds, extending across the Jolly property and neighbouring farms. If highly skilled hoaxers had created these circles, they would certainly have been wasting their time – as the patterns were visible only from the air or from the high seats on a harvester. Practical jokers would also have had considerable difficulty in compressing the soil into a rock-hard state.

Few aspects of UFOs are so tantalising as the circular marks they purportedly leave in the soil, snow and sand, probably of every nation on earth. Saucer rings and nests have been photographed and analysed countless times. The burns, the compressed or fluorescing earth, the whirlpools of flattened grass or swamp weeds, all powerfully suggest that some incongruous craft has landed – or at the least that someone wants us to believe such an event has occurred.

UFO rings and nests conform to several basic, almost predictable patterns. Sometimes the intruder leaves its imprint with a fanfare that frightens the cattle. At other times it signs its namelessness fairly quietly. One intriguing pattern of rings, whose appearance was preceded by an aerial overture, was reported from Mount Garnet, south of

Mareeba, Queensland. As on the Jollys' farm the evidence comprised five perfect circles. The largest was six metres in diameter; the other four, which were equidistant from it, were each one metre. A boy, who had been collecting bottles, found the circles in a hollow invisible from the road. Stuart Keene, editor of the *Tableland Advertiser*, investigated. He found that a nearby tree had been knocked over. Residents said their dogs had been behaving strangely for days – and that television and radio reception had been shredded by static.

Fear among animals and television interference are classic symptoms associated with the reported sighting or presumed presence of a UFO. Other manifestations include interference with cars' electrical systems and, in humans, headaches, rashes and bodily twinges which may persist for weeks.

Australian pilots have had brushes with UFOs since the earliest days of aviation – although they lacked a label to attach to them until the term 'flying saucer' was coined. One credible skywitness was Mark Muscat, a pilot of 12 years experience, who survived a close encounter with six 'pale orange objects' over Semaphore, South Australia. On Wednesday 3 June 1998, Mark, 37, chartered a Piper Arrow light aircraft to show a German tourist Adelaide by night. At 9.00 p.m., after 40 minutes in the air, he decided to return to Parafield Airport.

'I was at 2,000 feet [600 metres] and on autopilot in controlled airspace when I saw six pale orange lights directly in front of us,' he recalled. 'At first I thought they might be fishing boats in the Gulf – but then one of them moved very quickly and I realised they were in the air with me.' Thinking he might have encountered aircraft without a clearance, Mark checked with Air Traffic Control – but they advised that nothing else was in the vicinity.

At this point the encounter became alarming. The lights swarmed steadily toward the tour plane, momentarily appearing to move aside to let it through, but then closing ranks again. 'As they drew closer there was no noise (and) no navigation lights,' Mark Muscat told the *Sunday Mail.* He did not know at the time that people on the ground around Semaphore were also watching the standoff. Several rang police to report that the strange orange objects were advancing on the plane, stopping to allow their companions to catch up, then moving forward again.

As the objects hurtled toward him at an estimated 200 kilometres per hour, Mark Muscat got an increasingly clear view. 'They were about the size of a large car,' he said. 'They had no navigation lights and appeared to be travelling like an aircraft – but I couldn't discern wings.

'I decided this could be a life-threatening situation – and guided my aircraft through the group of lights. I hoped they were not part of a large object, because I'd hit it if it was. For some reason I gambled against my better instincts and won. We looked at each other with our mouths open, relieved and excited.' As he flew past the intruders, Mark heard no noise. 'Normally, when you pass another aircraft you get wake turbulence, but there was nothing – no hissing on the radio, nothing.'

The relieved pilot checked again with Air Traffic Control, who repeated that there was 'nothing' on their instruments.

He was up there alone. This advice was not only at odds with what the pilot and his passenger saw, but also with police records of reports from people on the ground, and with sightings forms submitted to South Australia's UFO Investigation Society. Aviation authorities did not seek to interview the two people who had been aboard the Piper Arrow. As with most other UFO incidents the government was (apparently) not concerned.

Mark Muscat had never been particularly curious about flying saucers before, but he came out of this experience considerably disturbed. He admits that in the midst of the encounter he began thinking about the young pilot Frederick Valentich, who vanished over Bass Strait after radioing that an unknown aircraft was orbiting his Cessna (see page 83). He expressed dismay at the lack of an official reporting mechanism for a UFO event – whereas, if he'd hit a bird he would have been required to file a report.

Where flying saucers are concerned Australian officialdom is little different from its counterparts in other countries. It is simply not interested in investigating UFO incidents – not publicly, at any rate.

While it's easy for UFO enthusiasts to complain about 'cover-ups' it is a different matter when our government can be *proved* to have suppressed information. It's hard to find such proof – but an incontrovertible case did occur half a century ago. In August 1953 a Civil Aviation Department employee in New Guinea saw a bullet-shaped object flying at high speed over Port Moresby. As aircraft were his bread-and-butter he knew precisely what kind of planes were using the territory's airspace. This perplexing object fitted no known category. Serendipitously the man happened to be shooting a home movie at the time. He pointed his camera skyward and, using a telephoto lens, took a 16-millimetre colour film of the bullet-craft in flight.

The amateur cameraman handed his footage to the RAAF representative in Port Moresby and waited with great interest to hear what the object might have been. There was silence.

The following month Australia's Minister for Air, Mr William McMahon (a future prime minister) admitted that the RAAF had indeed taken possession of the UFO footage and had sent it to the United States Air Force (USAF) for evaluation. Neither the RAAF nor the USAF issued any report on their findings. Eventually they began to deny knowledge of the sighting.

However, in 1978 – a quarter-century after the Port Moresby UFO was filmed – the cover-up was exposed. Using the Freedom of Information Act the USAF's former astronomical adviser, Professor J. Allen Hynek, prised 13,134 official UFO reports out of the United States government. One of them encompassed the allegedly non-existent Port Moresby film under the classification 'Insufficient Data'.

Hynek – a reformed debunker himself – gave officially-mocked flying saucers increased respectability in the public's eyes – even encouraging retired astronauts to admit to their experiences with UFOs, both during space voyages and on earth. One was Colonel Gordon Cooper, who testified to an extraordinary incident witnessed by scores of air force personnel. The report created a sensation, especially when the respected space traveller made his now-famous statement:

> *The saucer landed on a dry lakebed near Edwards Air Force Base. We all saw it and a crew took film.*

As with the Port Moresby footage, the United States government denied that film's existence. But by the 1970s governments worldwide, including Australia's, were having increasing difficulty explaining away the frequent and continuing UFO sightings – especially as many citizens, armed with video-recorders, were now collecting visual evidence. And the nature of the UFO experience had gradually begun to change. An element of weirdness was creeping into some reports.

In August 1996, for example, a cigar-shaped craft dropped a cloud of cobweb-like material on a Queensland railway terminus. Among UFO investigators this case was classified as an impressive multiple-witness encounter. The incident began at about 3.00 a.m. when a 12-man work-gang, loading coal at the Hay Point facility, downed tools to stare up at a mist-shrouded cigar-shaped craft floating above them. As they watched, a cloud of cobweb-like material fell from the UFO.

All the equipment immediately malfunctioned and the coal train lost its compressed air. One of the workers, Gary, said: 'Near the middle of the cigar was a bubble-like protrusion with rectangular observation windows. I saw shadows standing in the viewports, looking down at the facility. The craft had no wings. At its rear was a bank of what could have been jets.

'A dull hum came from the UFO – and when it passed directly above us, the radio went wild. Everyone started shouting at once. The next we knew, the craft dropped sheets of a cobweb-like substance. When we tried to touch the stuff it turned into a watery liquid. After a minute or so, the thing flew away. The train still had no compressed air – and we had to recharge it before work could go on.'

In 1996 I received a hauntingly memorable letter from James Driscoll of Bowen, Queensland, in which he described extraordinary events at a New Year's Eve rabbit-trapping party:

*We were on my parents' property near Redcliffs, Victoria. We were spotlighting the rabbits – and instead of using guns we'd run down to the beam's edge and grab the blinded animals. This activity had attracted a lot of people. There were about 16 cars and more than 70 people in the 4,000-hectare paddock. Among the spotlighters were two off-duty police and the local Anglican minister. At that time I was a 19 year-old final year apprentice.*

*It was an uncomfortably warm night, but towards 12 a cloud seemed to drift across the moon and the temperature began to plunge, so fast that we all started to shiver violently. I looked up and was amazed to see a crescent of light created by the moon illuminating the leading edge of a huge object above us.*

*It was egg-shaped, probably 2,000 metres long by 500 metres wide. And it was hanging there in total silence. No-one seemed scared. We started shining our spotlights at the object – but the beams went only so far, then stopped. Having done a lot of reading on the subject since then, I've come to believe that it was a craft of some sort that absorbed light. There were certainly no lights on its hull, or anything reflecting from it.*

*As we watched, the egg began to head due east, in line with the sand ridge on the property. Eventually the moon reappeared and the craft began to blank out tracts of stars as it moved in silence across the sky. Then the UFO seemed to shrink – and we assumed it had accelerated away at great speed. As soon as it vanished the temperature shot back up. Everything returned to normal and it was a typical summer night in the Mallee again.*

*We welcomed the New Year in with songs, then returned to the woolshed where the women had prepared a barbecue. They'd seen the craft too and had also felt the unseasonable chill. They told us they'd been alerted by our sudden silence and the strange spectacle of all our spotlights shining upward.*

*All up, more than 100 people saw that craft – and not one person was even slightly scared. I believe the UFO deliberately displayed itself to us.*

From the 1970s onward there were increasing numbers of cases in which UFOs were said to have impinged physically on both animals and humans. Cases of cattle mutilation, for a long time virtually unknown in Australia, have now been reported, albeit in small numbers, from every state.

One eyewitness to a mutilation was George Kampanellis, manager of a farm in Burekup, Western Australia.

One morning, in September 1973, George went out to start milking and found one of his 'best cows' dead. He told me: 'She was lying in a very strange position – and I naturally assumed an intruder had shot her. But I had to discard that theory when I could find no trace of blood. The death wound seemed to be a neat hole, a centimetre in diameter, under her front right leg. I started searching the paddock for a sharp object she might have stumbled on, but there was nothing.'

George called in a vet, who dismembered the cow and found that the hole penetrated its body for 2 centimetres, stopping near the belly. 'The vet kept shaking his head,' George recalled. 'He couldn't believe that not even a drop of blood had been lost. He agreed that it couldn't have been a gunshot – that would have made a mess. As it was, the hole was very neat – and I was able to push my finger into it.'

At that time George had read little about UFOs and nothing on cattle mutilations. But an incident that had occurred several days earlier caused him to wonder if there might be a link. 'A young bloke had come to work at the farm during his school holidays,' he recalled. 'One morning he turned up looking pale. He said he'd had a bad experience the previous night when he got up to go to an outside toilet. As he came out of the back door he was bathed in light. He looked up and saw it came from an enormous orange object hovering over the house. He never went to the loo that night. He just raced back to bed and lay there shaking.'

Most UFO events resonate with others. The mutilation described by George Kampanellis prefigures several American cases in my records. In July 1990 a heifer was found in Lee County, Mississippi, with a 'bloodless hole' bored cleanly through from its foreleg to the heart. Between May and December that year, seven similarly mutilated heifers were found in Clark County, Washington State. All the carcases contained neat 'drill-holes' with no blood loss. They were dissected by the Denver pathologist John Altshanler, who reported: 'The cells were intact. This suggests that the skin may have been cut by lasers at very high temperatures.'

In 1996 veterinarians tried to make sense of a rash of cattle mutilations in north-western Queensland, where stockmen were finding cows stripped of flesh – their brains and sex organs bloodlessly excised.

And then there are the Australians who say that they too have been physically impinged upon. One case that received wide media coverage concerned Bronte Lloyd who owned a farm in Spalding, South Australia. He produced photographs of his 'branded' face to back up his account. According to Bronte the nightmare began in the dark early morning hours of 18 June 1988.

'I woke up, unable to open my eyes, with the feeling I was floating above my bed,' he said. 'I wondered if I was dead. Then I felt intense pain, as if large insects were biting my cheeks. I put my hands up to brush the things away, then realised they weren't insects but a pair of hard tubes buried in my skin. When I tried to rip the tubes out they writhed in my hands like snakes. Soon after that, everything went black.'

Next morning, said Bronte, he realised the experience had been no dream. When he tried to shave, his blade encountered painful pairs of pinpricks on either cheek. He found four more tiny wounds on the side of his nose. 'By that evening my face was so swollen it was unrecognisable,' he said. 'When the swelling finally went down I was left with huge red markings on my cheeks and nose. Three weeks after that I got a glimpse of what I believe was the source of the pain.

'It was near nightfall. My son and I were ploughing when we heard the dogs barking at a grove of trees 50 metres from our back door. We crept close and were astonished to see a shining circular aircraft of some kind, sitting there on struts. We rushed into the house to telephone the rest of the family, who were at a nearby farm. Before we could get to the phone we saw two small dark creatures hurtling through the house in a blur of speed. The next thing we remembered was waking up in our beds.

'The police came to the farm and found that a large object had disturbed the ground beneath the trees.'

Bronte Lloyd's wounds would not heal. 'I've had a swag of pathology tests, but the medics can't guess what the marks are,' he said. 'What really throws them is the way the patches move around. One specialist photographed the cheek he'd taken samples from. He couldn't believe it the next week, when the mark had moved half an inch to the left.'

Bronte Lloyd said he knew other farmers who had been

'branded' in a similar way. 'A lady living north of here had a floating experience much the same as mine,' he said. 'Now she has triangular marks on her skin.'

Bizarre as this report may seem, it is not isolated. In 1993 the South Australian social scientist Keith Basterfield established a telephone hotline to help people who believe themselves to be UFO victims. 'I was a total sceptic about alien abductions,' he told me. 'Then I attended a conference at the Massachusetts Institute of Technology. Health professionals described to the meeting how they'd psychiatrically examined people making these claims. They'd found the overwhelming majority to be sane. Some Australian victims fear for their sanity. But in most states, psychologists, working alongside UFO researchers, are now helping these people come to terms with whatever has happened.'

Some people on Keith Basterfield's books claim to have had their first experiences in early childhood. A Queensland man recalled being kidnapped by 'beings' when he was between four and six years old. The remembered intruders were blue-grey in colour with large heads and eyes and no ears. While talking to the boy they placed him on a low table, then moved a box the size of a cigarette pack across his body. 'Then they inserted something like a needle up my nose,' the man said. 'It was painful. Throughout my life I've associated these events with seeing a blue light outside the window.'

Mysteriously missing time is a recurring theme in many of the cases studied by Keith Basterfield. A Finnish couple, Ben and Helen K., set out from Rockhampton Queensland to drive to Gladstone. They were amazed on arrival to find that 40 minutes had passed and that they had no memory of the towns they had driven through. However, they did recall seeing 'an unusual green light'. And something strange had happened to their 1971 Valiant sedan. It had unusual marks on the bonnet and was covered with a film of odourless oil.

Fourteen months before farmer Bronte Lloyd was attacked, a young South Australian woman described a comparable 'branding' experience to Colin Norris, president of International UFO Research Inc. Jillian Kass Ross of Mitchell Park reported: 'At about 2 o'clock one morning in April 1987 I woke from a deep sleep feeling utterly terrified. A blazing orange light, which seemed as hot as sunlight on the beach, was shining on my face. I tried to open my eyes to see what was going on but the lids wouldn't budge. Eventually I went back to sleep.

'The next morning I noticed three pinpricks in a vertical row in the centre of my forehead. I didn't think too much about them until that evening, when my face ballooned up. My doctor couldn't work out what was wrong – and neither could the specialist he referred me to. There had been no bite and the tests showed no sign of poison. After about a week the swelling subsided – but then I was distressed to see there were three deep triangular scars on my forehead.'

At this point Jillian's testimony enters the realms of the uncanny ...

'Several days later,' she said, 'I took off to Egypt for a holiday. Everywhere I went, Egyptians would stare at my forehead, then clasp their hands in a praying mode and bow. As I didn't understand the language I couldn't ask why they were doing it.'

While travelling through the Middle East, Jillian said, she began to have vivid recurring dreams: 'One became so familiar I almost knew it by heart. I'd be standing in the streets of a strange city watching a big fireworks display. The flashes of light kept illuminating a minaret-like building on the skyline. I didn't understand the significance of it until I was watching the television news one night, several years later.

*'To my amazement an image appeared that was exactly what I'd seen in my dreams – missiles exploding over Baghdad and that domed building lighting up.'*

Jillian Kass Ross had foreseen the first Gulf War.

When Jillian returned to Australia she began spending weekends at a small farm she owned outside Adelaide. 'While strolling around the property one afternoon I came across a deep six metre-diameter circle burned into the grass,' she said. 'At that moment the pieces began falling into place. I wondered if all the odd experiences were somehow related to UFOs.'

Another 'branding' victim – also living in South Australia – was Andrew L., a 21 year-old electronics apprentice. His doctor took photographs of a triple triangle inside a circle, which had appeared on the left side of his body. Again, the doctor could find no explanation for the mark which, as in Jillian's case, was caused neither by a bite nor a tattoo needle. Andrew and his family said that their house had been 'troubled' for more than two years by grey entities that sped through the building 'like bullets'.

Andrew described how he had sustained the marks on his skin: 'I woke up and saw a grey figure standing in what seemed to be a shimmering haze. I heard a woman's voice in my head telling me to roll over. My brain felt disengaged and I obeyed. Next I felt two sharp jabs – one in my neck at the base of my skull, the other in my left side. During the following week my neck was incredibly painful. Then I noticed a small scab where I'd been poked. When the scab fell away I saw in the mirror a small circle with three triangles inside. I found an identical circle on my left side.'

Among the most fascinating cases on Keith Basterfield's files is the testimony of a Melbourne woman, a graduate in psychology. 'I told my husband one morning that an interesting thing had happened overnight,' she said. 'I'd woken to find the bedroom filled with a brilliant, blinding light. I was lifted up into the light, somehow getting the feeling that I shouldn't be afraid. Next, I was lying on a table surrounded by strange beings. I got the mental impression that they were saying, "This will be uncomfortable, but not painful."

'Then I felt something probing my stomach – and I sensed they were going to take eggs from an ovary. They told me not to be frightened and said, "You're going back now – but you won't feel this really happened." Next thing I knew, I was wide awake in bed, remembering everything. I never believed for a moment that the experience was a dream. It was stark and very real.'

UFOs constitute one of the profoundest mysteries facing Australia and the world. Tens of thousands of witnesses, in this country alone, have seen and – often unwittingly – photographed them. Over the decades the phenomenon has increased in complexity – becoming more, rather than less, puzzling. Will we ever discover what these aerial enigmas are, and where they're from? There are numerous theories on that subject, but the French physicist Dr Jacques Vallee's answer is: probably not. Vallee believes that the UFO is part of 'a program created by a superior, albeit finite, consciousness' – a program designed to extend humanity's mental reach, forcing us to look infinitely outward, beyond our petty selves.

## Australian Snaps 'Boomerang' Above the Moon

On 4 June 1969 a member of Ballarat's Astronomical Society took an astonishing photograph. It shows a huge curved object apparently orbiting the moon.

The 'space boomerang', which is casting a black shadow, is estimated to be at least 500 kilometres long – and seems to be radiating light. Coincidentally it appeared just 46 days before astronaut Neil Armstrong became the first human to set foot on the lunar surface.

The picture was developed by the Victorian Railways, as the film also contained images of a train accident in Ballarat. The Astronomical Society asked

Ballarat's School of Mines and several photographers to analyse the anomalous lunar image. All declared it genuine. A second Astronomical Society member also photographed the crescent. In his two shots it was surrounded by haze.

According to Maurice Chatelain, a former NASA scientist, Armstrong himself may have seen UFOs on the moon's surface. Chatelain claims that Armstrong radioed Mission Control to say he could see two saucer-shaped craft perched on the lip of a crater. 'They're here before us,' he said. Armstrong's reports were blacked out for security reasons, Chatelain claimed.

He further alleged that astronaut Buzz Aldrin had photographed the alien craft from inside Apollo 11 – but the film was labelled top-secret. NASA dismissed Chatelain's claims – but they later received unexpected support from Moscow. In 1975 Soviet space program director Dr Vladimir Azhaza said: 'I am convinced Armstrong and Aldrin did see alien ships and that NASA censored the incident.'

*1. The author thanks Richard Tambling, a former Royal Air Force photographer, who broke the news of the lunar photographs in his 1978 book Flying Saucers – Where do they Come From?*

# Mystery of the Murdered Model

*The beautiful young woman's makeup, credit cards and other personal belongings were found strewn in frenzied confusion around a Sydney suburb. Aside from these grim mementoes, there was no indication of where she was or what had befallen her. Police and the coroner believed she had been murdered. Or did it simply look like murder?*

SYDNEY IN THE SPRING OF 1994 was alive with conflicting rumours about the fate of Revelle Balmain. At 22, the private school-educated dancer, with her exceptional ability and good looks, had seemed on the brink of a professional breakthrough. She had danced with cabaret companies in Japan, advertising agencies were increasingly engaging her to promote their clients' products – and she had even been anointed as a cover-model by the sophisticated magazine *Oyster*.

But there was an aspect of Revelle's working life that neither her family nor her public knew anything about. In her early days of struggle to establish herself in showbusiness, the young model had accepted work with a companionship firm – and she was still on its books. But she was quietly convinced that she would soon be finished with all that. She had told friends that the booking she accepted on the afternoon of 5 November would be her last. And shortly after completing it she would be flying to Japan again, for her fourth cabaret tour.

At 4 o'clock on that ominous afternoon Revelle – using her agency alias of 'Mischa' – knocked at the door of a client in Kingsford in south-eastern Sydney. In accordance with her employers' instructions she was clutching a $60 bottle of champagne. When the two-hour stint was over she planned to meet her friend Kate Brentnell for a drink. After that she would be seeing her new boyfriend, a 28 year-old man who was starting out as a film director.

At 7.15 p.m. Revelle rang Kate to say she was just about to leave her client and suggested they meet at the Royal Hotel, Paddington. She did not keep the appointment.

Next day Revelle Balmain's bag, make-up, diary, credit cards and the keys to her Bellevue Hill flat were found scattered around several Kingsford streets. Chillingly, one of her shell-studded platform shoes was retrieved from one street; its counterpart from another. Police interviewed the 31-year-old client, who said he had driven the young woman to the nearby Red Tomato Inn at about 7.00 p.m. Detectives also questioned the agency's owners. None of the enquiries resulted in charges being laid.

Weeks dragged by without any substantial clue to Revelle's whereabouts. The New South Wales government offered a $100,000 reward to anyone who could point police to her killer. No-one claimed the money. But there was no shortage of people who swore they had heard, 'through friends', what really had become of her. One widely-circulated story was that she had run off with an Arab sheikh who had long been in love with her.

Revelle's parents, Jan and Ivor Balmain, were devastated by their daughter's disappearance. 'Whenever the phone rings I think it's finally going to end,' Ivor told a newspaper reporter. 'I'm afraid we may never know what happened, although we strongly suspect murder was involved.'

In May 1999 the Deputy State Coroner, John Abernethy, handed down an open finding into Revelle's presumed death. He said he 'could not ascertain' how she had died, as her body had never been found. He offered condolences to the Balmains, saying he was 'sorry we don't have any more answers'.

Jan and Ivor Balmain were inconsolable. 'This has been harder than the first day she disappeared,' Ivor said. 'What kept us going was that justice was going to be done. It hasn't. But we'll never give up.'

# Death from a Distance
# Uncanny Power of the Killing Bone

*It is no more than a simple shard of bone, whittled to a point at one end and plaited with human hair at the other. Yet people at whom it is pointed have been known to plunge into coma or die. How does the ancient Aboriginal practice of bone-pointing work? And why does the mere threat of its use strike such terror into potential victims?*

FOR THOUSANDS OF YEARS Aboriginal communities used the *kundela*, or killing bone, to injure enemies and to punish those who had disobeyed tribal law. Education and the diffusion of western beliefs have reduced the incidence of bone-pointing and the dire results it can produce. But even today, the *kundela* is still imbued, in the minds of many indigenous Australians, with an awesome power.

In his book *The Australian Aboriginal*, published in 1925, anthropologist Dr Herbert Basedow wrote:

> *A man who discovers that he is being boned by an enemy is indeed a pitiable sight. He stands aghast, with his eyes staring at the treacherous pointer, and with his hands lifted, as though to ward off the lethal medium which he imagines is pouring into his body ... He attempts to shriek, but usually the sound chokes in his throat and all one might see is froth at his mouth.*
>
> *His body begins to tremble and the muscles twist involuntarily. He sways backwards and falls to the ground, and for a short time appears to be in a swoon; but soon after he begins to writhe in mortal agony, and covering his face with his hands, begins to moan ... From this time onwards he sickens and frets, refusing to eat and keeping aloof from the daily affairs of the tribe. Unless help is forthcoming in the shape of a counter-charm, administered by the hands of the*

> Nangarri, *or medicine man, his death is only a matter of a comparatively short time. If the coming of the medicine man is opportune, he might be saved.*

One tragic victim of bone-pointing was Kinjika, who had defied a law of his Arnhem Land tribe. Australian and international newspapers reported in 1953 that the man had been flown, 'in a terminal condition', to a Darwin hospital. Doctors could find no wounds, injuries or signs of disease – but his vital systems were closing down. In the words of a hospital administrator he was 'exhibiting the signs of a person dying of extreme old age'.

A young friend, who had accompanied Kinjika to Darwin, told medical staff that the sick man had been summoned to appear before the tribal council several days earlier. He had responded by running away.

Angry elders, unaccustomed to such disobedience, promptly sentenced him to death. In the fugitive's absence the *milangwa* (tribal executioner) performed a ceremony in which he loaded a killing bone with deadly energy, powerful enough to span vast distances. The executioner then conducted another ritual in which he passed the bone to the *kurdaita*, the tribe's specialists in punishing wrongdoers who had escaped justice. They 'fired' the bone at the fleeing man, who, by now, was several hundred kilometres away. When their grisly task was complete they destroyed the *kundela* in a ceremonial fire. The death-bone is seldom used more than once.

Despite intense efforts to save him, Kinjika died on his fifth day in the hospital. His slow and agonising end aroused sympathy across Australia. Newspapers published photographs of a rapier-like *kundela*, with its lank strands of human hair affixed to it by spinifex gum – describing the Aboriginal belief that once it was pointed, there was no escape from its sinister effect.

Psychologists countered by assuring readers and radio listeners that a killing bone had no intrinsic power. The entire process depended on the mindset of the victim. If he believed strongly enough that he would fall ill and die, his body would produce precisely that effect. This theory was borne out three years later when a young Aborigine, Laia Wolumu, became mortally ill following another 'death ceremony' (also in Arnhem Land).

Laia was unable to eat, drink or even swallow. When his breathing became laboured, the hospital placed him in an iron lung. A doctor was eventually able to convince him that he could be healthy again almost immediately, if only he believed it was possible. The young man found the argument persuasive. He recovered within hours.

Purportedly magical procedures which maim and kill from a distance are not confined to Australia. In the British magazine the *Spectator* (6 July 2002) journalist Hugh Russell described the plight of a 26 year-old Zambian man who stole a shopping bag from an elderly woman in the northern town of Luansha. Finding that the bag contained dressmaking materials he caught a bus to the larger town of Ndola, where he tried to sell the booty at an open-air market. Police arrested him and took him to the station. During interrogation, the hapless thief's testicles began to swell.

Hugh Russell writes:

*Don't jump to conclusions. This was not the result of rigorous police examination with rubber truncheons. No, the testicles just began to swell. Soon, reports police chief Musumba, they were as big as oranges. The suspect knew immediately what was happening to him and why. He had been 'witched' – presumably by his victim, the old lady who had lost her shopping bag. He pleaded to be taken back to Luansha so that he could return the goods and have the spell removed. But the police pointed out that they had no idea who the woman was or where she lived. Instead, they took the suspect to hospital, where doctors removed his underpants and examined him. By now the testicles were so big that the man was unable to put his underpants back on.*

The 'witching' practised by Australian Aborigines can also be grimly effective – merely psychological as it may be. In the Northern Territory in 1990 a teenage boy fell for a girl who had been promised to an elder from another tribe. On behalf of the old man, several tribeswomen gathered to 'sing', or curse, the offending youth to death. The boy lapsed into a coma, from which doctors were unable to revive him. Only when he was 'unsung' by an elder from his own tribe did the victim regain consciousness.

One of Australia's most celebrated bone-pointing dramas began in 1969, when a full-blooded member of the Arunta was attacked by a fellow-tribesman. During the struggle a rifle went off and the attacker died. A court found that the death had been accidental and declared the surviving Aborigine not guilty of manslaughter. But his people disagreed. A delegation met him outside the courtroom and reminded him that the penalty for killing a member of one's own tribe was death.

The man fled from Alice Springs in a van, with his wife, children and dogs. Undaunted by the fact that he had vanished, seemingly untraceably, into the outback, the *kurdaita* pointed the bone at him. Journalists who managed to speak to the bone victim during the years that followed reported that he was working at odd jobs to feed his family, never staying in one place for more than a few days. He was constantly on the verge of mental breakdown, sleeping with a gun at his side and fearful that he might die at any moment. However, he managed to survive in the outback for 11 years, before slipping off the newspapers' radar.

He became the first Aborigine in recorded history to survive, unaided, the terrifying sentence of death-by-bone.

# Strange Saga of the Mahogany Ship

*In 1992 the Victorian government offered a $250,000 reward to anyone who could produce physical evidence of a Portuguese caravel, known to have been wrecked off Warrnambool more than four centuries ago. The will-o'-the-wisp Mahogany Ship, buried somewhere in drifting sand dunes, proves elusive. But archaeologists are still determined to solve the mystery of the vessel's final burial place.*

WHEN *BULLETIN* EDITOR J.F. ARCHIBALD died in 1919 he bequeathed numerous gifts to his young nation. Best-known was the portrait prize that bears his name. But among the other treasures and curiosities he left behind was a length of polished wood that captured the national imagination.

It was, Archibald asserted in his will, a chunk of decking from the Mahogany Ship – a four-masted ocean caravel which (if an ancient Portuguese map can be believed) was wrecked on the Warrnambool coast in 1522. For centuries the stricken vessel had lain amid the wind-whipped dunes, slowly becoming buried beneath a mountain of sand.

Archibald accurately believed that if the elusive mahogany hulk could be found again, historians would be obliged radically to rewrite Australia's history. The wreck would offer first-hand evidence that Europeans discovered the east coast of *Terra Australis Incognito* two and a half centuries before Captain Cook.

The first recorded sighting by whites of the ruined Mahogany Ship was in 1836. Two sealers were walking along the beach between Warrnambool and Belfast (now Port Fairy) when they happened upon 'the half-buried remains of a vessel high up in the sand dunes'. On arrival at Belfast, which at that time was a tiny whaling station, they reported the discovery to Captain J.B. Mills. The old seaman, who would later become harbourmaster, immediately visited the wreck and took a bearing of its position, which, he vaguely pronounced, was 'the iron church in line with the Tower Hill peak, well in the hummocks'. To the frustration of searchers then unborn, he offered no cross-bearing. Mills climbed on to the deck and tested the timber with a blade. The result surprised him. 'My claspknife glanced over the wood as though it were a bar of iron,' he wrote.

As a seasoned sailor Captain Mills was intrigued by the vessel's 'ancient appearance, and a design of a kind I had never seen'. He could not have been expected to be familiar with the Portuguese caravel, the two-decked ship used by Columbus on his first Atlantic voyage and by Portuguese and Spanish explorers of the 1500s. The captain was also perplexed by the fact that the vessel lay more than 90 metres inland. Later analysts surmised that the ocean had receded over the centuries, leaving the ship stranded far up in the sandhills.

But what intrigues researchers most is Mills' description of the impenetrable deck timber. This dovetailed with early settlers' memories of old whalers' huts in the area being floored with mahogany – a wood which was, to the Portuguese shipbuilder, what oak was to the English. The alien and outdated look of the wreckage appeared also to explain the Spanish and Portuguese coins which had been turning up on Warrnambool's beaches for as long as locals could remember.

Captain Mills, a historian by inclination, questioned elderly local Aborigines about the Mahogany Ship. They had no memory of that particular vessel being wrecked.

Their legends said nothing about it either. As far as they knew, the ship had always been there.

Over the decades the wreck began slowly to vanish from sight – occasionally rearing from the dunes again during gales and storms. Eventually it disappeared completely into its tomb of sand. However, recollections of the caravel remained vivid.

A detailed eyewitness report was published in the Melbourne *Argus* in April, 1876. Captain John Mason of Belfast wrote:

> *Sir, Riding along the beach from Port Fairy to Warrnambool in the summer of 1846, my attention was attracted to the hull of a vessel embedded high and dry in the Hummocks, far above the reach of any tide. It appeared to have been that of a vessel about 100 tons burden, and from its bleached and weather-beaten appearance must have remained there many years.*
>
> *The spars and deck were gone, and the hull was full of drift sand. The timber of which she was built had the appearance of cedar or mahogany. The fact of the vessel being in that position was well-known to the whalers in 1846, when the first whaling station was formed in that neighbourhood and the oldest natives, when questioned, stated their knowledge of it extended from their earliest recollection.*
>
> *... Mr McGowan, the superintendent of the Post-office ... informed me that it was supposed to be one of a fleet of Portuguese or Spanish discovery ships, one of them having parted from the others during a storm.*

*He referred me to notice of a wreck having appeared in the novel* Geoffrey Hamlyn, *written by Henry Kingsley ... One of the characters, a doctor, [says] the English should never sneer at [Portugal and Spain] – they were before us everywhere.*

*The wreck lies about midway between Belfast and Warrnambool, and is probably by this time entirely covered with drift sand ... During a search made for it within the last few months, it was not to be seen.*

*Yours &c.,*
*John Mason*

From the 1880s onward, hundreds of search parties visited Warrnambool, all believing they would be the ones to rediscover the Mahogany Ship. The would-be excavators used tools as disparate as sounding rods, divining wands and plain spades. But the ancient vessel, thought to be buried no more than 10 metres beneath the shifting dunes, declined to show itself.

During the Depression the *Herald* suggested that the government pay squads of unemployed men to dig the dunes. The federal government liked the idea, but lacked money to implement it. The greatest impetus to exploration came in 1992 when the Victorian government offered a $250,000 prize to anyone who could produce physical evidence pointing to the wreck's whereabouts.

The Portuguese government considered matching this offer (but never did). By the 1990s some historians concluded that the Mahogany Ship was one of three caravels under the command of the Portuguese explorer

Cristovao de Mendonca, who is thought to have charted Australia's north and east coasts in 1522. In his book *The Secret Discovery of Australia*, the maritime historian Kenneth McIntyre describes the Dauphin Map, drawn 14 years after Mendonca's expedition. Parts of it could be interpreted as representing the Australian coastline.

The map abruptly ends west of a bay, which could be Port Phillip Bay – possibly indicating that Mendonca abandoned his expedition after one of his ships ran aground at the future location of Warrnambool.

The $250,000 prize attracted scores of searchers. But they located no wreck and collected no money. Perhaps they should have saved their time. Even the Commonwealth Scientific and Industrial Research Organization (CSIRO) scientists, using ground-penetrating radar, had earlier failed to find the legendary vessel.

There were always people who imagined that the caravel would be easy to trace. On 30 October 1933 the *Herald* interviewed one of them: Mr Calloway, a Warrnambool sewerage construction surveyor. It should, he said, be 'a simple matter' to survey the dune-scape described in 1836 by Captain Mills and 'reduce the area of search to a very small one'. The buried ship's deck would lie no more than 25 feet [75 metres] below the sand's surface, he predicted.

*If bores were put down at regular intervals over the plotted area, it should not be hard to locate the hull,' he said. 'Digging would be easy, and the whole operation – surveying, boring and excavation – would not cost more than £200.*

Sadly, Mr Calloway was just another optimist. The Mahogany Ship continues to defy every effort to find it. Several generations, and several hundreds of thousands of dollars later, it still lies undisturbed in the darkness beneath Warrnambool's dunes.

## Did the Chinese Beat Cook to Australia?

Deep in the tribal memory of Aborigines in the Warrnambool district lie images of 'yellow-skinned men' who arrived in gigantic ships from an unknown place.

One of the earliest recorded reports of this ancient recollection can be found in the 3 June 1890 edition of the *Warrnambool Standard*.

More than a century later a historian has asserted that the tribal legends are firmly rooted in fact. In a lecture to the Royal Geographical Society, Gavin Menzies produced what he claimed to be evidence that Chinese explorers and cartographers, in gigantic teak ships as big as aircraft carriers, landed on Australia's west and east coasts in 1422. If this is correct it means the Chinese explored and mapped Australia almost three and a half centuries before Captain Cook.

Menzies' controversial assertion was immediately picked up by the Chinese satellite television station Phoenix, followed by America's ABC and NBC. In

2002 he published a controversial book on the subject – *1421: the Year China Discovered the World*. He quotes an 'eyewitness' to the voyages – a young Venetian aristocrat Nicola da Conti, who published detailed accounts. He has also produced a map, drawn in 1542 by the French cartographer Jean Rotz. Apparently using Chinese data it accurately depicts parts of the Australian coastline, describing the landmass as 'Greater Java'.

According to Menzies, the 15th century Chinese expedition, headed by Admiral Zheng, travelled in a fleet of massive teak ships, with about 1,000 sailors aboard each one. The fleet was serviced by factory vessels which grew rice and vegetables and raised animals for the sailors' consumption. Even the men's libidos were catered for, by a squad comprising hundreds of prostitutes, equipped with aphrodisiacs and sexual aids.

But some sailors also entered into longterm partnerships. Menzies believes they settled in several places, including Arnhem Land, where they and their descendants melted into Aboriginal tribes. Evidence of the Chinese invasion was commented upon by the earliest European settlers. Without understanding the significance of their discoveries they reported that they had found ceramics, figurines and Chinese jade in the bush. It was – allegedly – a two-way traffic. The Chinese emperor kept kangaroos in his zoo.

The explorers' principal motive was to search for minerals. According to Menzies they built villages, equipped with observation platforms for surveying, in what are now Eden (New South Wales) and Gympie (Queensland). Their search was successful. The ships returned home with cargoes of precious stones, silver and lead.

The Chinese, says Menzies, would have colonised Australia, had it not been for one man's history-changing decree. While Admiral Zheng was at sea the expansion-minded emperor Zhu Di was dethroned by his son Zhu Ghaozi. He had no interest in empire-building – and commanded that there be no further voyages of discovery.

Western and Chinese scholars are hostile to Menzies' theories, which also suggest that other 'pioneering' European voyages were mere re-runs of Asian forays centuries earlier. 'It's impossible to claim Columbus discovered America, Cook discovered Australia and Magellan was the first to circumnavigate the world,' Menzies defiantly asserted. 'Anyone who looked at the evidence objectively couldn't say that. You'd have to be a crank to believe it.'

## Who Was 'H' – the Unknown Explorer?

Chiselled into a sun-scorched boulder in the remote Pilbara region is the weather-worn initial 'H' – accompanied by a date, 1771.

Underneath the cryptic inscription, found 248 kilometres from the Western Australian coastline, is an engraving of a sailship's wheel. The find has created controversy among archaeologists. Some believe the markings might have been made by a shipwrecked sailor who struggled inland 17 years before Captain Arthur Phillip established the first penal colony in New South Wales.

Robert Bednarik, who found the rock carving, believed Aborigines must have helped the engraver make the perilous journey inland. Dr Paul Tacon of the Australian National Museum agreed – but pointed out that there could be 'other explanations' for the design.

The Pilbara rock is not the only evidence that Europeans might have settled in Australia before Phillip, Cook and even Tasman. Late in the 20th century unexplained wagon wheel tracks were discovered in central Australia. Richard White, a senior lecturer in Australian history at Sydney University, is convinced that Captain Cook was pre-empted.

'Certainly, 1788 wasn't the first time Europeans were living on Australian soil,' he said. 'The British found the west coast inhospitable and tended to ignore it. Of course, it's the winners who write the history.'

And who was the traveller who carved his initial at the heart of a searing sunscape? Almost certainly, his name will never be known.

## What Did the Future King See?

During the 18th and 19th centuries, numerous sailors swore they had seen the *Flying Dutchman*, the phantom East Indiaman that purportedly sailed the world's oceans, bringing ill-luck wherever she went.

The tales of these credulous men were easy to discount. But one report, officially made aboard HMS *Bacchante* on 11 July 1881, has long given nautical historians cause to reflect.

Bacchante was en route at the time from Melbourne to Sydney. In her log a 16-year-old Royal Navy midshipman wrote:

> *At 4.00 a.m. the* Flying Dutchman *crossed our bows. A strange red light, as of a phantom ship all aglow, in the midst of which the masts, spars and sails of a brig two hundred yards distant stood out in strong relief as she came up on the port bow. The lookout man on the forecastle reported her as close on the port bow, where also the officer of the watch from the bridge clearly saw her, as did also the quarterdeck midshipman,*

*who was sent forward at once to the forecastle; but on arriving there no vestige nor any sign whatever was to be seen, either near nor right away to the horizon, the night being clear and the sea calm.*

*Thirteen persons altogether saw her, but whether it was* Van Diemen *or the* Dutchman *must remain unknown. The* Tourmaline *and* Cleopatra, *who were sailing on our starboard bow, flashed to ask whether we had seen the strange light.*

The young sailor's name was George. He would later become better known as George V, King of England. Standing beside him on the deck had been his brother, the Duke of Clarence, who made a similar entry in his journal.

Royal Navy records show that the sailor who first reported the phantom vessel later fell from the foremast and was killed.

# Stones that 'Fell from Nowhere'

*The bizarre phenomenon was witnessed by scores of visitors, scientific observers and journalists. It defied all their attempts at explanation. At the centre of the mystery was a distressed young farmworker who was being daily plagued by a gentle downpour of round warm stones, of unknown origin. And he could not escape them. Even when he took refuge in his employer's house, the 'stones from nowhere' continued to fall ...*

ON 22 MARCH 1957 Britain's *Daily Express* newspaper published an unusual report. On an Australian property a young farmworker was beside himself with fear because showers of warm stones were softly falling on him – and no-one could imagine how or why it was happening.

The property, Corabin, at Pumphrey, Western Australia, was owned by Alan Donaldson, whose first thought had been that someone was playing a rather sinister practical joke. But as days passed and the stone-fall showed no sign of stopping, he was forced to admit that something inexplicable was happening. The news spread and an assortment of neighbours, sightseers and newspaper reporters began to arrive at the farm.

Everyone agreed that although the stones seemed to be falling from above, there was definitely nobody up there dropping them. It was typically fine March weather. A plane or helicopter would immediately have been visible in the cloudless sky. In the wake of press reports, scientific 'experts' descended on the farm. They were intrigued by the phenomenon's seemingly nonsensical nature – particularly the fact that whenever the young man retreated into the farmhouse, the stones followed him. There were no holes in the roof, but – impossibly – the stones continued to fall as though there was no roof at all. Desperate for an explanation – any explanation – one scientist opined that 'freak winds' were probably causing it all. This prompted two witnesses to swear that while they were in a tent with the young man, stones had fallen at their feet. Weather at the time had been still – and windless.

For several days, visitors discussed the case as though it were unique. But it wasn't. At another farm, Boyup Brook, about 350 kilometres away, a similarly mysterious skyfall, witnessed by hundreds, had been in progress for almost two years. The drama began in May 1955, when stones rained down on a shack occupied by the Smiths, a family of Aboriginal farm employees. Dogs belonging to the farm's owners, the Hack family, panicked, broke their chains and fled into the darkness.

Hugh Schmitt, a journalist with the weekly magazine, *Post*, reported that as he drove toward the farmhouse a stone thumped the roof of his car. At dinner in the kitchen, several stones clattered on to the table. They were smooth and warm to the touch. And the stones were ubiquitous – even nestling in bowls and hurricane lamps.

The phenomenon was apparently infectious. After visiting Boyup Brook, the Smiths' friends, the Krakovers, returned to their camp on the adjoining property Lynford Hill – and were almost immediately subjected to a similar bombardment.

Skyfalls are not peculiar to Australia. The British authors John Mitchell and Robert Rickard have collected thousands of international newspaper reports spanning two centuries, most of which describe the enigma in broadly similar terms. Typical is a report in London's *Times*, dated 1 May 1821. 'Showers of stones,' says the article, 'continue to pour on a house in Truro, Cornwall, despite many days of guarding and investigation by the mayor, soldiers and others.' On 4 September 1886, page 5 of the American daily, *Charleston News and Courier*, reports that stones, 'found to be warm' have bounced on a pavement outside the newspaper's own building. The editor testifies that he witnessed several showers – and saw the stones 'emerging from a point overhead, strangely confined to an area of about 75 square feet [22.5 metres].'

Almost half a century has passed since warm stones descended on two farms in Western Australia. Where the stones came from, and why they fell, remains as deep a puzzle today as it was then.

**'Silver Rain' Nonplusses Police**

Ipswich (Queensland) police had never investigated a case remotely like it. The date was 6 February 1989 – and for an hour, *thousands of sardines* had been falling 'like a sheet of silver rain' on houses around Rosewood. It was a calm summer day. There were no winds that could have lifted the sardines from a body of water and in the clear sky there was no sign of an aircraft that might be dropping them.

One couple gathered a bowlful of the flapping fish for their cat. Kookaburras swooped to enjoy the unusual feast. Police estimated that the fishfall was confined to an area of two acres (0.8 hectares). When a reporter asked if they had any theories about what had caused the sardine downpour a sergeant replied. 'We've got no theories whatever.'